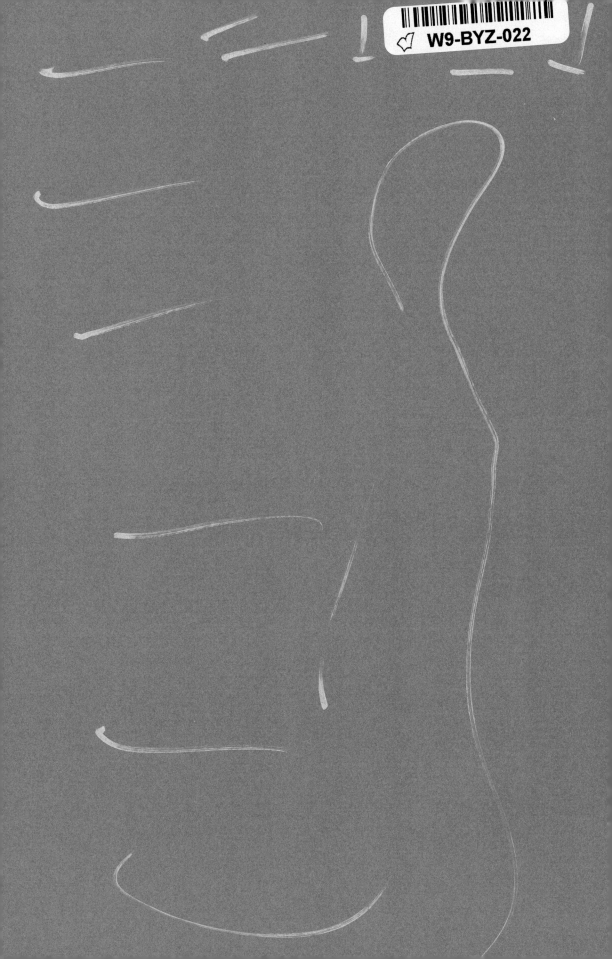

W9-BYZ-022

THE CENTER FOR CARTOON STUDIES PRESENTS

CHARLOTTE BRONTË
before JANE EYRE

GLYNNIS FAWKES

with an introduction by **Alison Bechdel**

LOS ANGELES   NEW YORK

Text and illustrations copyright © 2019 by the Center for Cartoon Studies
Introduction © 2019 by Alison Bechdel

All rights reserved. Published by Disney • Hyperion, an imprint of Disney Book Group. No part of this book may be reproduced or transmitted in any form or by any means, electronic or mechanical, including photocopying, recording, or by any information storage and retrieval system, without written permission from the publisher. For information address Disney • Hyperion, 125 West End Avenue, New York, New York 10023.

First Hardcover Edition, September 2019
First Paperback Edition, September 2019
10 9 8 7 6 5 4 3 2 1
FAC-029191-19179
Printed in Malaysia

Font created from Glynnis Fawkes's hand-lettering
Remaining text set in Adobe Caslon Pro/Fontspring
Designed by Jamie Alloy

Library of Congress Cataloging-in-Publication Data

Names: Fawkes, Glynnis, author. • Bechdel, Alison, 1960- writer of introduction. • Title: Charlotte Brontë before Jane Eyre / Glynnis Fawkes with an introduction by Alison Bechdel. • Other titles: At head of title: Center for Cartoon Studies presents • Description: First hardcover edition. • Los Angeles ; New York : Disney-Hyperion, 2019. • Audience: Ages 10-14. • Identifiers: LCCN 2018057035 • ISBN 9781368023290 (hardcover) • ISBN 1368023290 (hardcover) • ISBN 9781368045827 (paperback) • ISBN 1368045820 (paperback) • Subjects: LCSH: Brontë, Charlotte, 1816-1855—Childhood and youth—Juvenile literature. • Women novelists, English—19th century—Biography—Juvenile literature. • Novelists, English—19th century—Biography—Juvenile literature. • Graphic novels. • Classification: LCC PR4168 .F39 2019 • DDC 823/.8 [B]—dc23 LC record available at https://lccn.loc.gov/2018057035

Reinforced binding
Visit www.DisneyBooks.com

The Center for Cartoon Studies
P.O. Box 125
White River Junction, Vermont 05001
Visit www.cartoonstudies.org

INTRODUCTION

BY ALISON BECHDEL

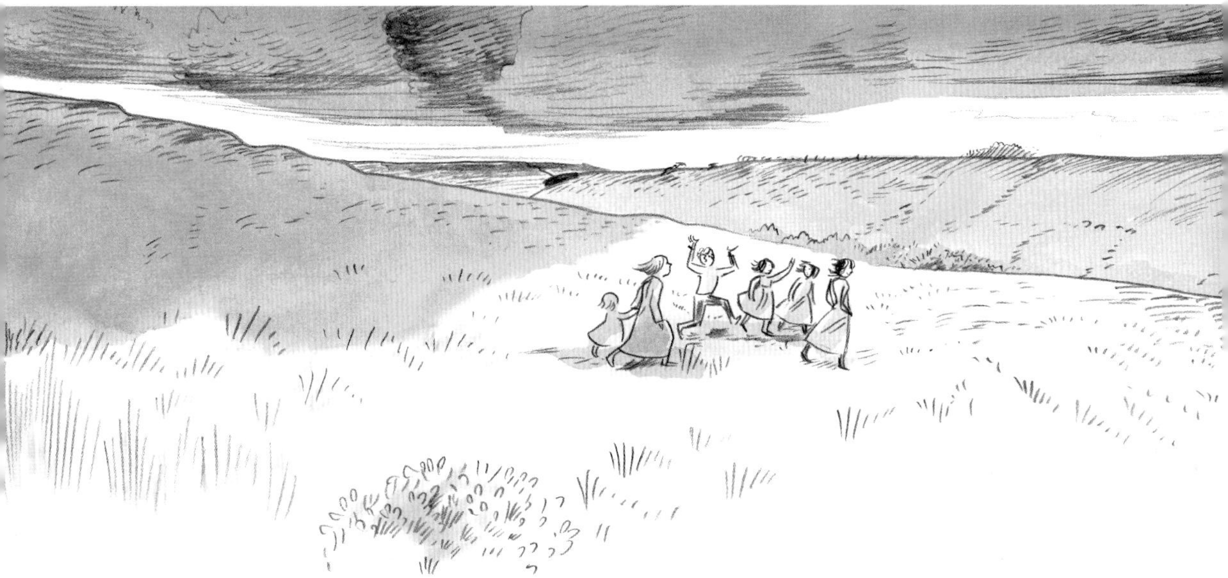

I first read *Jane Eyre* when I was eleven or twelve, in the form of a comic book. One day my dad brought home a box full of old, musty *Classic Comics*, great works of literature boiled down into a format that you could ingest in an hour or two. It would have taken me years to read all of the actual novels these comics were based on, so the idea of working my way through the entire literary canon in just a week or two appealed to the overachiever in me.

As I slammed back one badly illustrated and crudely abbreviated story after another, I did get a rough sense of their plots. But soon I would discover the pleasure of reading actual grown-up books, of being lost in a densely imagined fictional world for weeks at a time. It wasn't until I was in my twenties that I got around to *Jane Eyre* proper, but when I did, I was rewarded with one of my richest reading experiences yet. Riding the packed New York City subway to work every morning, I was as lost in Jane's story as anyone reading it in 1847 London. The struggle of a young woman trying to hang on to her sense of self in a hostile world felt completely contemporary. And almost four decades of reading later, I can say that not many books have topped it.

What I know now is that even though *Jane Eyre* is fiction, part of its power derives from the fact that Charlotte Brontë was drawing so directly on her own experience. Her struggle to make her name as a writer in a place and time where that was almost unheard of for a woman—especially one with no money—mirrors Jane's struggle for autonomy in a world stacked against her. I wasn't really thinking about that as I was reading *Jane Eyre* on the subway, though. I was just caught up in the twisting plot, the mysterious characters, and the foreboding atmosphere. But now I see that the beginning of *Jane Eyre* isn't just a gripping scene, it's also a vivid depiction of Brontë's own predicament as a woman writer in the early nineteenth century.

Young Jane is trying to get some peace from her bratty cousin John Reed by retreating behind a curtain in the window seat with a book. She has taken care to choose one "stored with pictures," Bewick's *History of British Birds*—a nice touch that reminds us that Jane is just a small child, heightening our horror at how badly she is mistreated by her relatives. But alone with her book, Jane was happy, "happy at least in my way," she tells us. "Each picture told a story." She's poring over engravings of solitary arctic seabirds and shipwrecks when John the bully finally finds her and begins teasing and hitting her. He makes her hand over Bewick, and when she does, he hurls it at her head.

That the inciting incident of *Jane Eyre* centers on access to a book is no random accident. Yes, John is just Jane's fourteen-year-old cousin, but it's not too much of a stretch to see him as a symbol of the oppressive patriarchal society that Charlotte herself struggled so mightily against in making her way as a writer. An early feminist book about Victorian women's writing is called *The Madwoman in the Attic*. The title is a reference to one of the characters in *Jane Eyre*. I don't think a spoiler alert is necessary—knowing there's a madwoman in the attic won't dampen the excitement of unraveling just what she's doing there when you read the book for yourself. But the authors of this work suggest that the confined madwoman is actually a double or twin of the character of Jane, as well as of Brontë herself. Brontë uses the madwoman to convey the plight of women in that era even more vividly, more baldly than she does with Jane's story—so vividly that it must be encoded, literally hidden, in order for her to get away with it.

This is the great thing about fiction. Would you rather read a book about the systemic patriarchal oppression of women in the nineteenth century? Or a book about a curious little girl who has the nerve to snap back at her older male cousin, saying, ". . . you are like a slave-driver—you are like the Roman emperors!"

When Glynnis Fawkes begins her virtuosic graphic biography of Charlotte Brontë with the scene of Charlotte's older sister Maria tucked up in the Haworth Parsonage library with Bewick's *History of British Birds* on her lap, this is not a random accident, either. It's a striking way of illustrating how real life and fiction were intertwined in this remarkable family of writers. Of course, I mean illustrating quite literally, and—unlike my old *Classics Comics* version of *Jane Eyre*—quite beautifully.

Fawkes's crisp, engaging drawings bring to life the boisterous camaraderie of the Brontë siblings, the windswept moor, a grim school dormitory, even the notoriously difficult to dramatize activities of reading and writing that Charlotte spent most of her time engaged in. We travel inside the imaginary worlds the children invented and we see the tiny, infinitesimally hand-lettered magazines that Charlotte and her brother collaborated on like mad, Victorian-era 'zinesters. Fawkes's infinitely nuanced expressions—sly, anguished, inspired,

bored, vexed—make these scenes of creativity feel almost animated.

It's true that it was hard to be a woman artist in the nineteenth century, and for that matter in the twentieth and the twenty-first. But it's also true that it's hard to be any kind of artist, at any time. The Brontë siblings had a feverish drive to create, but just as importantly, they had the discipline and determination necessary to perfect their craft. Fawkes shows us this, too—Charlotte concentrating, editing herself, lost in thought, writing in a frenzy. These interior actions read with as much energy and excitement as any superhero comic. And indeed, this tale of Brontë's life can be read as a kind of superhero origin story—just with frocks instead of spandex. Although I'm a cartoonist myself, I know

that the old adage about a picture being worth a thousand words is not necessarily true—otherwise we'd still be writing with hieroglyphics. There are many times when words are a much more efficient way of transmitting information, particularly in the interest of saving space. But Fawkes has achieved yet another remarkable feat here. In a mere ninety-one pages—about the length of two *Classic Comics*—she gives us not just a gorgeously illustrated version of Brontë's early life, but a densely detailed and finely textured one, in which nothing feels glossed over or unduly abbreviated. Like most of the luxuriantly immersive stories I have read, I didn't want this one to end. If you feel that way, too, when you're done, you're in luck. Just go find a copy of *Jane Eyre*, and jump in.

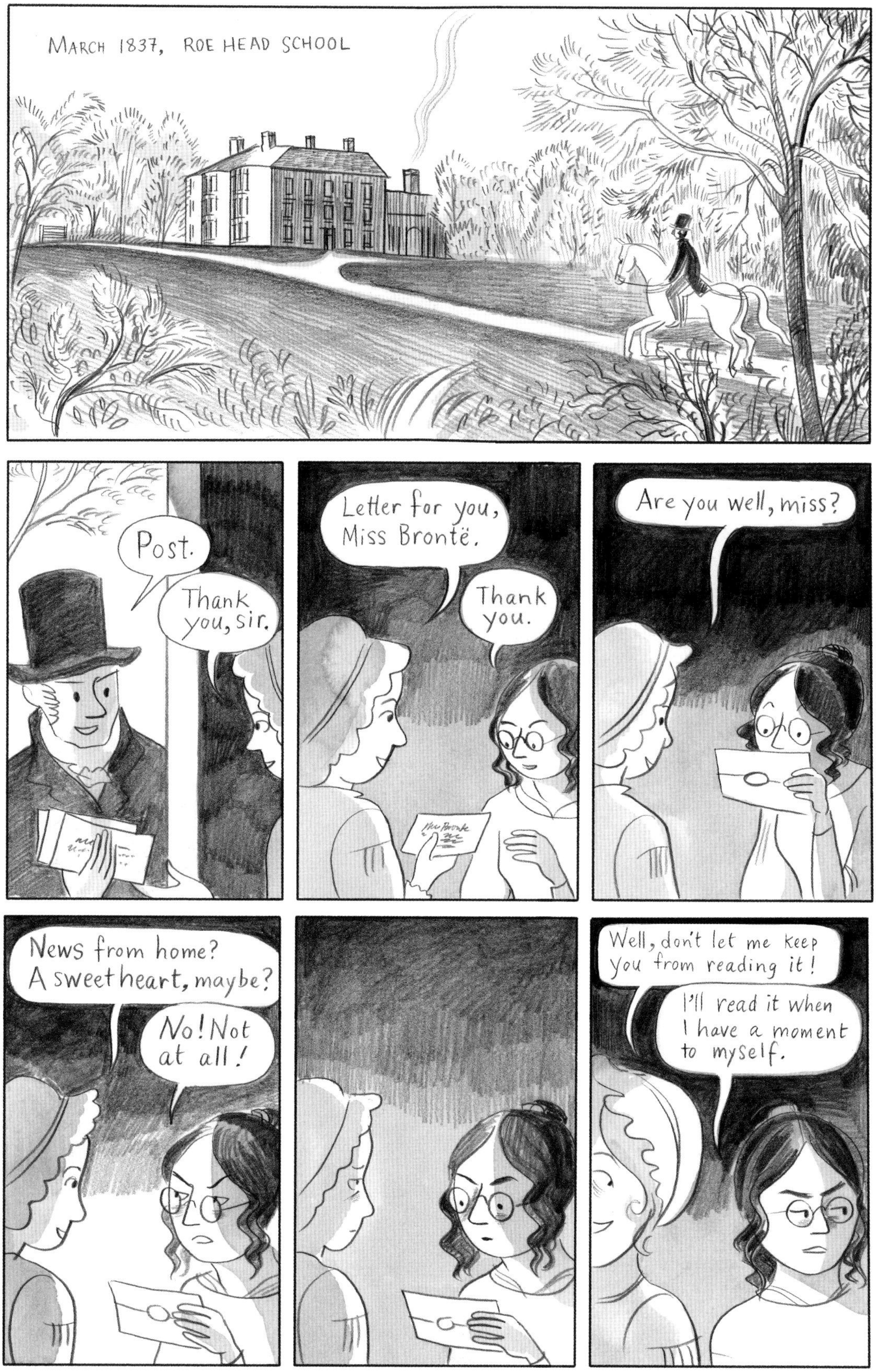
March 1837, Roe Head School
Post.
Thank you, sir.
Letter for you, Miss Brontë.
Thank you.
Are you well, miss?
News from home? A sweetheart, maybe?
No! Not at all!
Well, don't let me keep you from reading it!
I'll read it when I have a moment to myself.

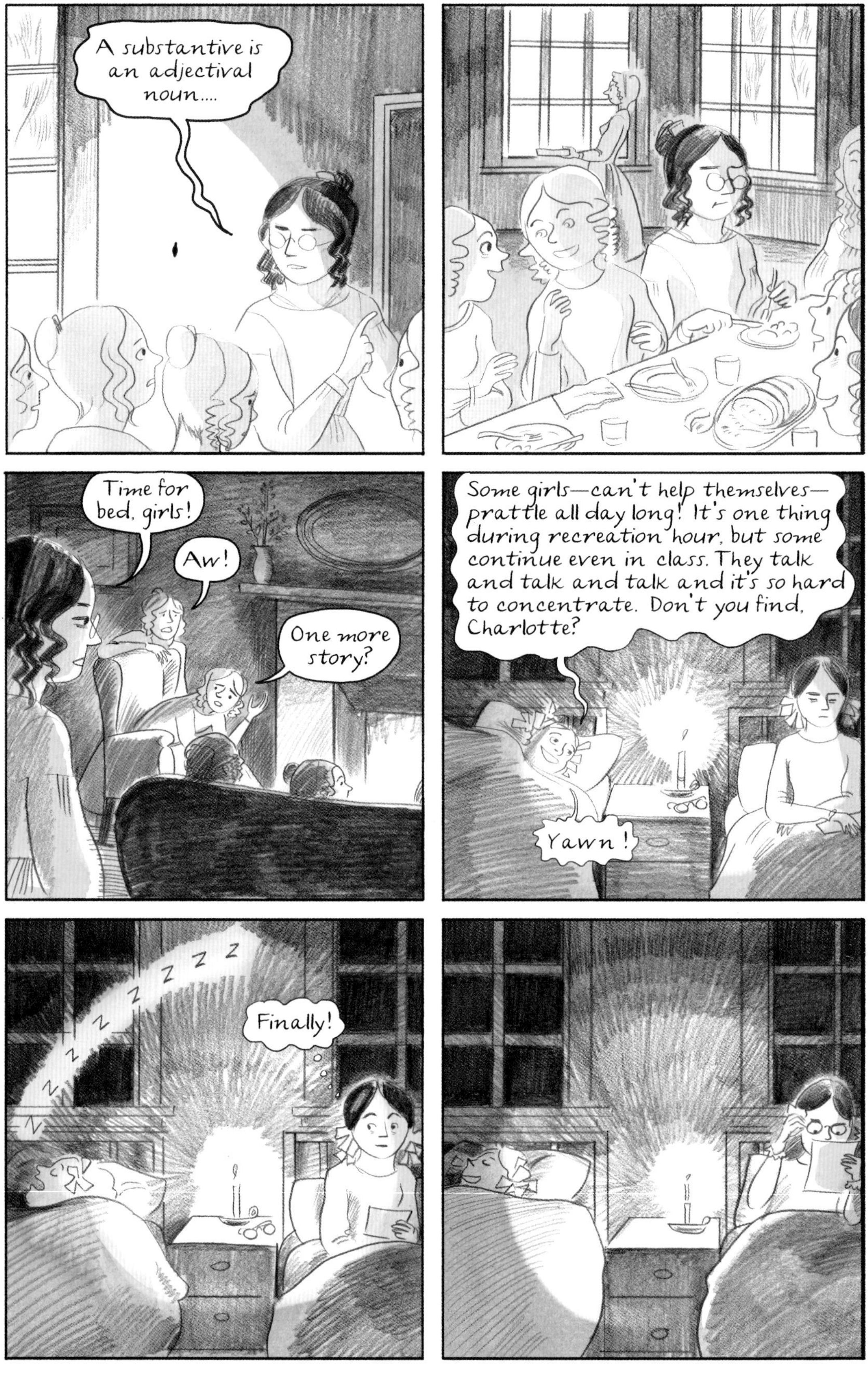
A substantive is an adjectival noun....
Time for bed, girls!
Aw!
One more story?
Some girls—can't help themselves—prattle all day long! It's one thing during recreation hour, but some continue even in class. They talk and talk and talk and it's so hard to concentrate. Don't you find, Charlotte?
Yawn!
Z Z Z Z Z Z Z Z Z Z
Finally!

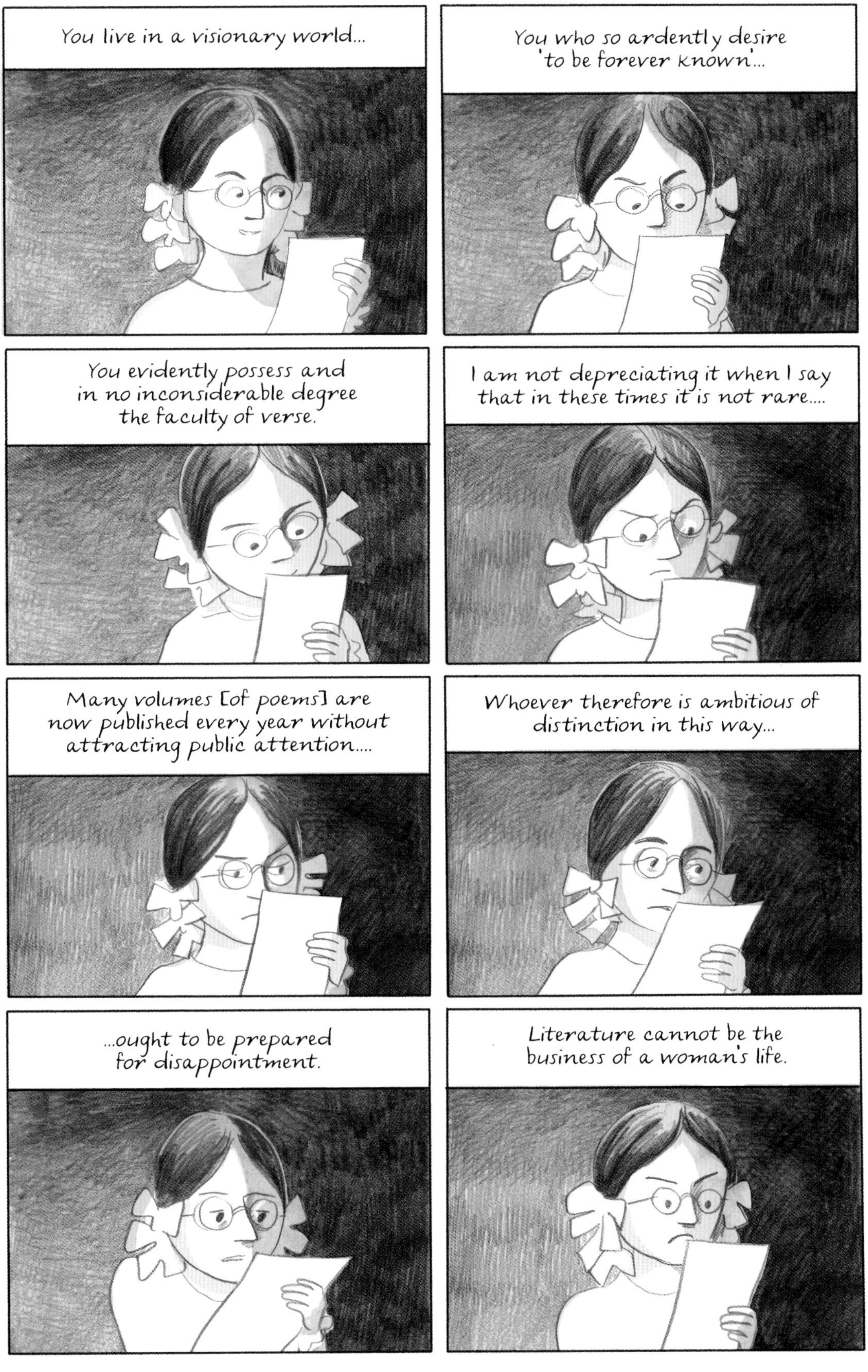
You live in a visionary world...
You who so ardently desire 'to be forever known'...
You evidently possess and in no inconsiderable degree the faculty of verse.
I am not depreciating it when I say that in these times it is not rare....
Many volumes [of poems] are now published every year without attracting public attention....
Whoever therefore is ambitious of distinction in this way...
...ought to be prepared for disappointment.
Literature cannot be the business of a woman's life.

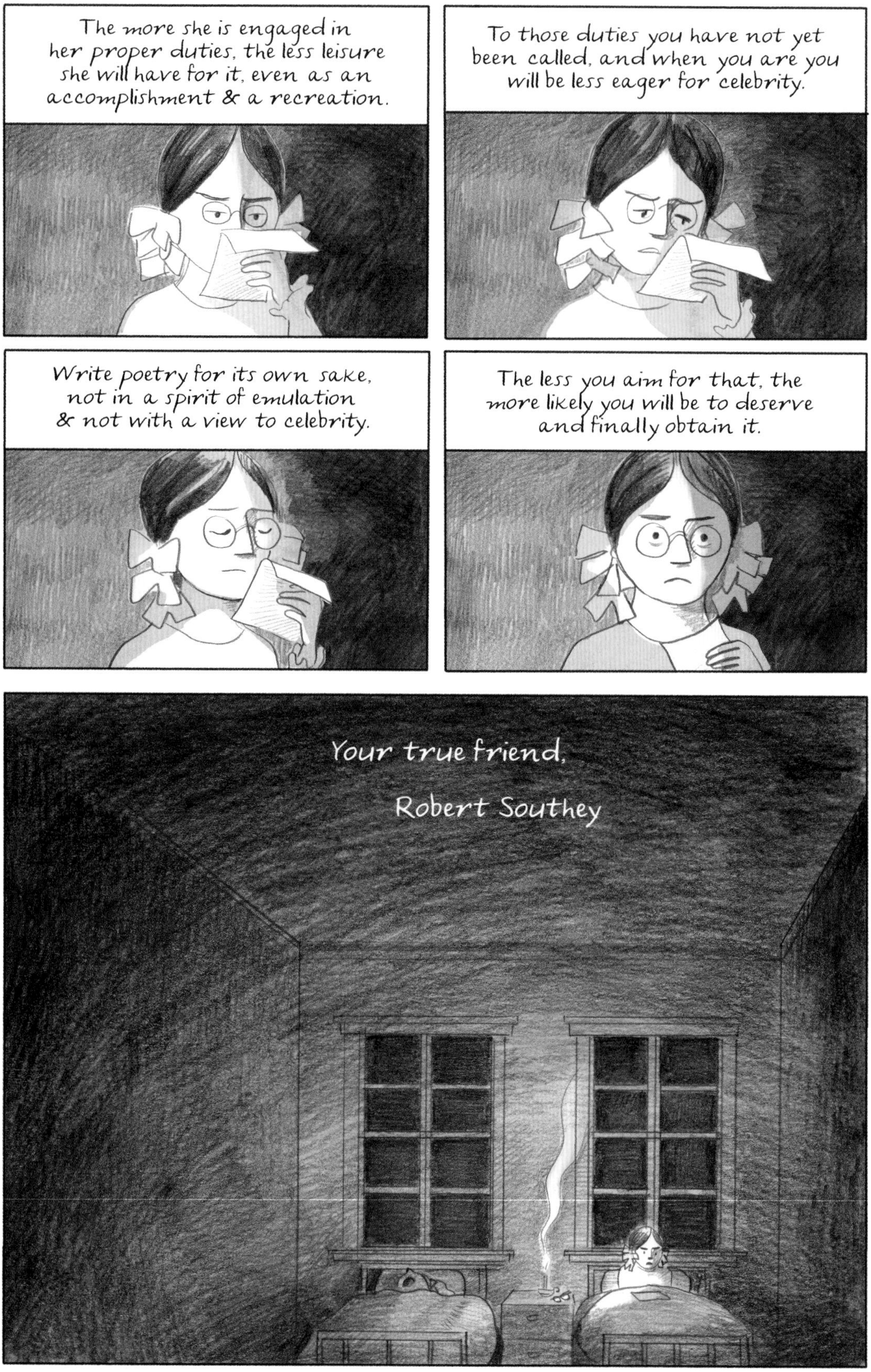
The more she is engaged in her proper duties, the less leisure she will have for it, even as an accomplishment & a recreation.
To those duties you have not yet been called, and when you are you will be less eager for celebrity.
Write poetry for its own sake, not in a spirit of emulation & not with a view to celebrity.
The less you aim for that, the more likely you will be to deserve and finally obtain it.
Your true friend,
Robert Southey

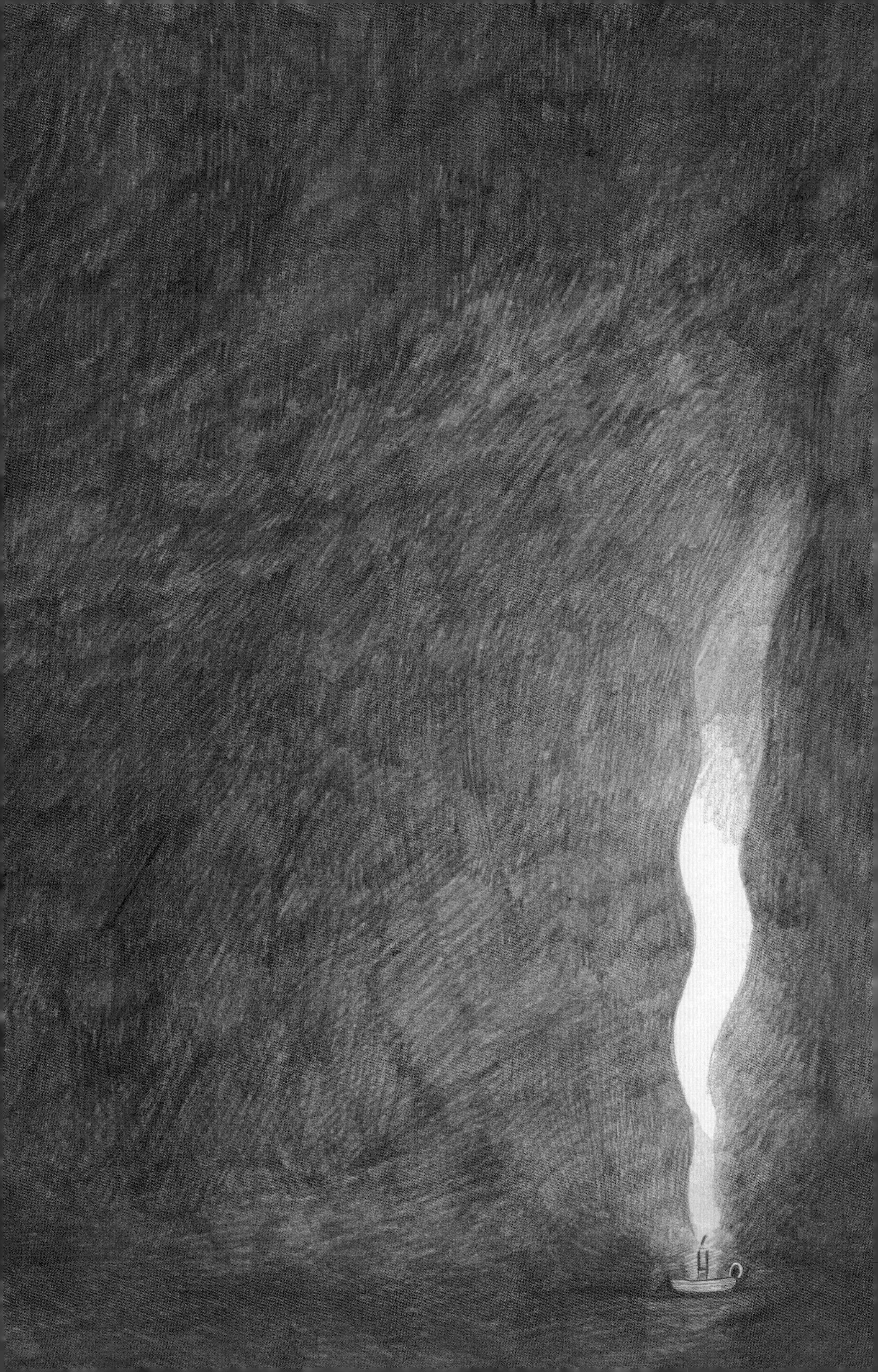

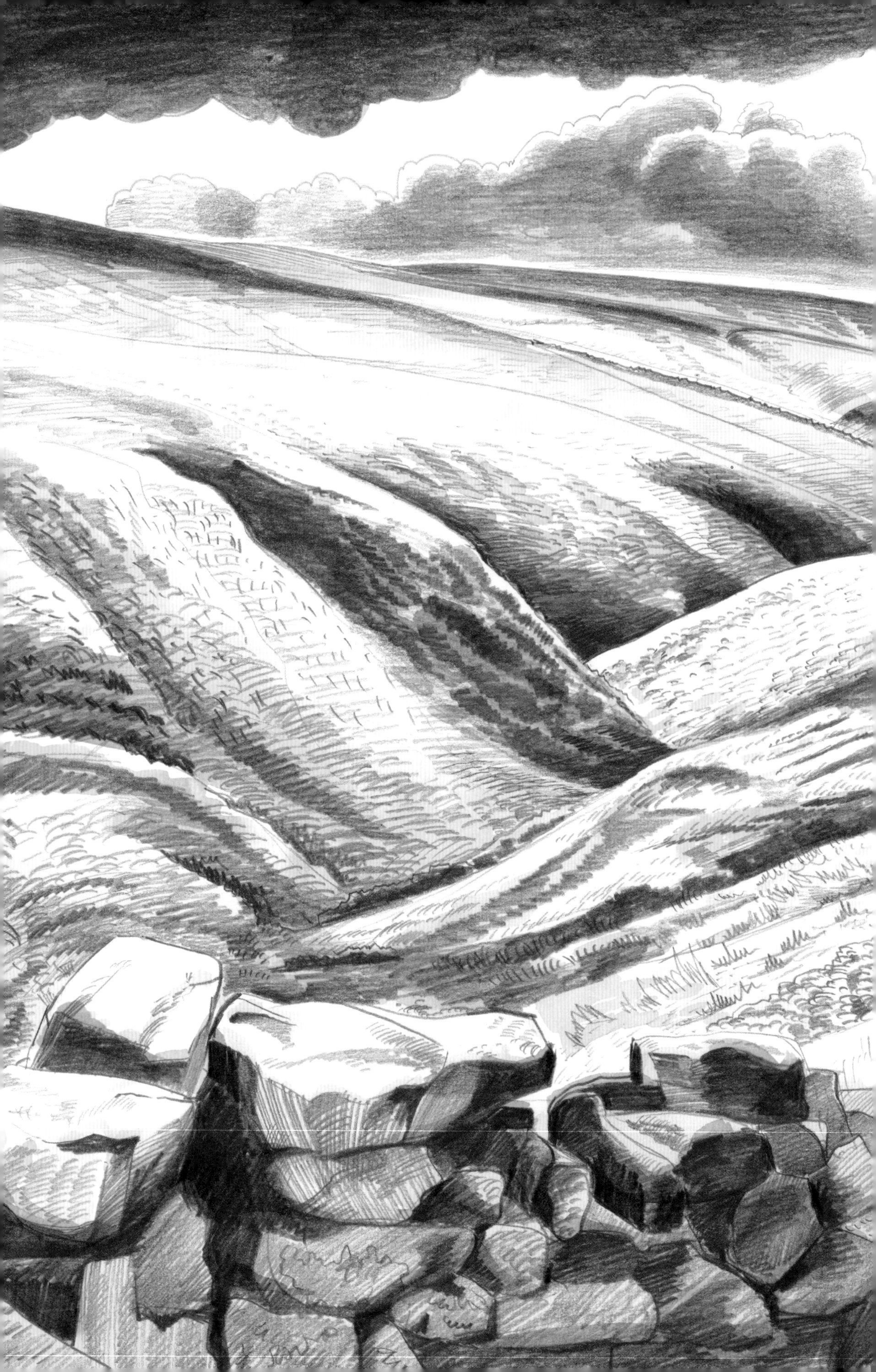

CHARLOTTE BRONTË
before JANE EYRE

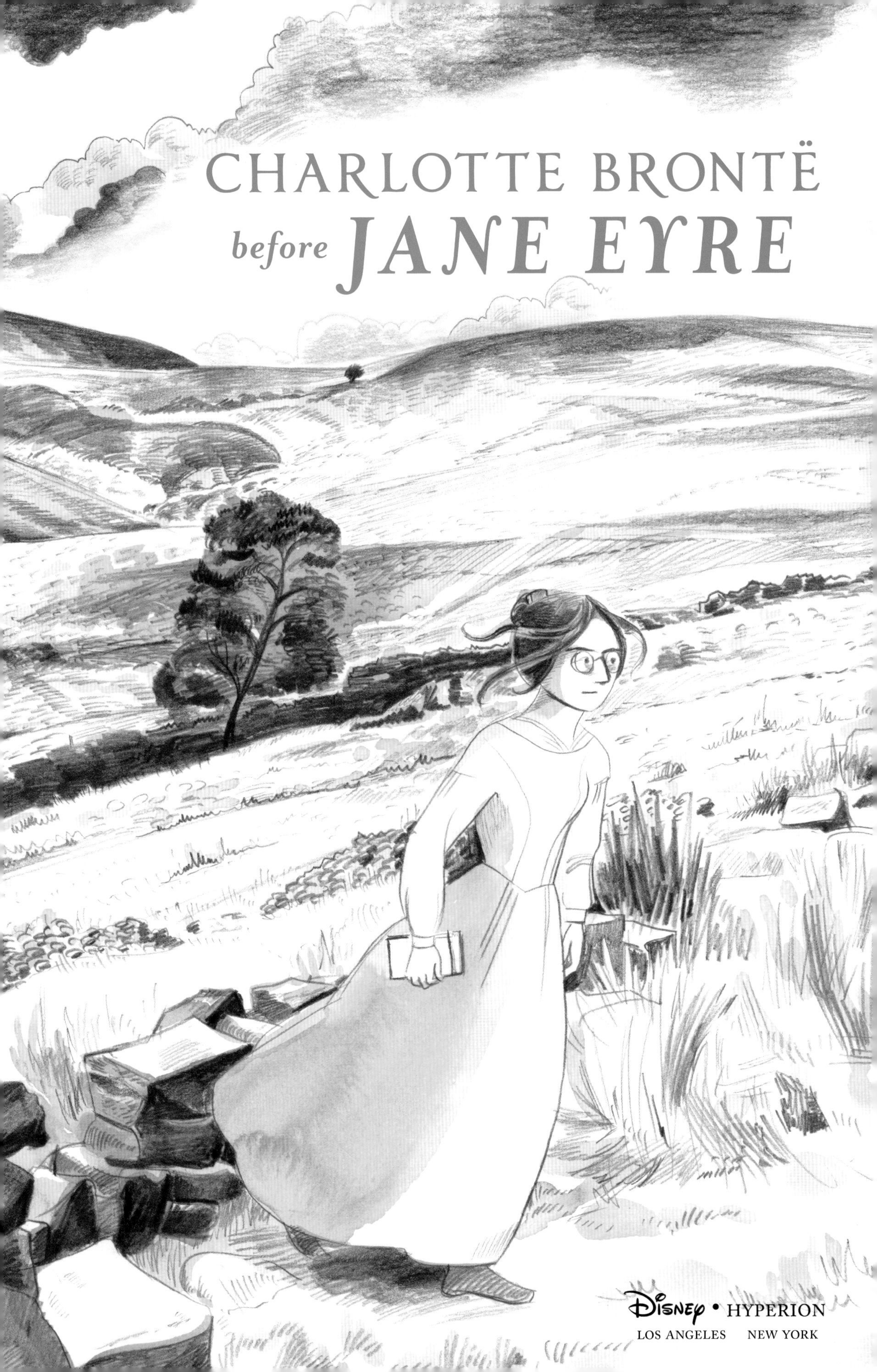

DISNEY • HYPERION
LOS ANGELES NEW YORK

SIXTEEN YEARS EARLIER, HAWORTH PARSONAGE, 1821

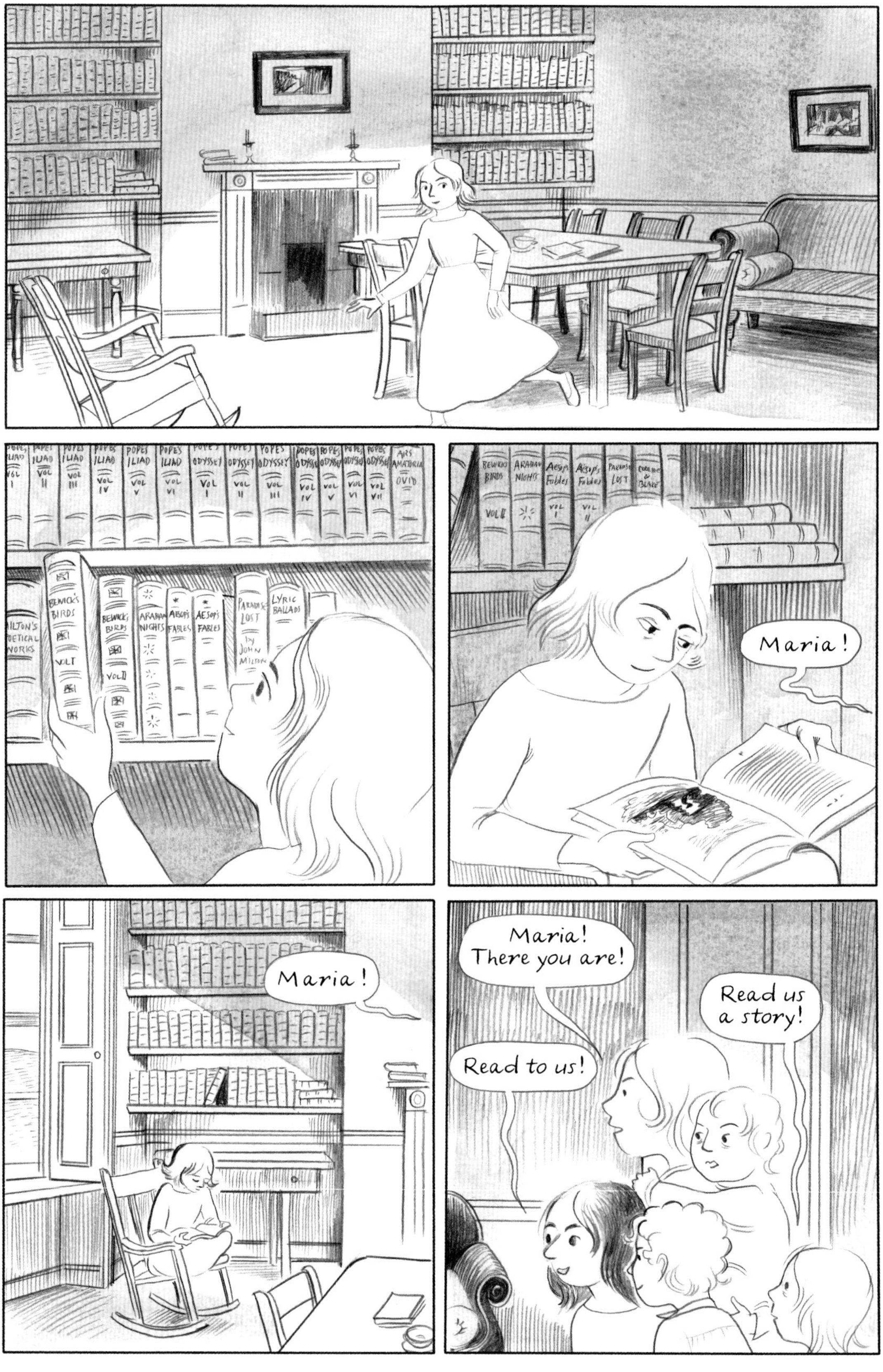
POPES ILIAD
POPES ODYSSEY
ARS AMATORIA OVID
BEWICK'S BIRDS
ARABIAN NIGHTS
AESOP'S FABLES
PARADISE LOST by JOHN MILTON
LYRIC BALLADS
Maria!
Maria!
Maria! There you are!
Read us a story!
Read to us!

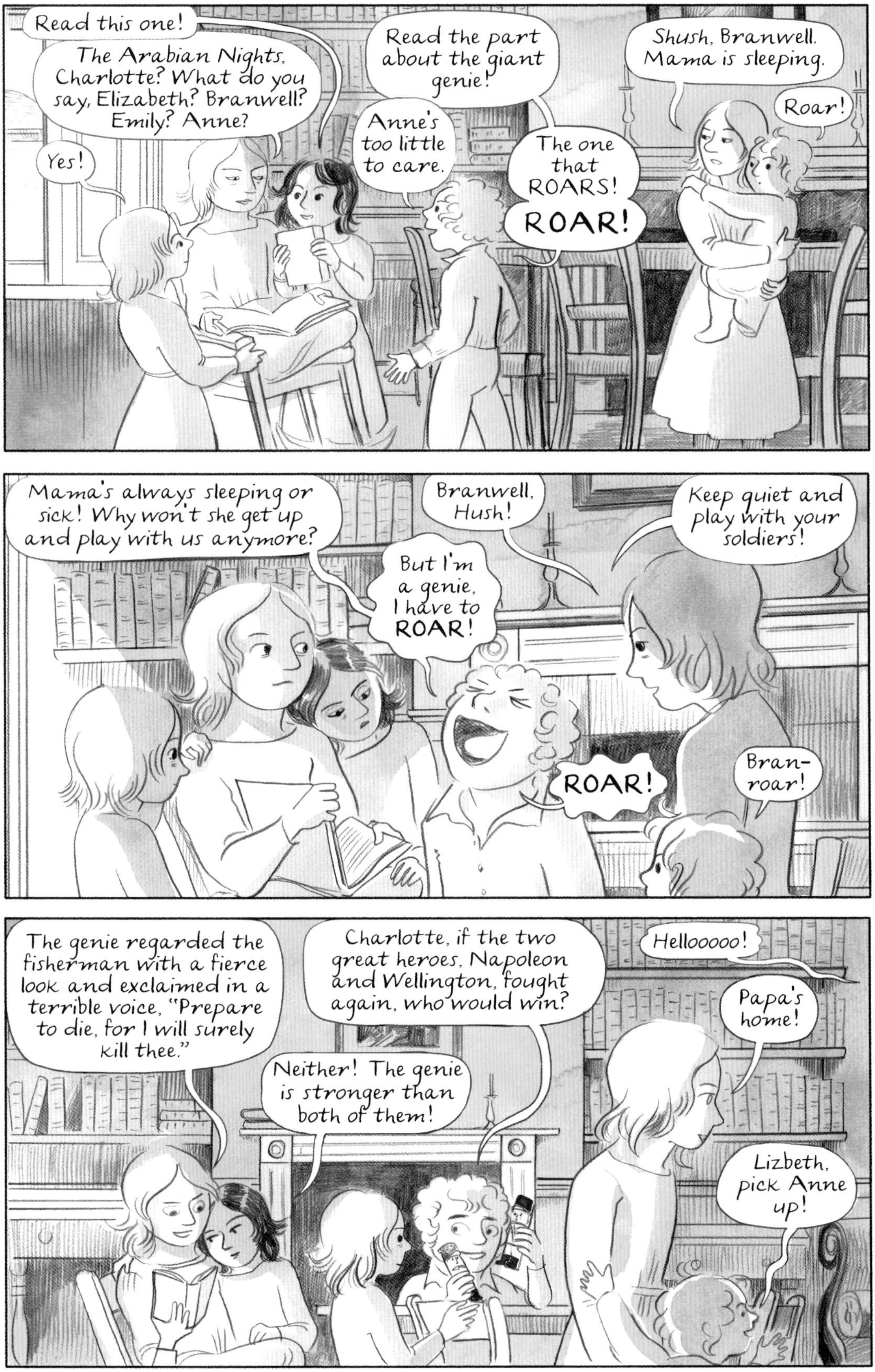
Read this one!
The Arabian Nights, Charlotte? What do you say, Elizabeth? Branwell? Emily? Anne?
Yes!
Anne's too little to care.
Read the part about the giant genie!
The one that ROARS!
ROAR!
Shush, Branwell. Mama is sleeping.
Roar!
Mama's always sleeping or sick! Why won't she get up and play with us anymore?
But I'm a genie, I have to ROAR!
Branwell, Hush!
Keep quiet and play with your soldiers!
ROAR!
Bran-roar!
The genie regarded the fisherman with a fierce look and exclaimed in a terrible voice, "Prepare to die, for I will surely kill thee."
Neither! The genie is stronger than both of them!
Charlotte, if the two great heroes, Napoleon and Wellington, fought again, who would win?
Hellooooo!
Papa's home!
Lizbeth, pick Anne up!

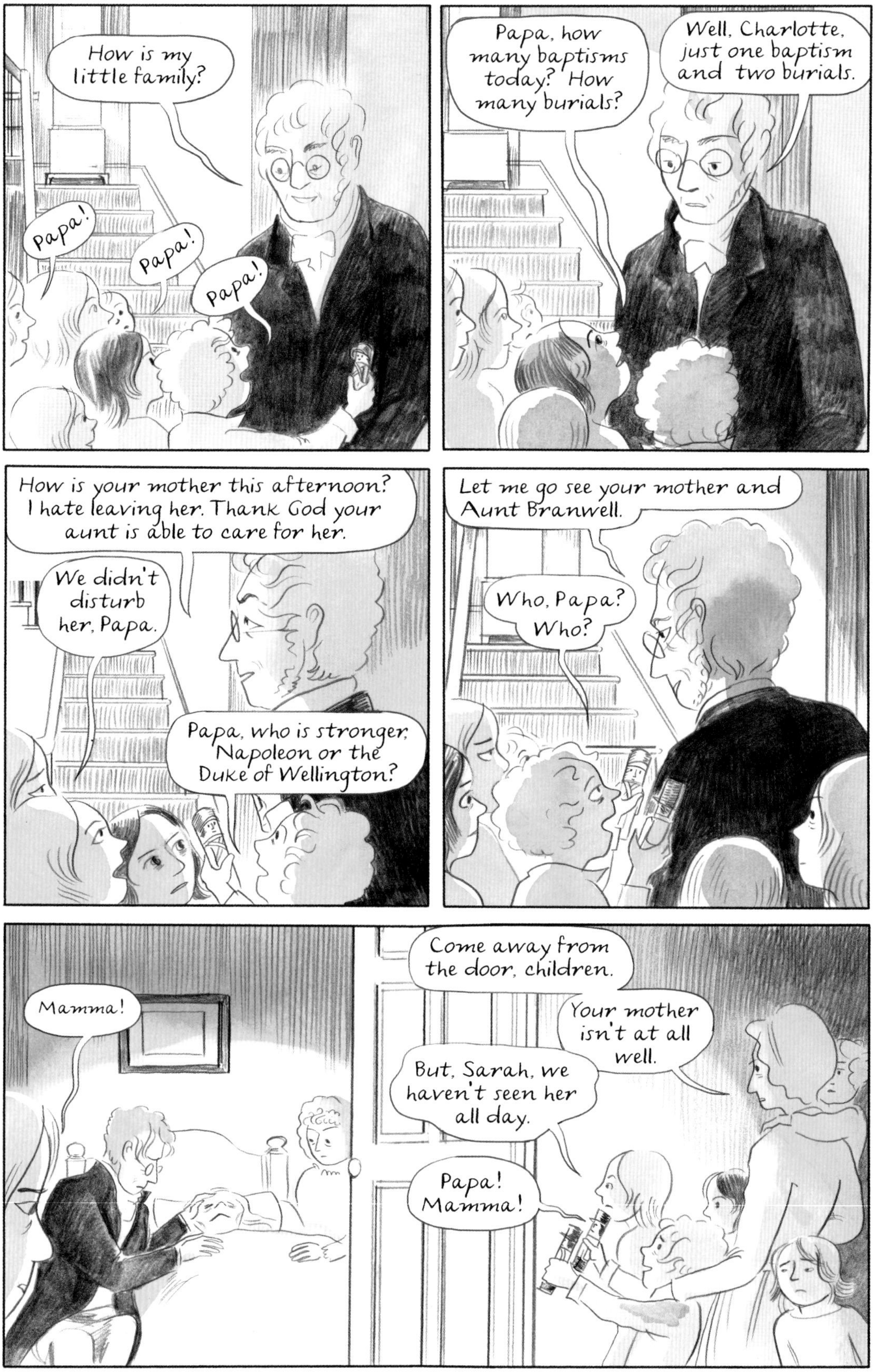
How is my little family?
Papa!
Papa!
Papa!
Papa, how many baptisms today? How many burials?
Well, Charlotte, just one baptism and two burials.
How is your mother this afternoon? I hate leaving her. Thank God your aunt is able to care for her.
We didn't disturb her, Papa.
Papa, who is stronger, Napoleon or the Duke of Wellington?
Let me go see your mother and Aunt Branwell.
Who, Papa? Who?
Mamma!
Come away from the door, children.
Your mother isn't at all well.
But, Sarah, we haven't seen her all day.
Papa! Mamma!

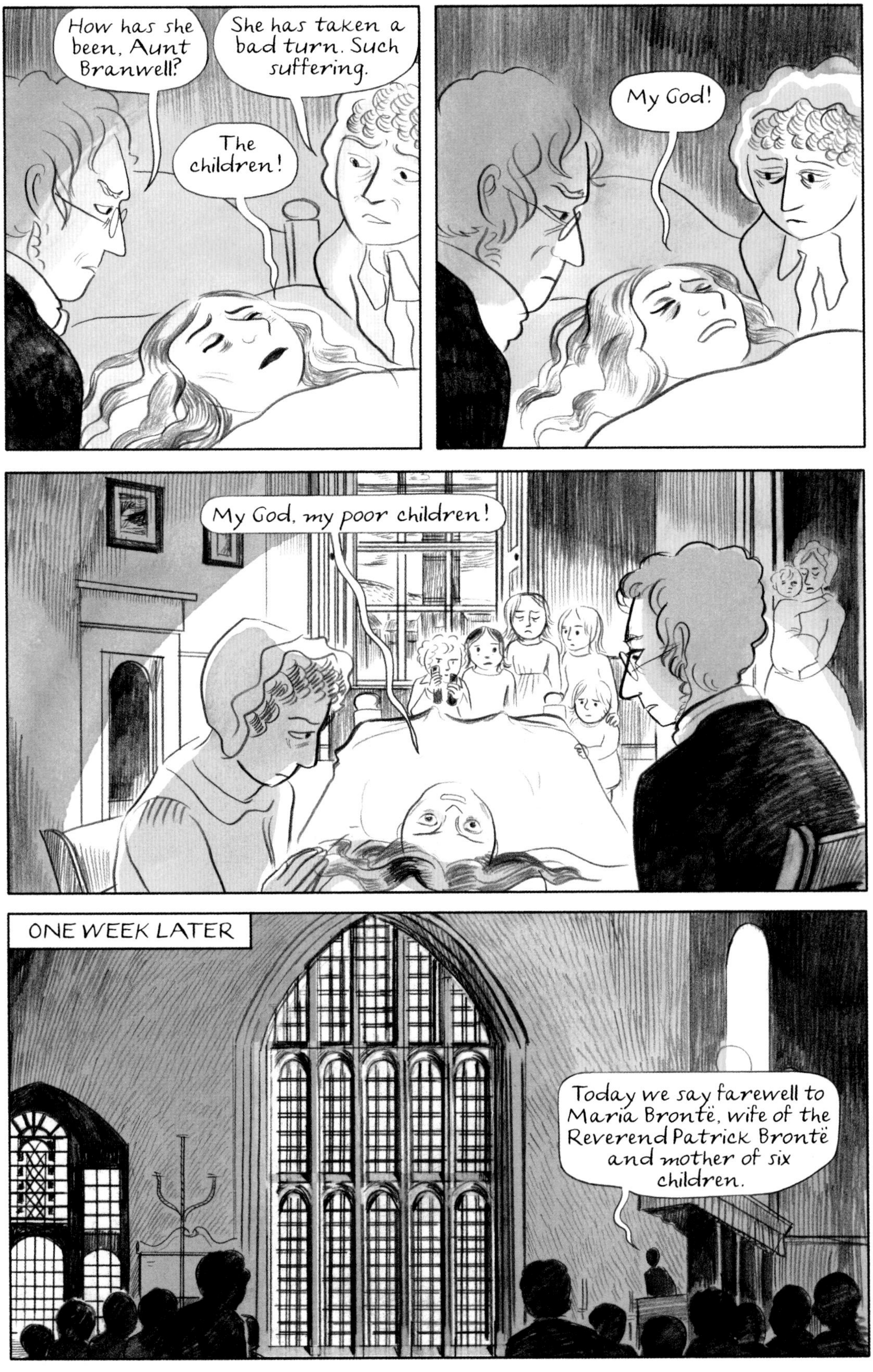
How has she been, Aunt Branwell?
She has taken a bad turn. Such suffering.
The children!
My God!
My God, my poor children!
ONE WEEK LATER
Today we say farewell to Maria Brontë, wife of the Reverend Patrick Brontë and mother of six children.

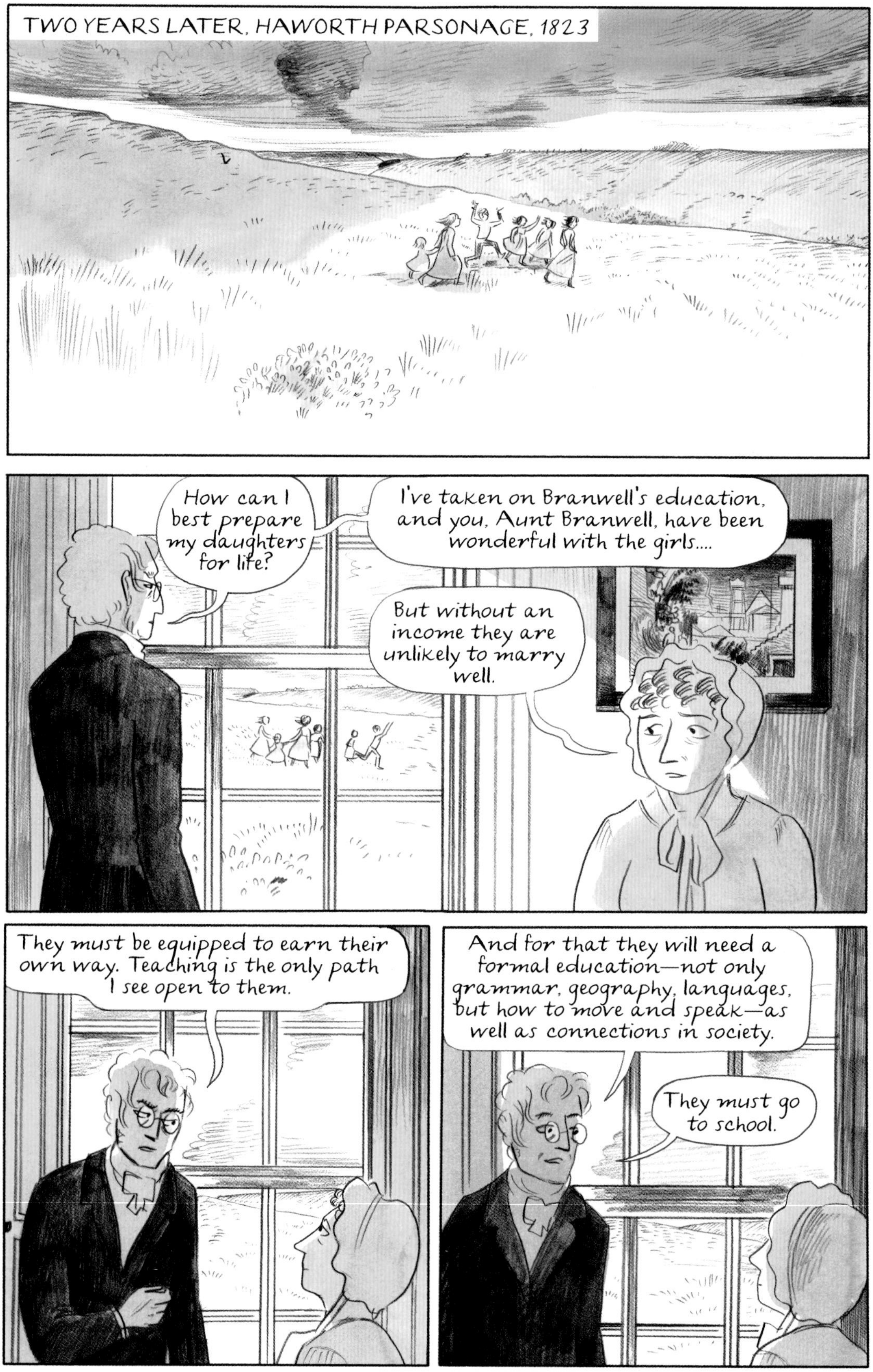
TWO YEARS LATER, HAWORTH PARSONAGE, 1823
How can I best prepare my daughters for life?
I've taken on Branwell's education, and you, Aunt Branwell, have been wonderful with the girls....
But without an income they are unlikely to marry well.
They must be equipped to earn their own way. Teaching is the only path I see open to them.
And for that they will need a formal education—not only grammar, geography, languages, but how to move and speak—as well as connections in society.
They must go to school.

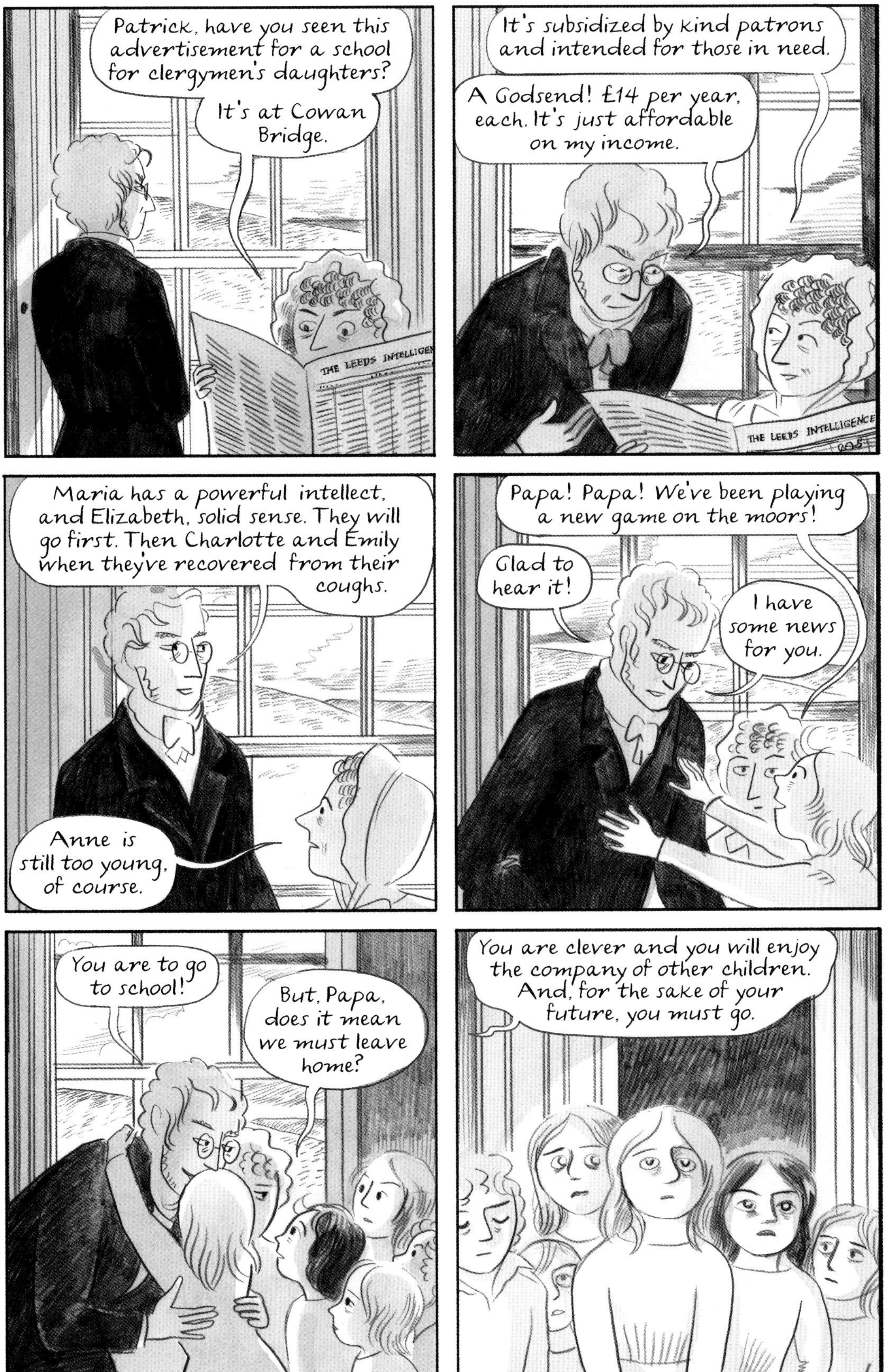
Patrick, have you seen this advertisement for a school for clergymen's daughters?
It's at Cowan Bridge.
THE LEEDS INTELLIGEN
It's subsidized by kind patrons and intended for those in need.
A Godsend! £14 per year, each. It's just affordable on my income.
THE LEEDS INTELLIGENCE
Maria has a powerful intellect, and Elizabeth, solid sense. They will go first. Then Charlotte and Emily when they've recovered from their coughs.
Anne is still too young, of course.
Papa! Papa! We've been playing a new game on the moors!
Glad to hear it!
I have some news for you.
You are to go to school!
But, Papa, does it mean we must leave home?
You are clever and you will enjoy the company of other children. And, for the sake of your future, you must go.

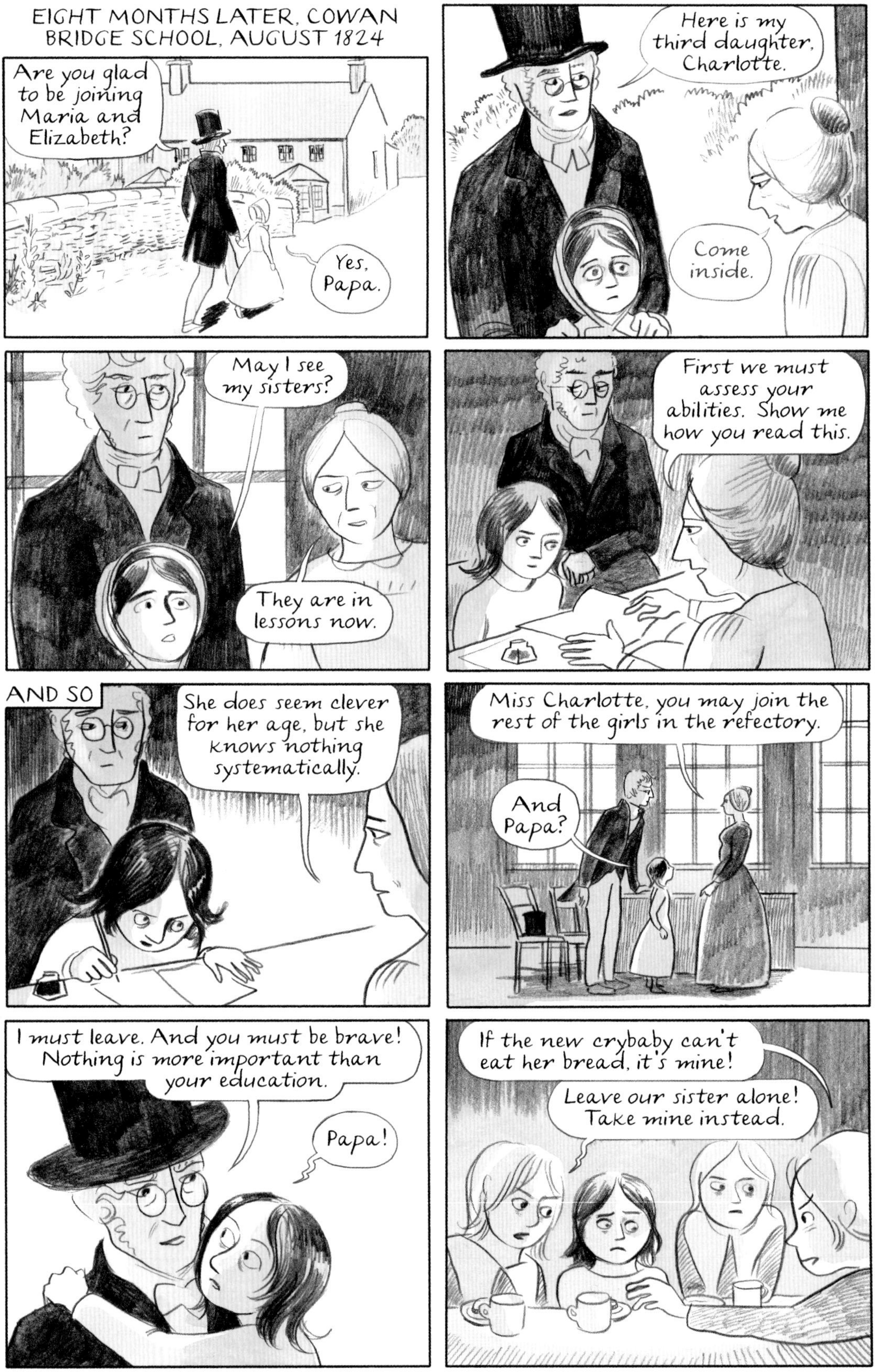
EIGHT MONTHS LATER, COWAN BRIDGE SCHOOL, AUGUST 1824
Are you glad to be joining Maria and Elizabeth?
Yes, Papa.
Here is my third daughter, Charlotte.
Come inside.
May I see my sisters?
They are in lessons now.
First we must assess your abilities. Show me how you read this.
AND SO
She does seem clever for her age, but she knows nothing systematically.
Miss Charlotte, you may join the rest of the girls in the refectory.
And Papa?
I must leave. And you must be brave! Nothing is more important than your education.
Papa!
If the new crybaby can't eat her bread, it's mine!
Leave our sister alone! Take mine instead.

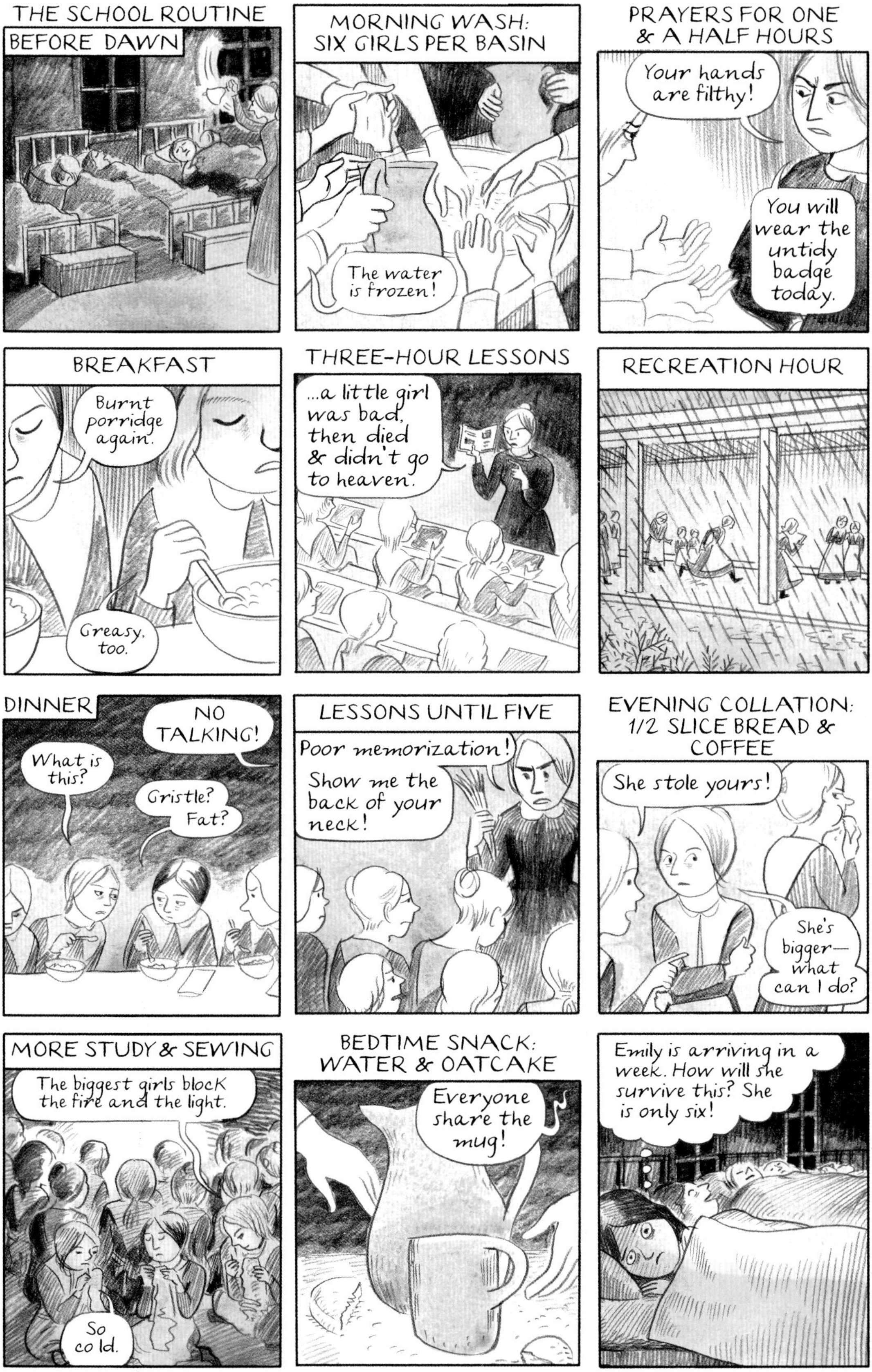
THE SCHOOL ROUTINE
BEFORE DAWN
MORNING WASH: SIX GIRLS PER BASIN
The water is frozen!
PRAYERS FOR ONE & A HALF HOURS
Your hands are filthy!
You will wear the untidy badge today.
BREAKFAST
Burnt porridge again.
Greasy, too.
THREE-HOUR LESSONS
...a little girl was bad, then died & didn't go to heaven.
RECREATION HOUR
DINNER
NO TALKING!
What is this?
Gristle? Fat?
LESSONS UNTIL FIVE
Poor memorization!
Show me the back of your neck!
EVENING COLLATION: 1/2 SLICE BREAD & COFFEE
She stole yours!
She's bigger— what can I do?
MORE STUDY & SEWING
The biggest girls block the fire and the light.
So cold.
BEDTIME SNACK: WATER & OATCAKE
Everyone share the mug!
Emily is arriving in a week. How will she survive this? She is only six!

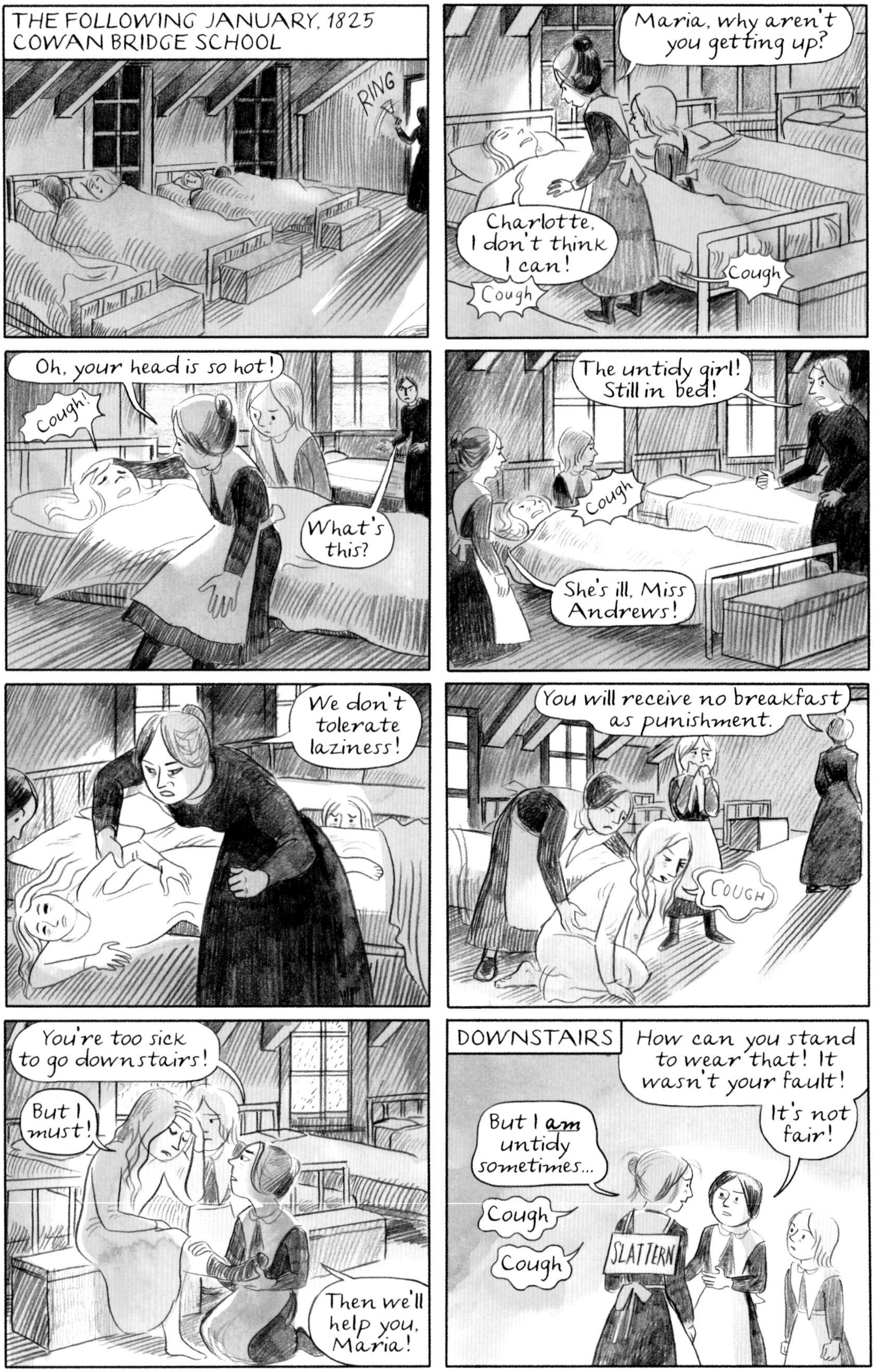
THE FOLLOWING JANUARY, 1825
COWAN BRIDGE SCHOOL
RING
Maria, why aren't you getting up?
Charlotte, I don't think I can!
Cough
Cough
Oh, your head is so hot!
Cough!
What's this?
The untidy girl! Still in bed!
Cough
She's ill, Miss Andrews!
We don't tolerate laziness!
You will receive no breakfast as punishment.
COUGH
You're too sick to go downstairs!
But I must!
Then we'll help you, Maria!
DOWNSTAIRS
How can you stand to wear that! It wasn't your fault!
It's not fair!
But I **am** untidy sometimes...
Cough
Cough
SLATTERN

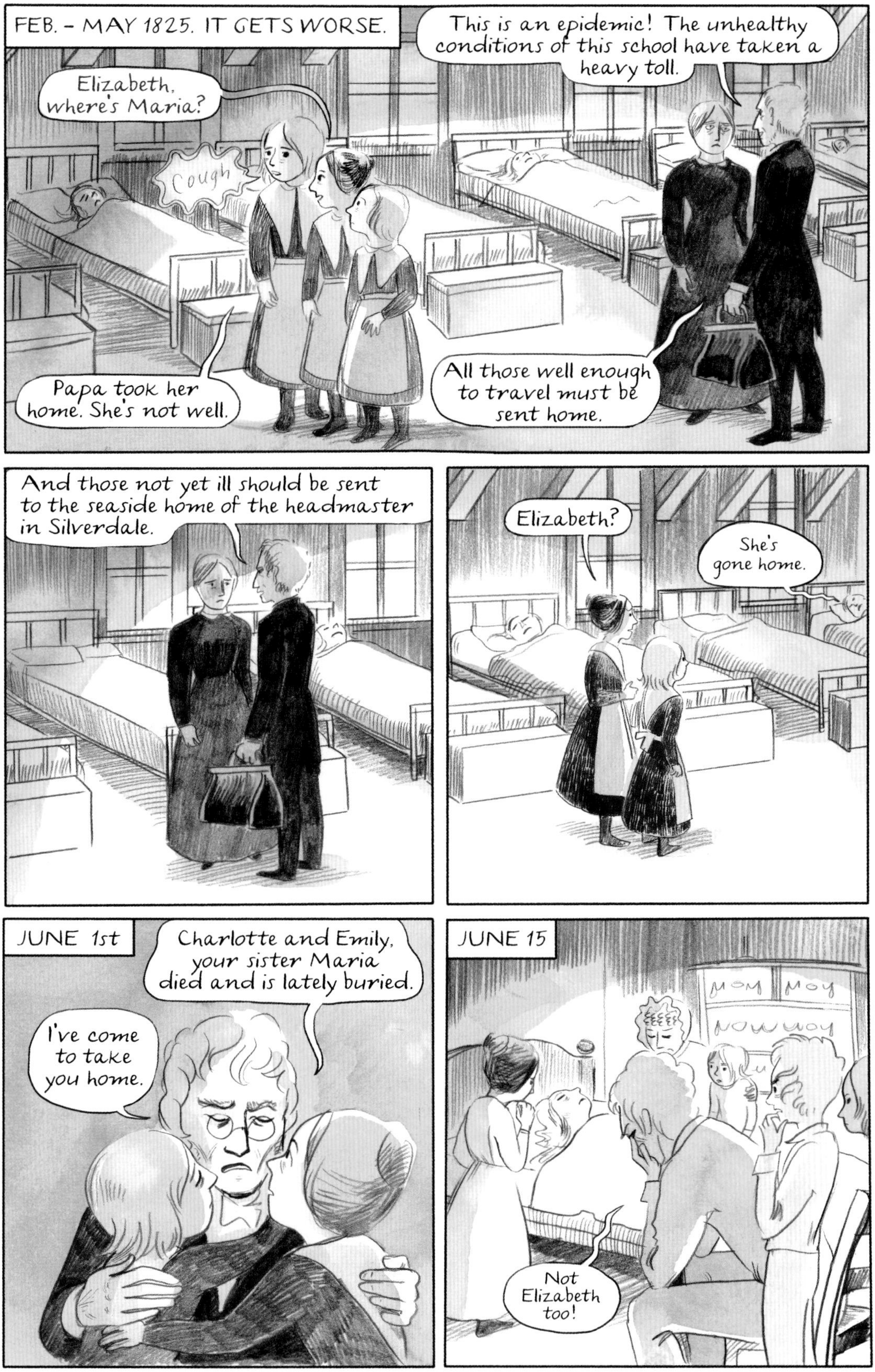
FEB. – MAY 1825. IT GETS WORSE.
Elizabeth, where's Maria?
Cough
This is an epidemic! The unhealthy conditions of this school have taken a heavy toll.
Papa took her home. She's not well.
All those well enough to travel must be sent home.
And those not yet ill should be sent to the seaside home of the headmaster in Silverdale.
Elizabeth?
She's gone home.
JUNE 1st
Charlotte and Emily, your sister Maria died and is lately buried.
I've come to take you home.
JUNE 15
Not Elizabeth too!

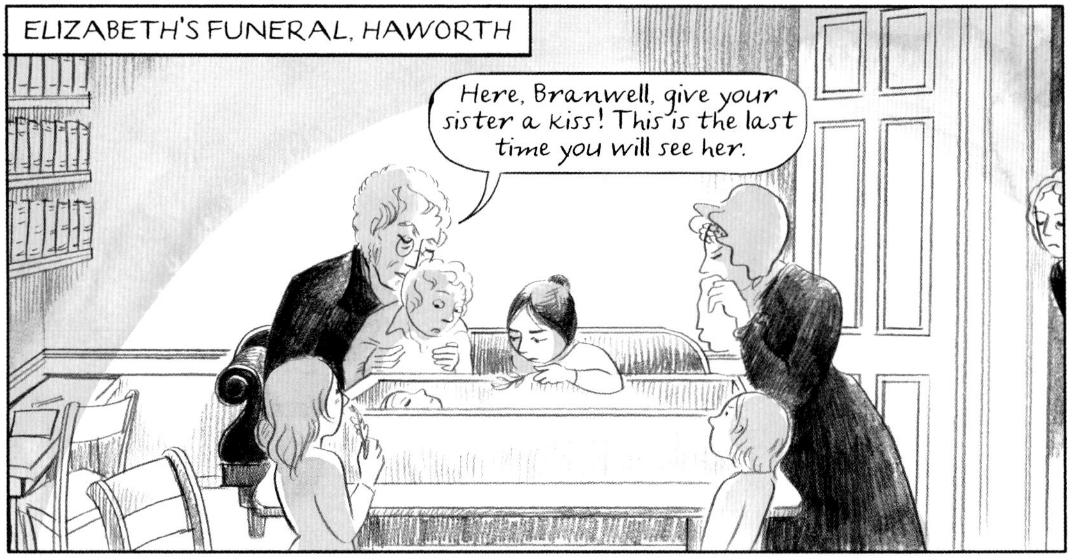
ELIZABETH'S FUNERAL, HAWORTH
Here, Branwell, give your sister a kiss! This is the last time you will see her.

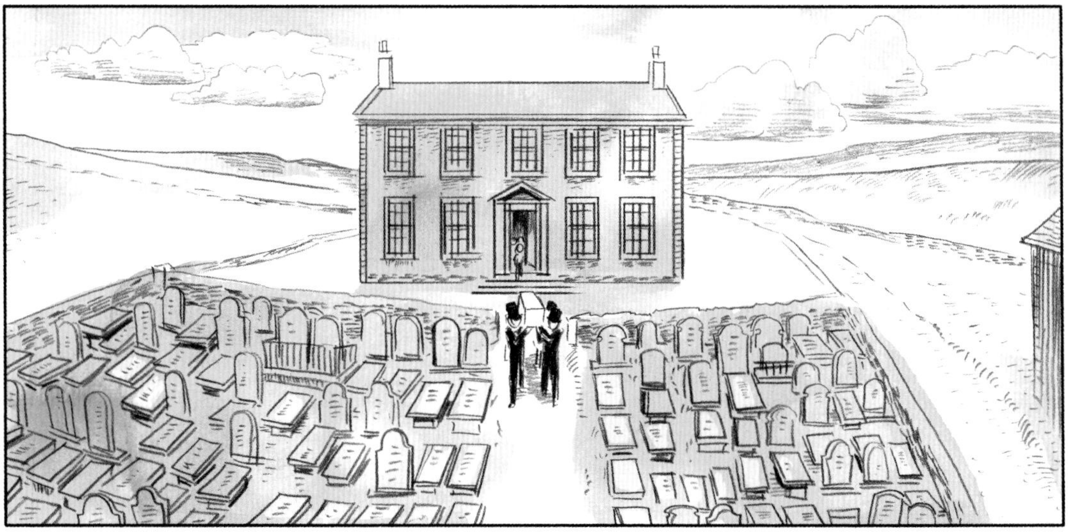

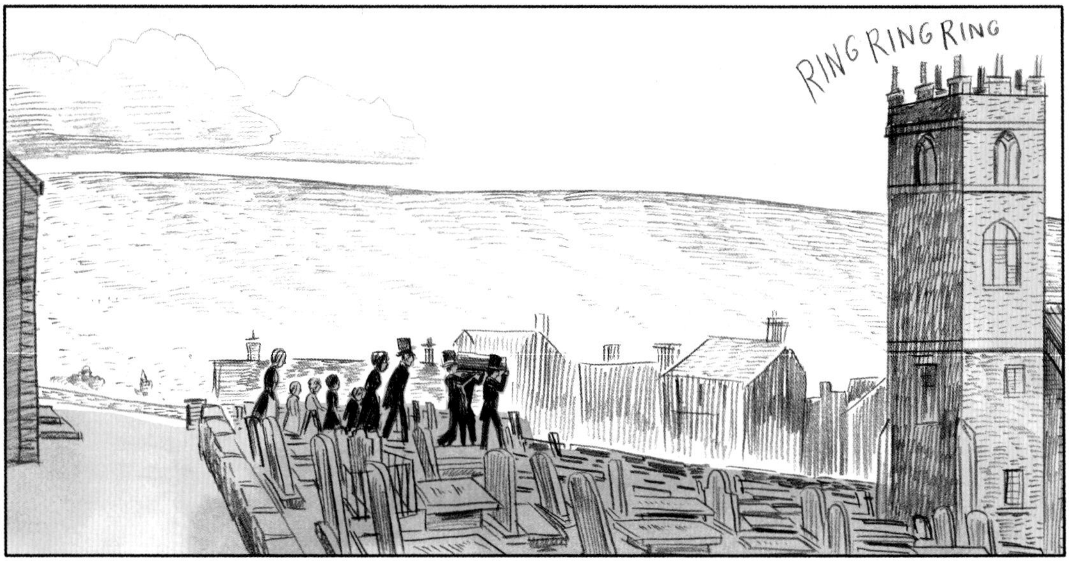
RING RING RING

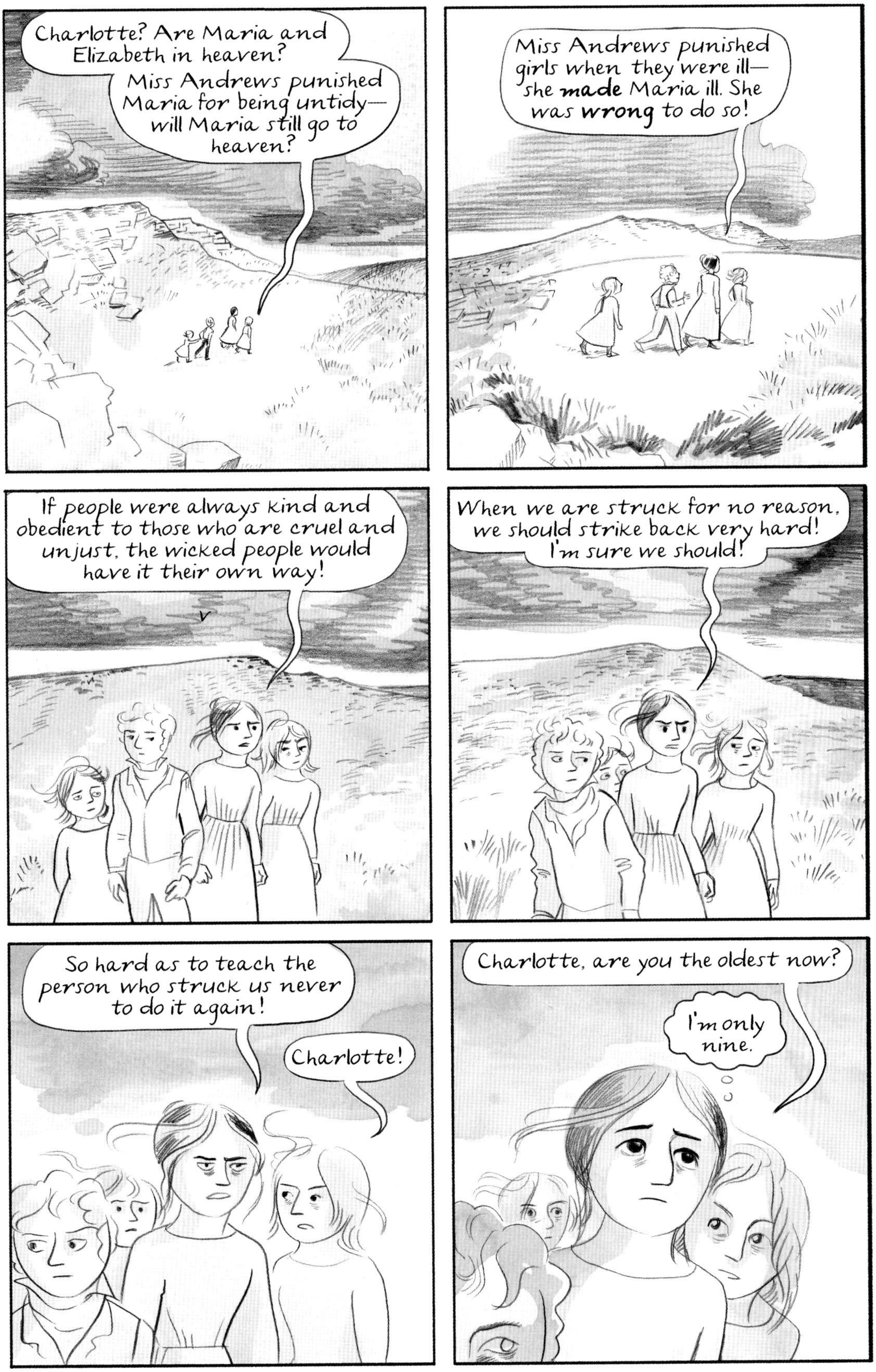
Charlotte? Are Maria and Elizabeth in heaven?
Miss Andrews punished Maria for being untidy— will Maria still go to heaven?
Miss Andrews punished girls when they were ill— she **made** Maria ill. She was **wrong** to do so!
If people were always kind and obedient to those who are cruel and unjust, the wicked people would have it their own way!
When we are struck for no reason, we should strike back very hard! I'm sure we should!
So hard as to teach the person who struck us never to do it again!
Charlotte!
Charlotte, are you the oldest now?
I'm only nine.

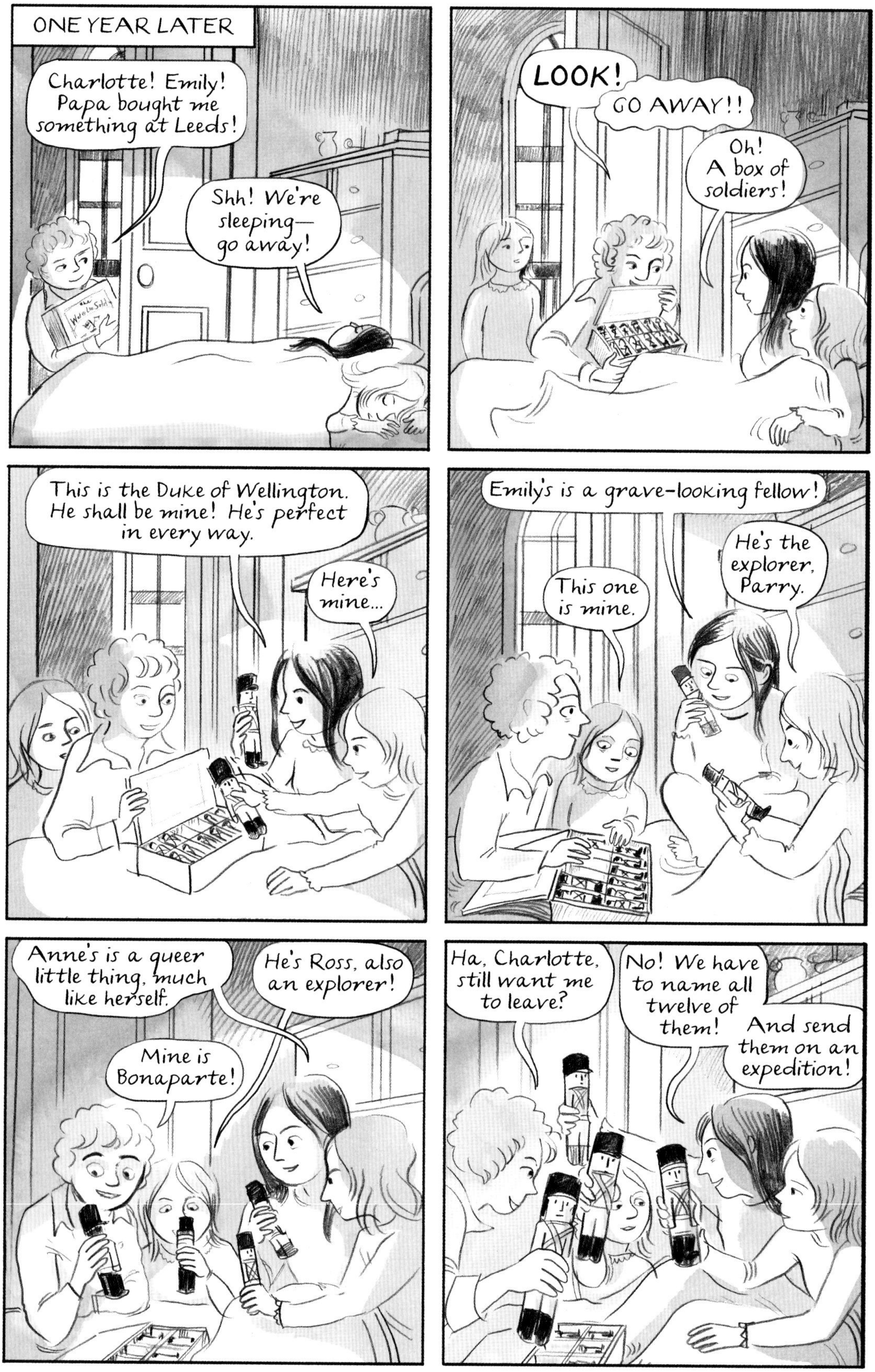
ONE YEAR LATER
Charlotte! Emily! Papa bought me something at Leeds!
Shh! We're sleeping—go away!
LOOK!
GO AWAY!!
Oh! A box of soldiers!
This is the Duke of Wellington. He shall be mine! He's perfect in every way.
Here's mine...
Emily's is a grave-looking fellow!
This one is mine.
He's the explorer, Parry.
Anne's is a queer little thing, much like herself.
He's Ross, also an explorer!
Mine is Bonaparte!
Ha, Charlotte, still want me to leave?
No! We have to name all twelve of them!
And send them on an expedition!

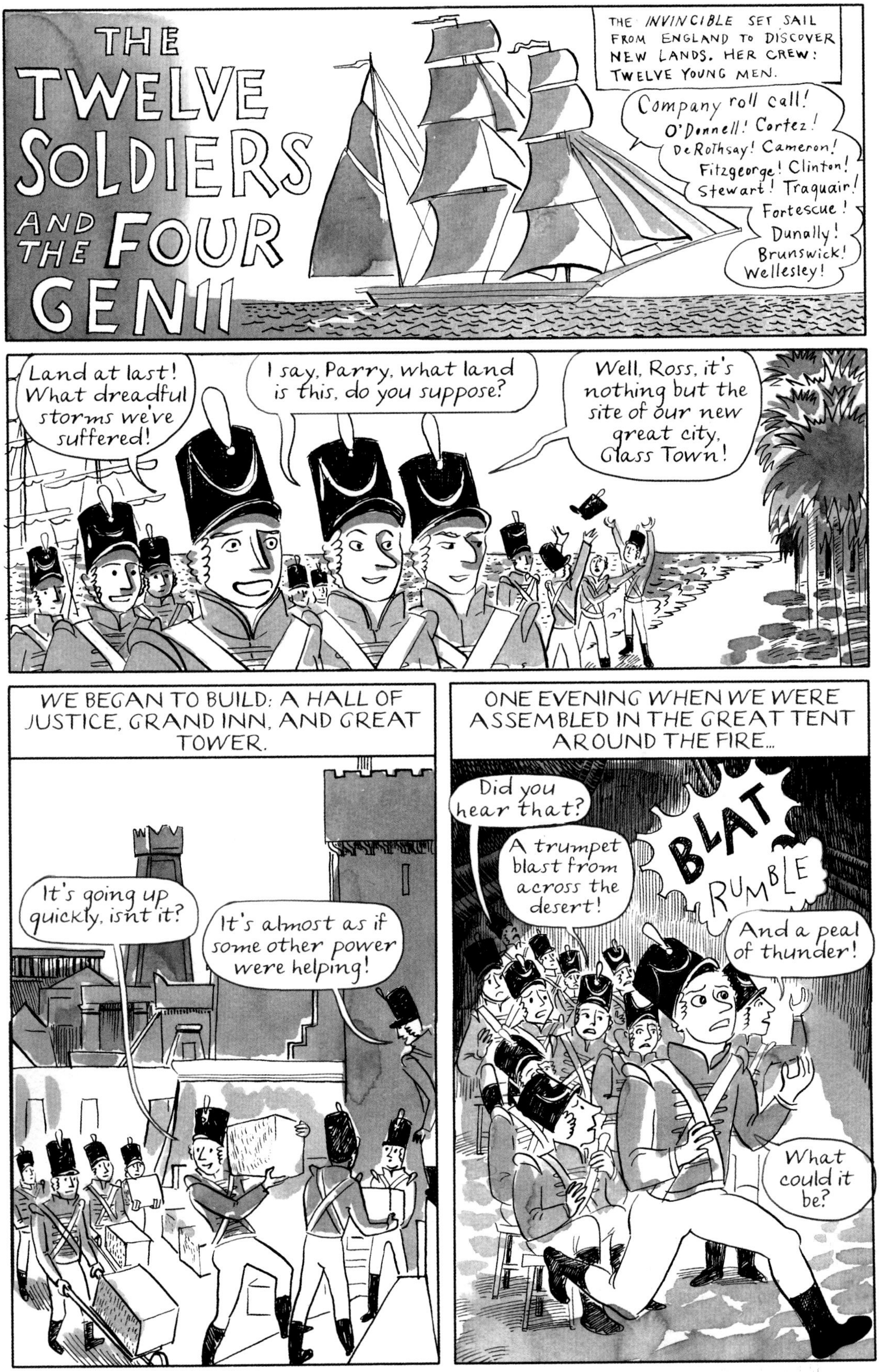
THE TWELVE SOLDIERS AND THE FOUR GENII
THE INVINCIBLE SET SAIL FROM ENGLAND TO DISCOVER NEW LANDS. HER CREW: TWELVE YOUNG MEN.
Company roll call! O'Donnell! Cortez! DeRothsay! Cameron! Fitzgeorge! Clinton! Stewart! Traquair! Fortescue! Dunally! Brunswick! Wellesley!
Land at last! What dreadful storms we've suffered!
I say, Parry, what land is this, do you suppose?
Well, Ross, it's nothing but the site of our new great city, Glass Town!
WE BEGAN TO BUILD: A HALL OF JUSTICE, GRAND INN, AND GREAT TOWER.
It's going up quickly, isnt it?
It's almost as if some other power were helping!
ONE EVENING WHEN WE WERE ASSEMBLED IN THE GREAT TENT AROUND THE FIRE...
Did you hear that?
A trumpet blast from across the desert!
BLAT
RUMBLE
And a peal of thunder!
What could it be?

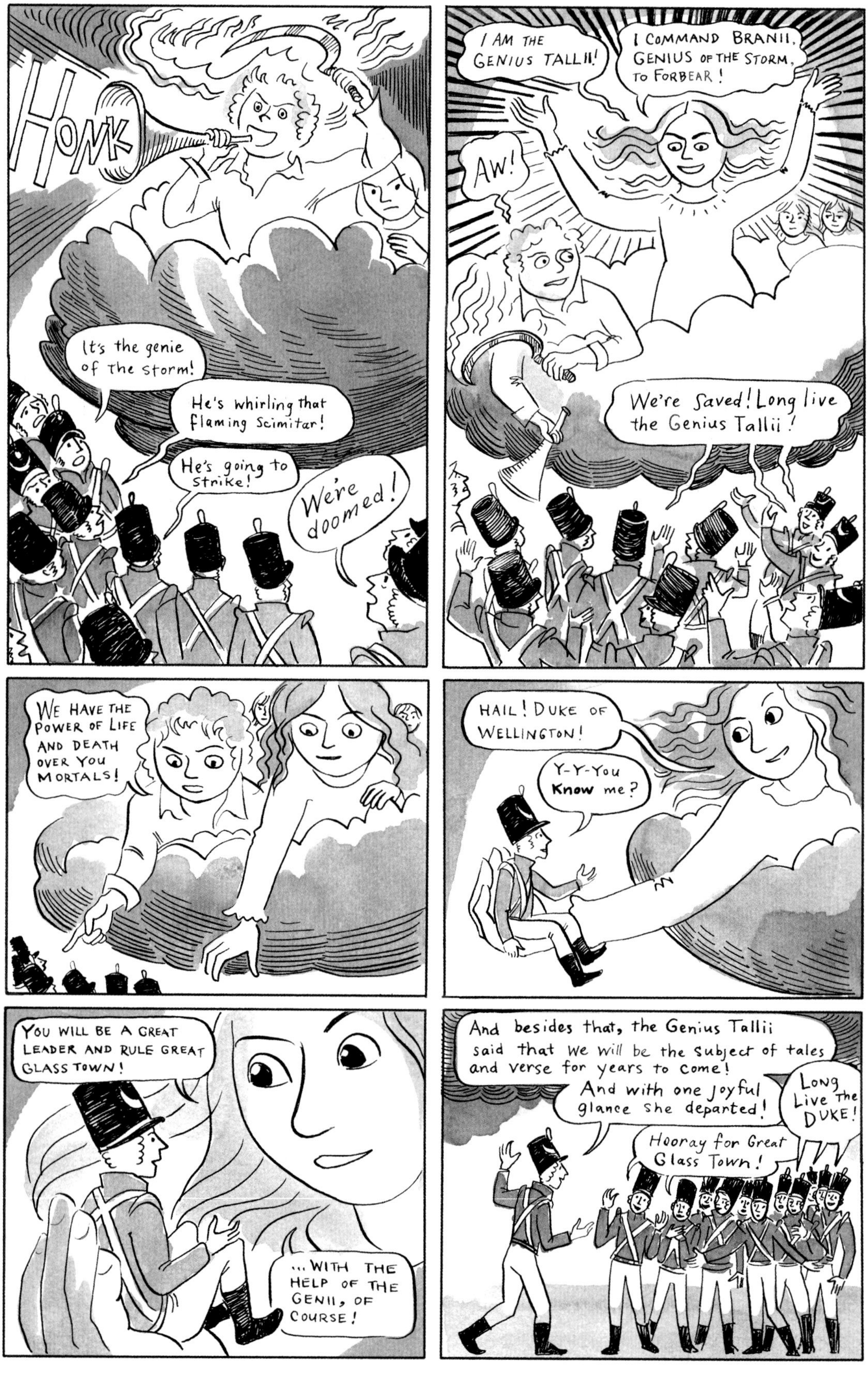
HONK
It's the genie of the storm!
He's whirling that flaming Scimitar!
He's going to strike!
We're doomed!
I AM THE GENIUS TALLII!
I COMMAND BRANII, GENIUS OF THE STORM, TO FORBEAR!
AW!
We're saved! Long live the Genius Tallii!
WE HAVE THE POWER OF LIFE AND DEATH OVER YOU MORTALS!
HAIL! DUKE OF WELLINGTON!
Y-Y-You **Know** me?
YOU WILL BE A GREAT LEADER AND RULE GREAT GLASS TOWN!
...WITH THE HELP OF THE GENII, OF COURSE!
And besides that, the Genius Tallii said that we will be the subject of tales and verse for years to come!
And with one joyful glance she departed!
Long Live the DUKE!
Hooray for Great Glass Town!

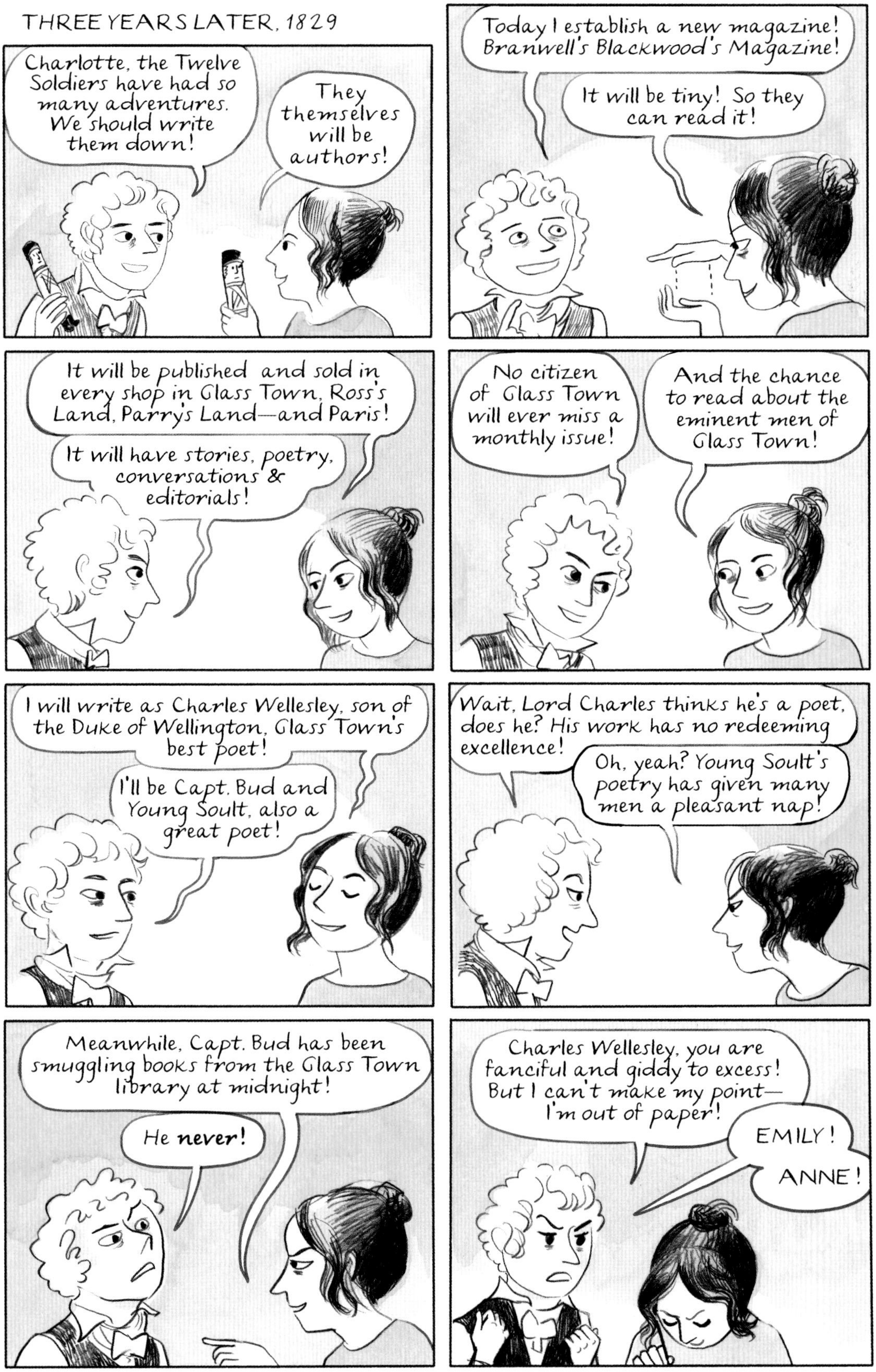
THREE YEARS LATER, 1829
Charlotte, the Twelve Soldiers have had so many adventures. We should write them down!
They themselves will be authors!
Today I establish a new magazine! Branwell's Blackwood's Magazine!
It will be tiny! So they can read it!
It will be published and sold in every shop in Glass Town, Ross's Land, Parry's Land—and Paris!
It will have stories, poetry, conversations & editorials!
No citizen of Glass Town will ever miss a monthly issue!
And the chance to read about the eminent men of Glass Town!
I will write as Charles Wellesley, son of the Duke of Wellington, Glass Town's best poet!
I'll be Capt. Bud and Young Soult, also a great poet!
Wait, Lord Charles thinks he's a poet, does he? His work has no redeeming excellence!
Oh, yeah? Young Soult's poetry has given many men a pleasant nap!
Meanwhile, Capt. Bud has been smuggling books from the Glass Town library at midnight!
He **never**!
Charles Wellesley, you are fanciful and giddy to excess! But I can't make my point— I'm out of paper!
EMILY!
ANNE!

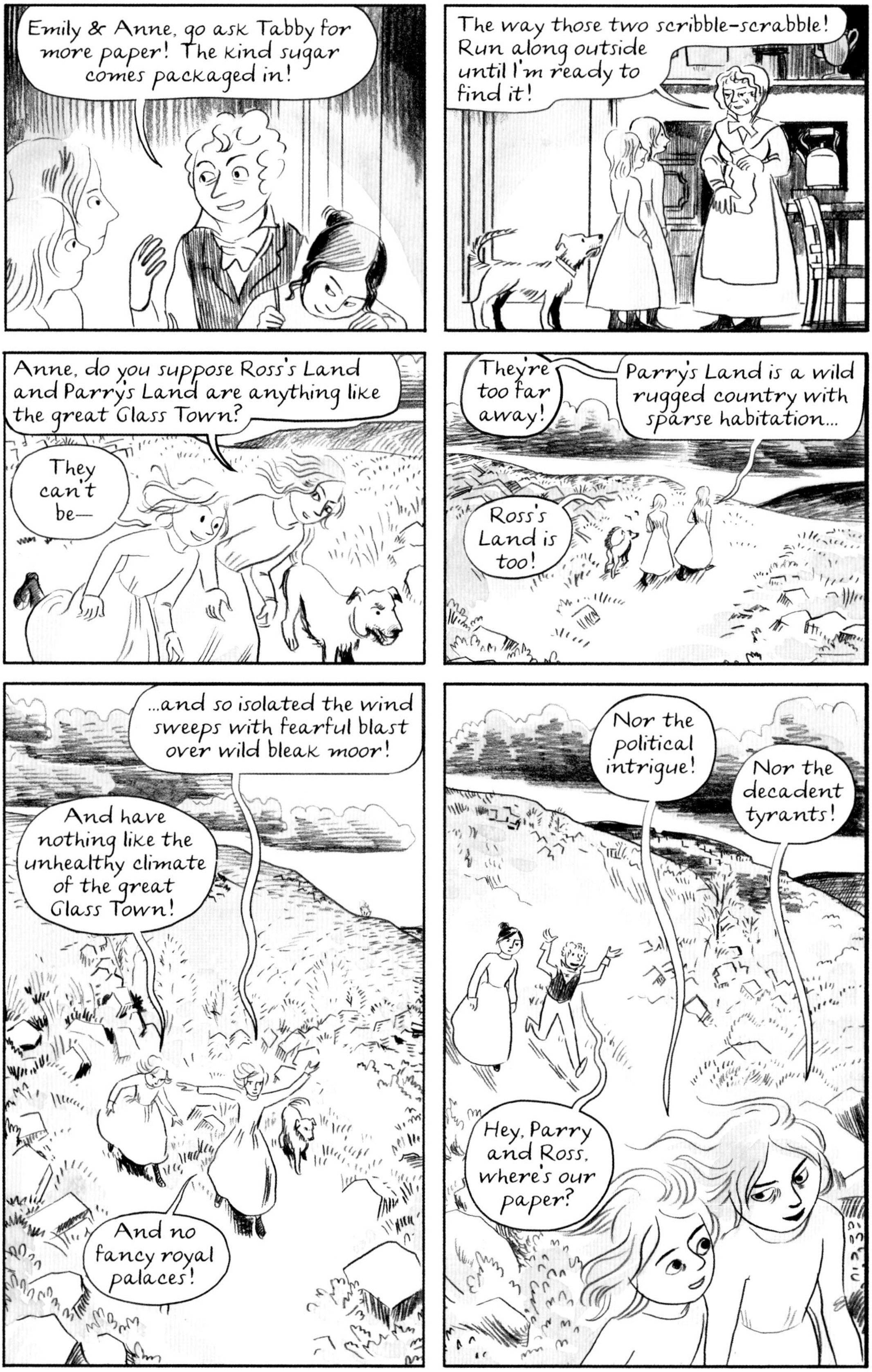
Emily & Anne, go ask Tabby for more paper! The kind sugar comes packaged in!
The way those two scribble-scrabble! Run along outside until I'm ready to find it!
Anne, do you suppose Ross's Land and Parry's Land are anything like the great Glass Town?
They can't be—
They're too far away!
Parry's Land is a wild rugged country with sparse habitation...
Ross's Land is too!
...and so isolated the wind sweeps with fearful blast over wild bleak moor!
And have nothing like the unhealthy climate of the great Glass Town!
And no fancy royal palaces!
Nor the political intrigue!
Nor the decadent tyrants!
Hey, Parry and Ross, where's our paper?

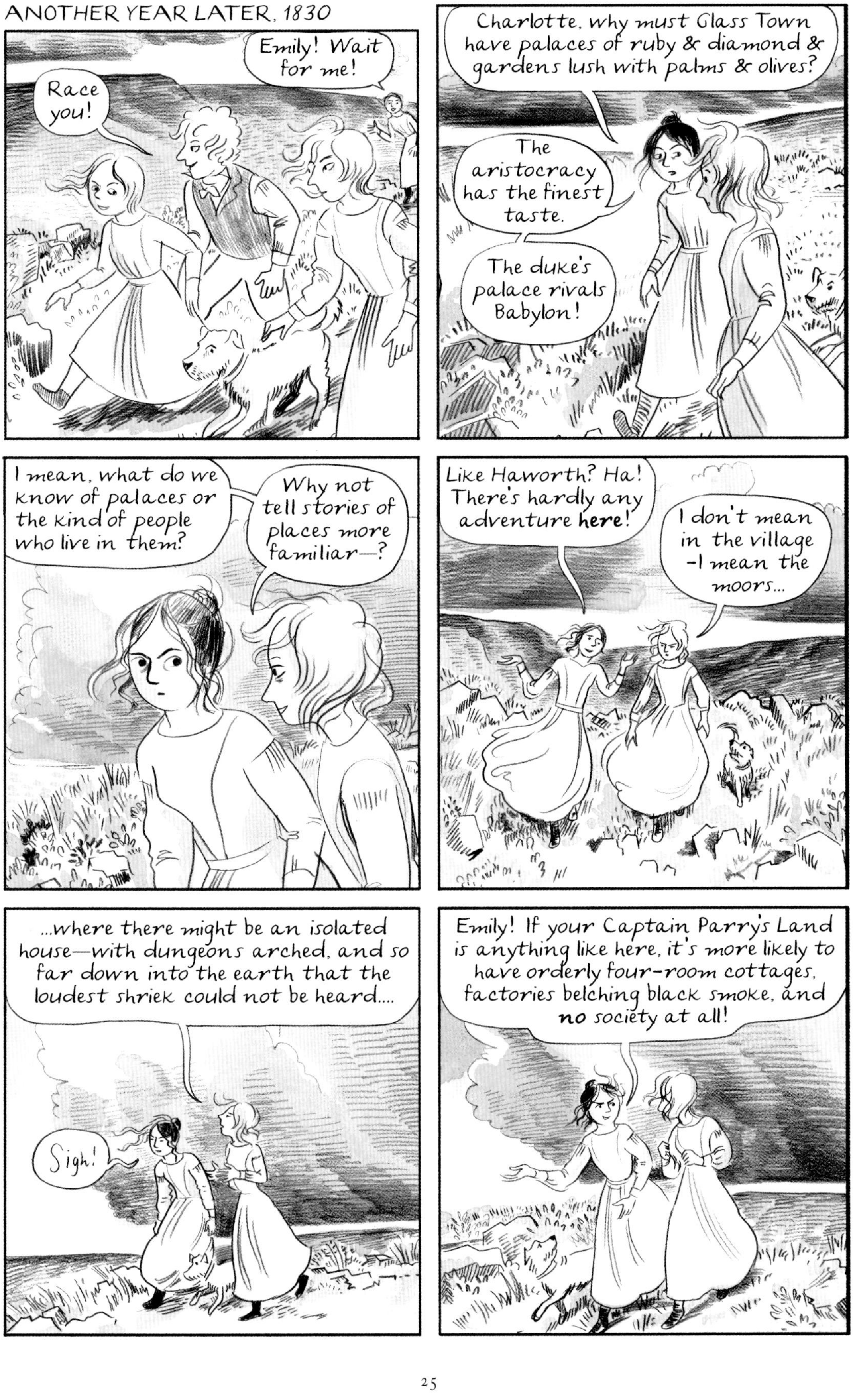

ANOTHER YEAR LATER, 1830
Race you!
Emily! Wait for me!
Charlotte, why must Glass Town have palaces of ruby & diamond & gardens lush with palms & olives?
The aristocracy has the finest taste.
The duke's palace rivals Babylon!
I mean, what do we know of palaces or the kind of people who live in them?
Why not tell stories of places more familiar—?
Like Haworth? Ha! There's hardly any adventure **here**!
I don't mean in the village -I mean the moors...
...where there might be an isolated house—with dungeons arched, and so far down into the earth that the loudest shriek could not be heard....
Sigh!
Emily! If your Captain Parry's Land is anything like here, it's more likely to have orderly four-room cottages, factories belching black smoke, and **no** society at all!

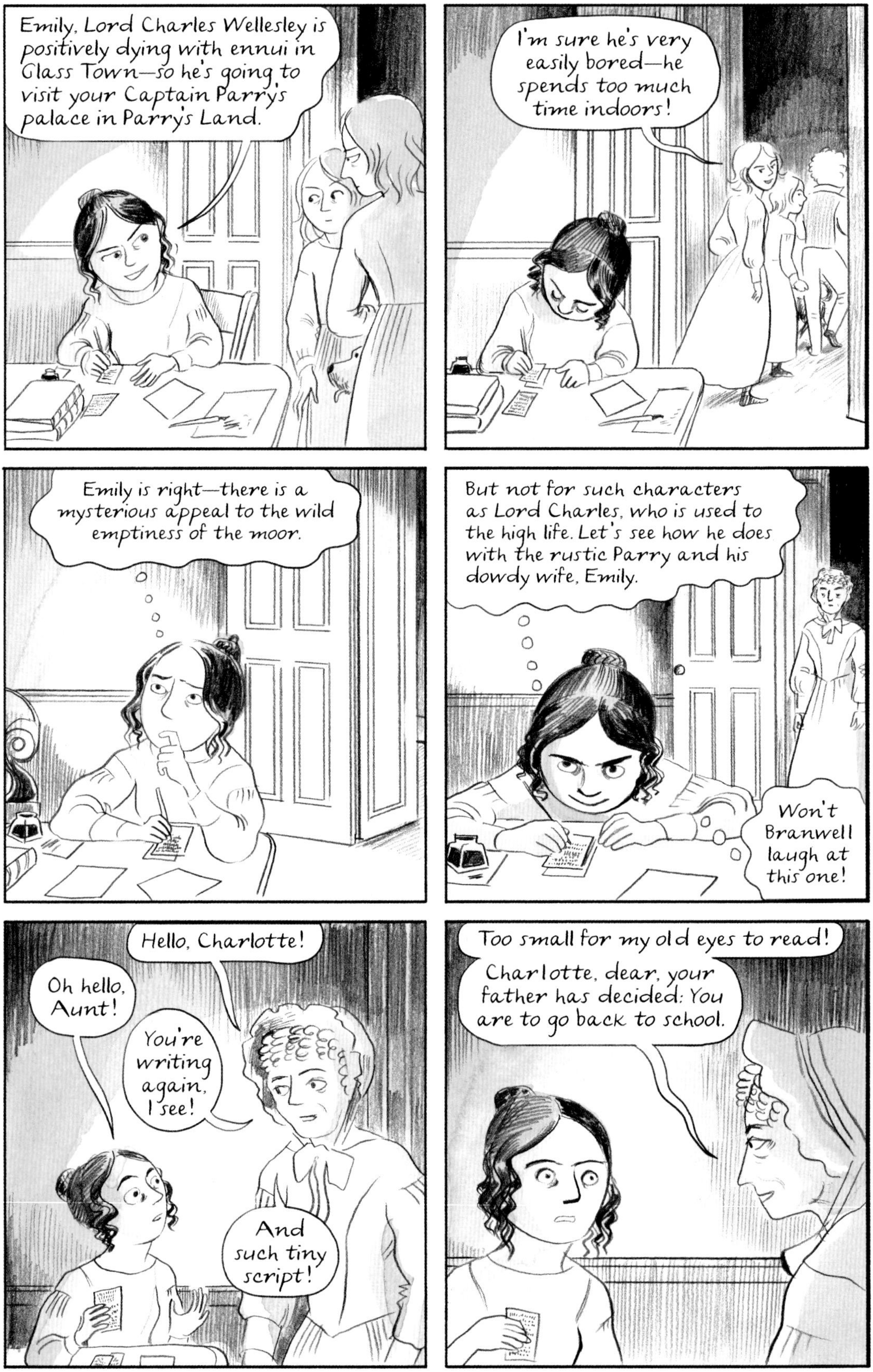

Emily, Lord Charles Wellesley is positively dying with ennui in Glass Town—so he's going to visit your Captain Parry's palace in Parry's Land.
I'm sure he's very easily bored—he spends too much time indoors!
Emily is right—there is a mysterious appeal to the wild emptiness of the moor.
But not for such characters as Lord Charles, who is used to the high life. Let's see how he does with the rustic Parry and his dowdy wife, Emily.
Won't Branwell laugh at this one!
Hello, Charlotte!
Oh hello, Aunt!
You're writing again, I see!
And such tiny script!
Too small for my old eyes to read!
Charlotte, dear, your father has decided: You are to go back to school.

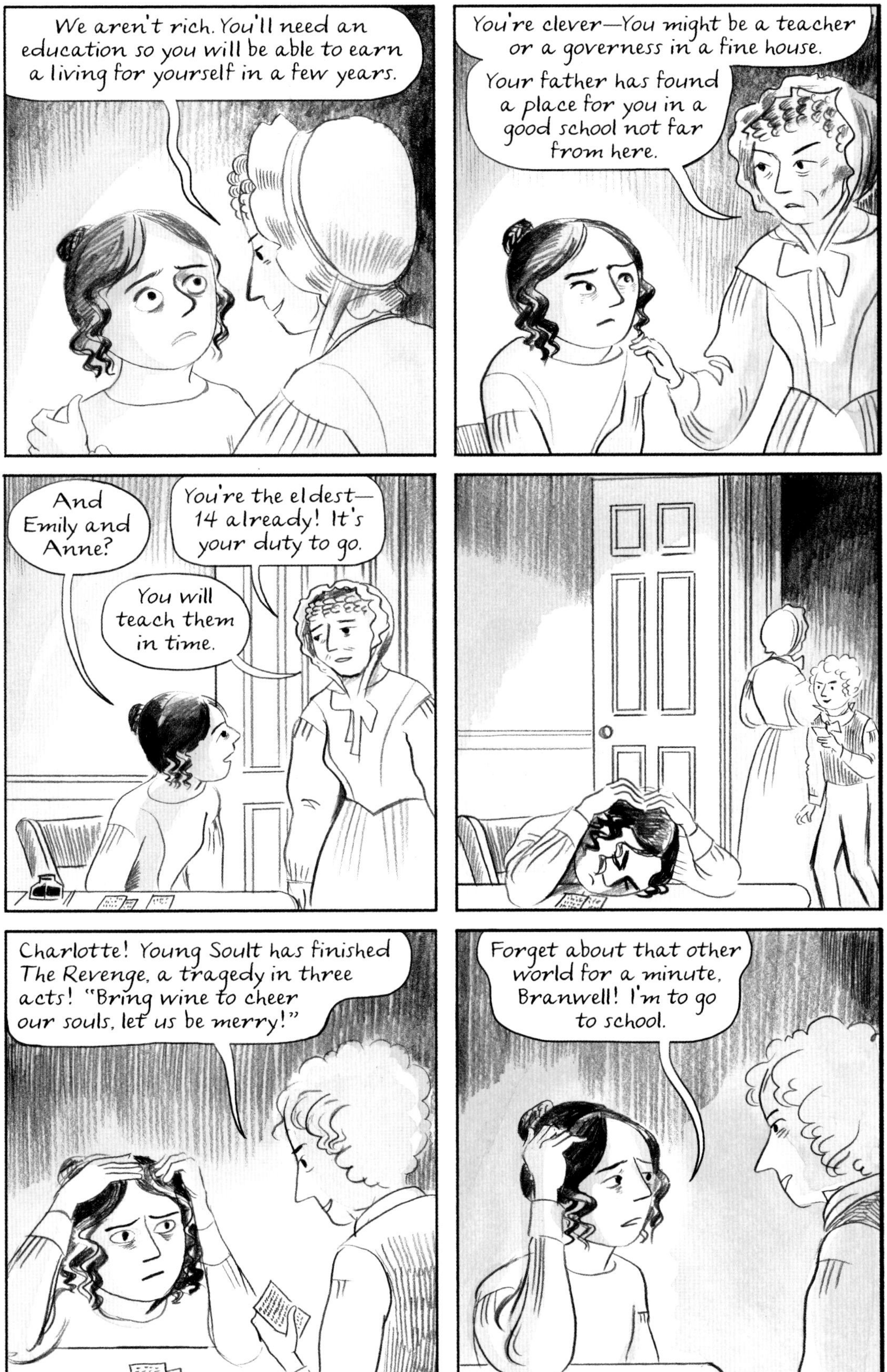
We aren't rich. You'll need an education so you will be able to earn a living for yourself in a few years.
You're clever—You might be a teacher or a governess in a fine house.
Your father has found a place for you in a good school not far from here.
And Emily and Anne?
You're the eldest— 14 already! It's your duty to go.
You will teach them in time.
Charlotte! Young Soult has finished The Revenge, a tragedy in three acts! "Bring wine to cheer our souls, let us be merry!"
Forget about that other world for a minute, Branwell! I'm to go to school.

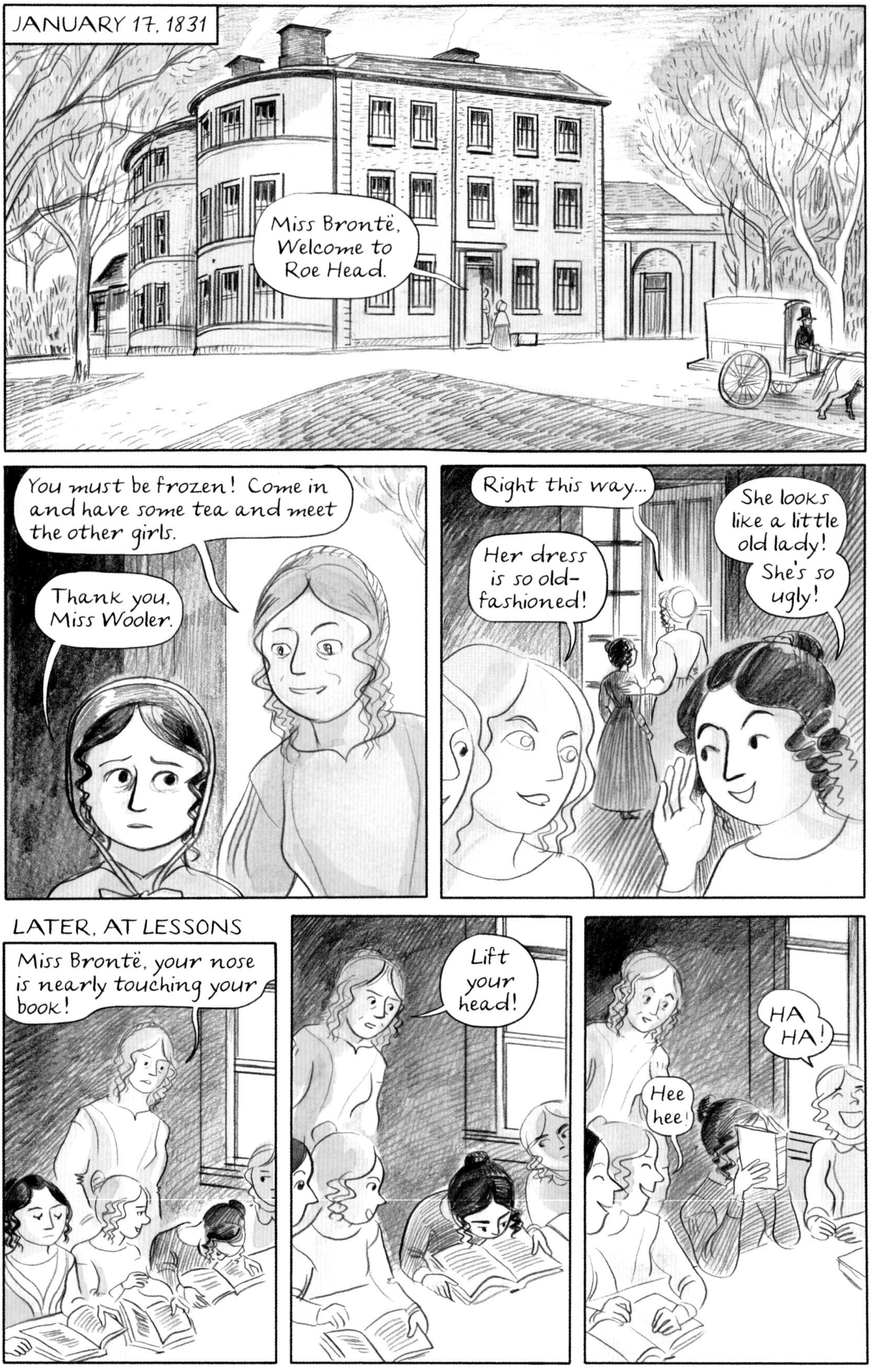
JANUARY 17, 1831
Miss Brontë, Welcome to Roe Head.
You must be frozen! Come in and have some tea and meet the other girls.
Thank you, Miss Wooler.
Right this way...
Her dress is so old-fashioned!
She looks like a little old lady!
She's so ugly!
LATER, AT LESSONS
Miss Brontë, your nose is nearly touching your book!
Lift your head!
HA HA!
Hee hee!

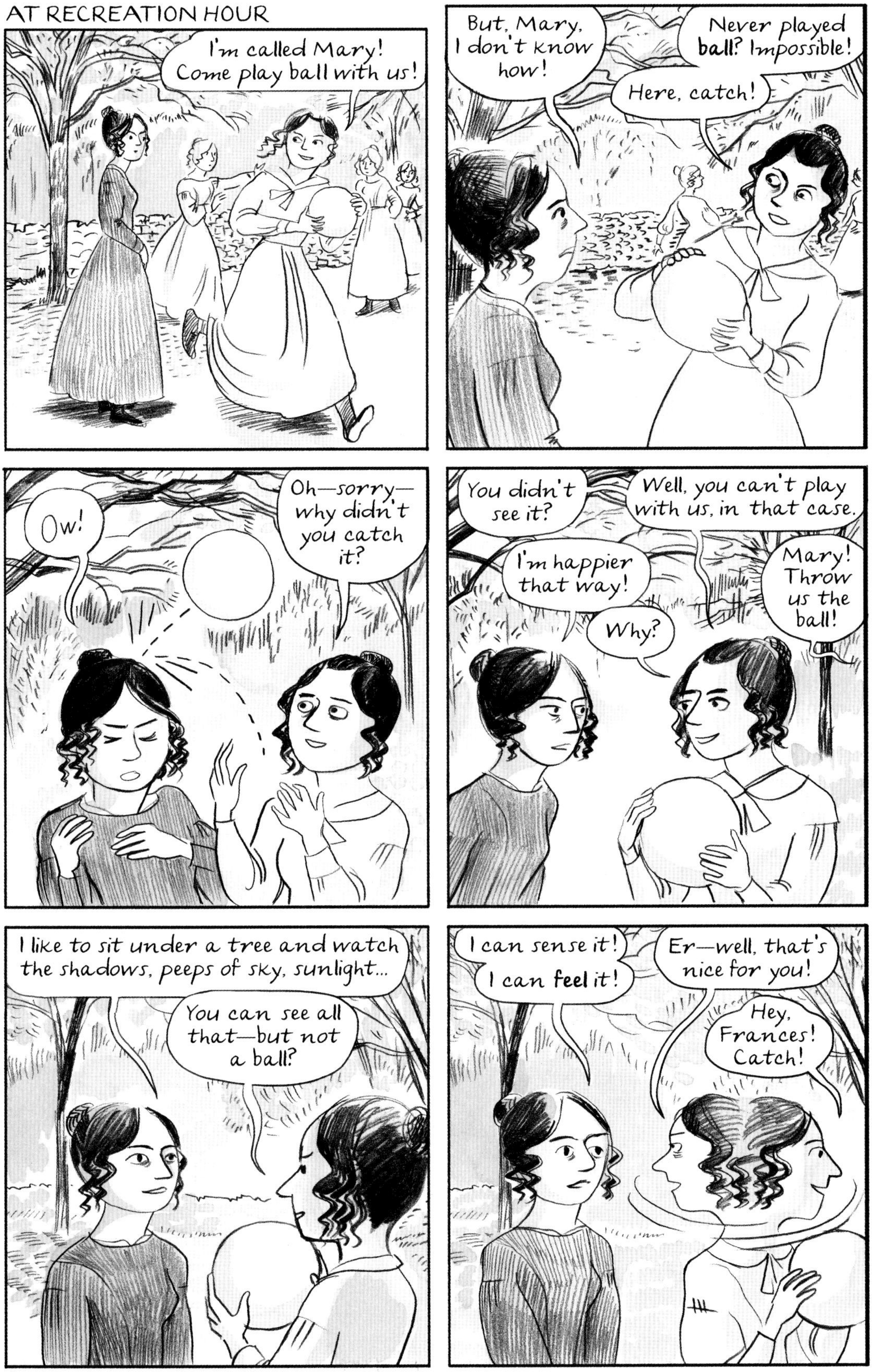
AT RECREATION HOUR
I'm called Mary! Come play ball with us!
But, Mary, I don't know how!
Never played **ball**? Impossible!
Here, catch!
Ow!
Oh—sorry—why didn't you catch it?
You didn't see it?
Well, you can't play with us, in that case.
I'm happier that way!
Why?
Mary! Throw us the ball!
I like to sit under a tree and watch the shadows, peeps of sky, sunlight...
You can see all that—but not a ball?
I can sense it!
I can **feel** it!
Er—well, that's nice for you!
Hey, Frances! Catch!

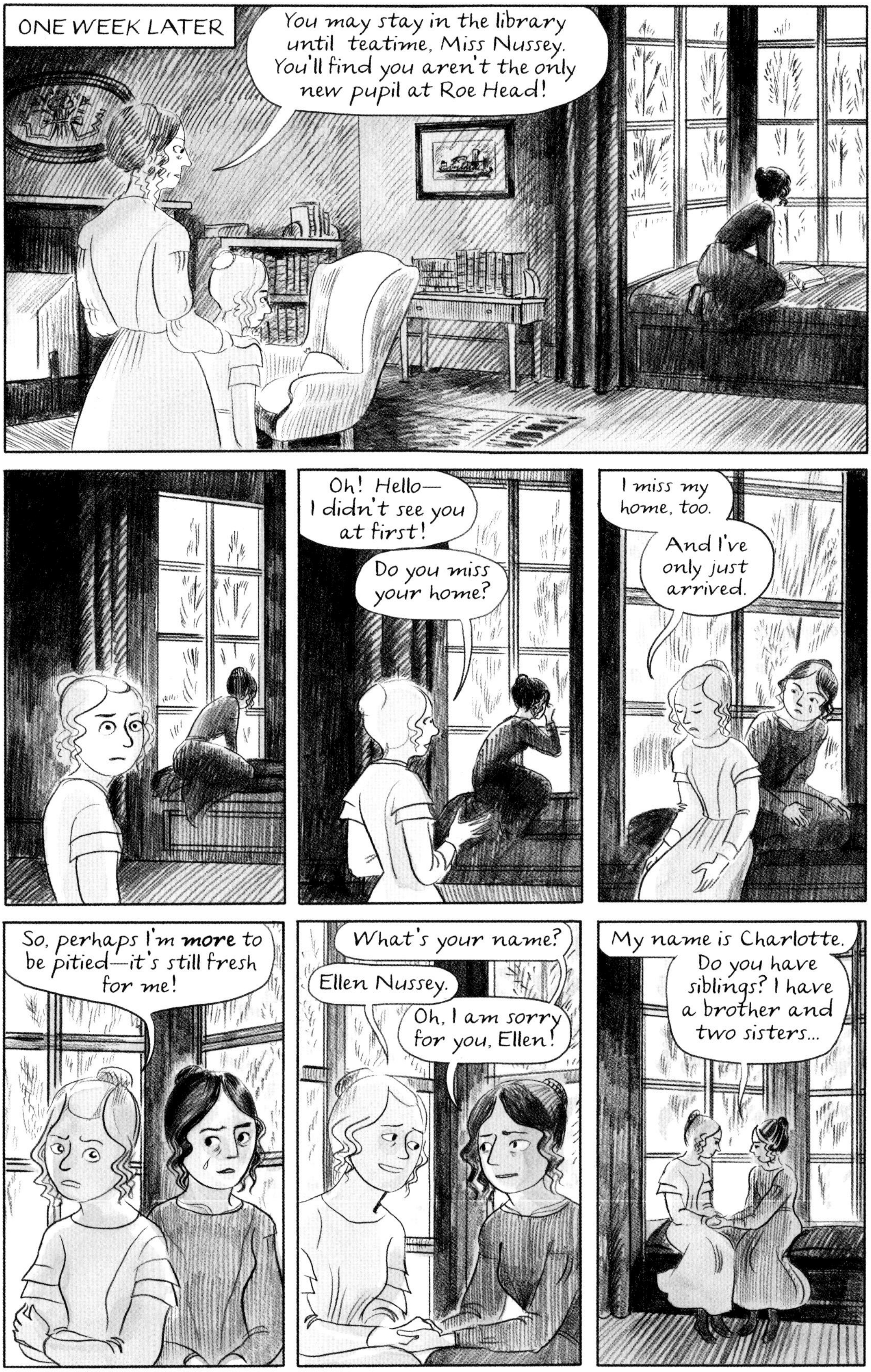
ONE WEEK LATER
You may stay in the library until teatime, Miss Nussey. You'll find you aren't the only new pupil at Roe Head!
Oh! Hello— I didn't see you at first!
Do you miss your home?
I miss my home, too.
And I've only just arrived.
So, perhaps I'm **more** to be pitied—it's still fresh for me!
What's your name?
Ellen Nussey.
Oh, I am sorry for you, Ellen!
My name is Charlotte.
Do you have siblings? I have a brother and two sisters...

SCHOOL WORK

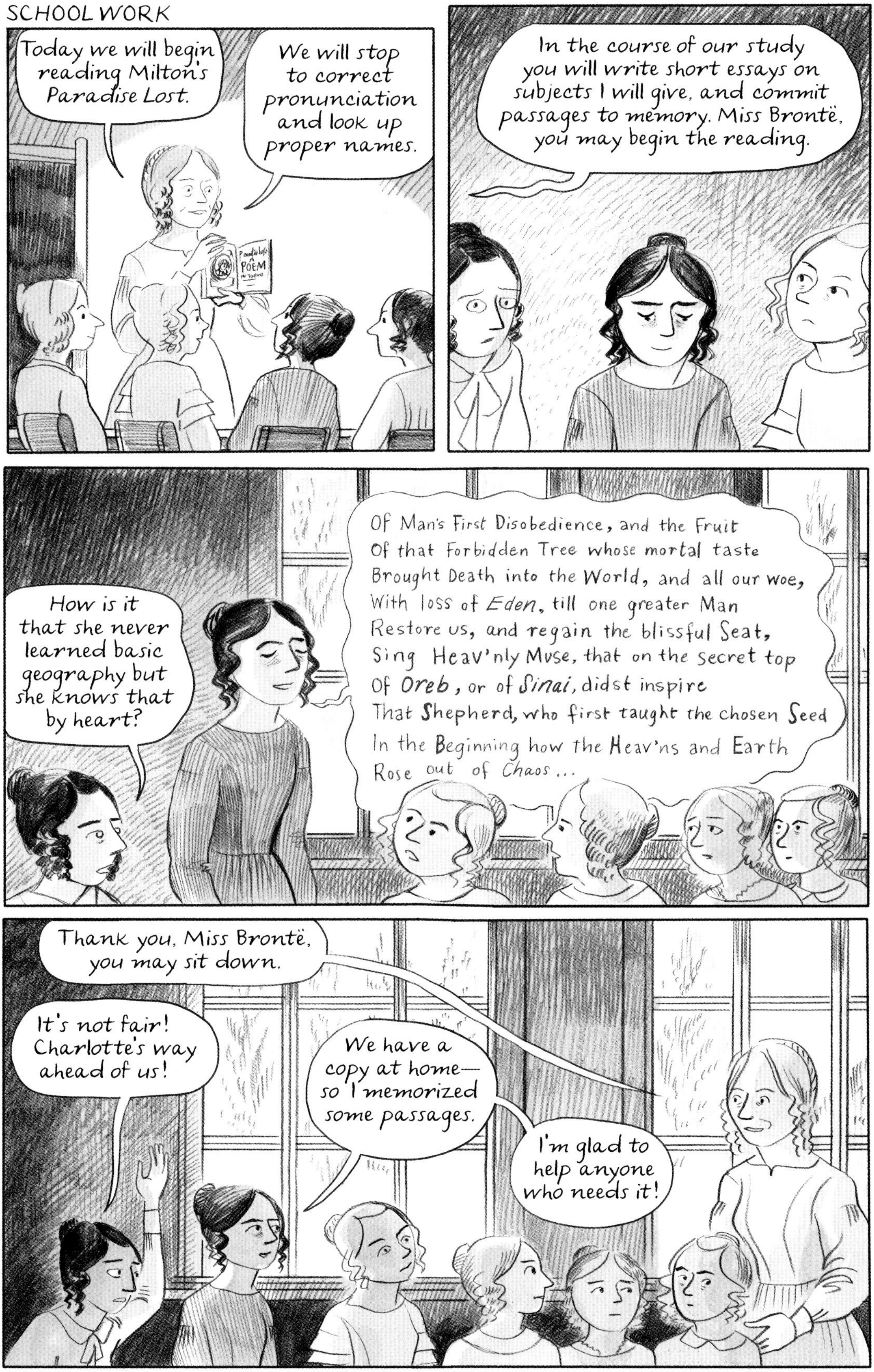
Today we will begin reading Milton's Paradise Lost.
We will stop to correct pronunciation and look up proper names.
In the course of our study you will write short essays on subjects I will give, and commit passages to memory. Miss Brontë, you may begin the reading.
How is it that she never learned basic geography but she knows that by heart?
Of Man's First Disobedience, and the Fruit
Of that Forbidden Tree whose mortal taste
Brought Death into the World, and all our woe,
With loss of Eden, till one greater Man
Restore us, and regain the blissful Seat,
Sing Heav'nly Muse, that on the secret top
Of Oreb, or of Sinai, didst inspire
That Shepherd, who first taught the chosen Seed
In the Beginning how the Heav'ns and Earth
Rose out of Chaos...
Thank you, Miss Brontë, you may sit down.
It's not fair! Charlotte's way ahead of us!
We have a copy at home—so I memorized some passages.
I'm glad to help anyone who needs it!

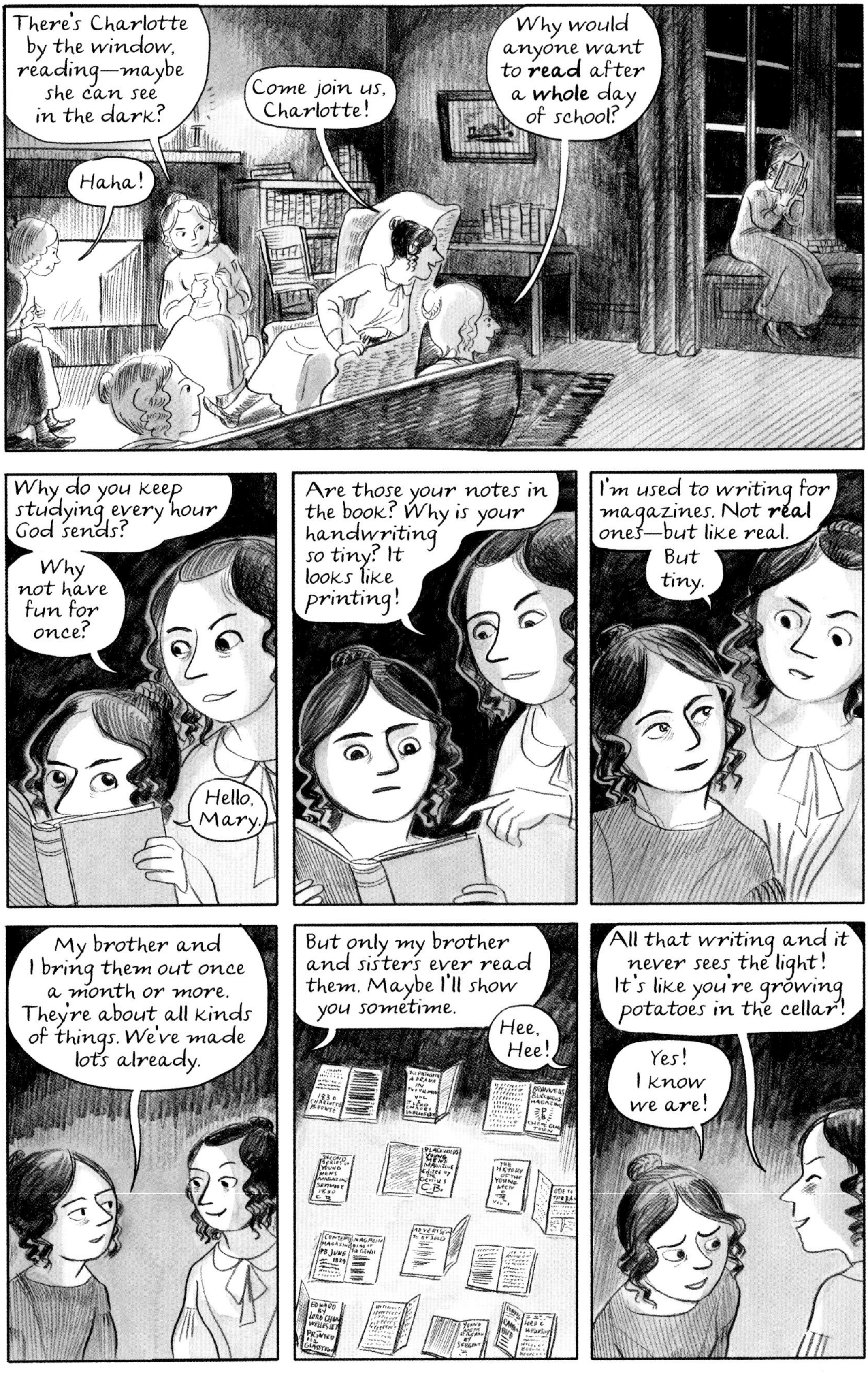
There's Charlotte by the window, reading—maybe she can see in the dark?
Haha!
Come join us, Charlotte!
Why would anyone want to **read** after a **whole** day of school?
Why do you keep studying every hour God sends?
Why not have fun for once?
Hello, Mary.
Are those your notes in the book? Why is your handwriting so tiny? It looks like printing!
I'm used to writing for magazines. Not **real** ones—but like real.
But tiny.
My brother and I bring them out once a month or more. They're about all kinds of things. We've made lots already.
But only my brother and sisters ever read them. Maybe I'll show you sometime.
Hee, Hee!
All that writing and it never sees the light! It's like you're growing potatoes in the cellar!
Yes! I know we are!

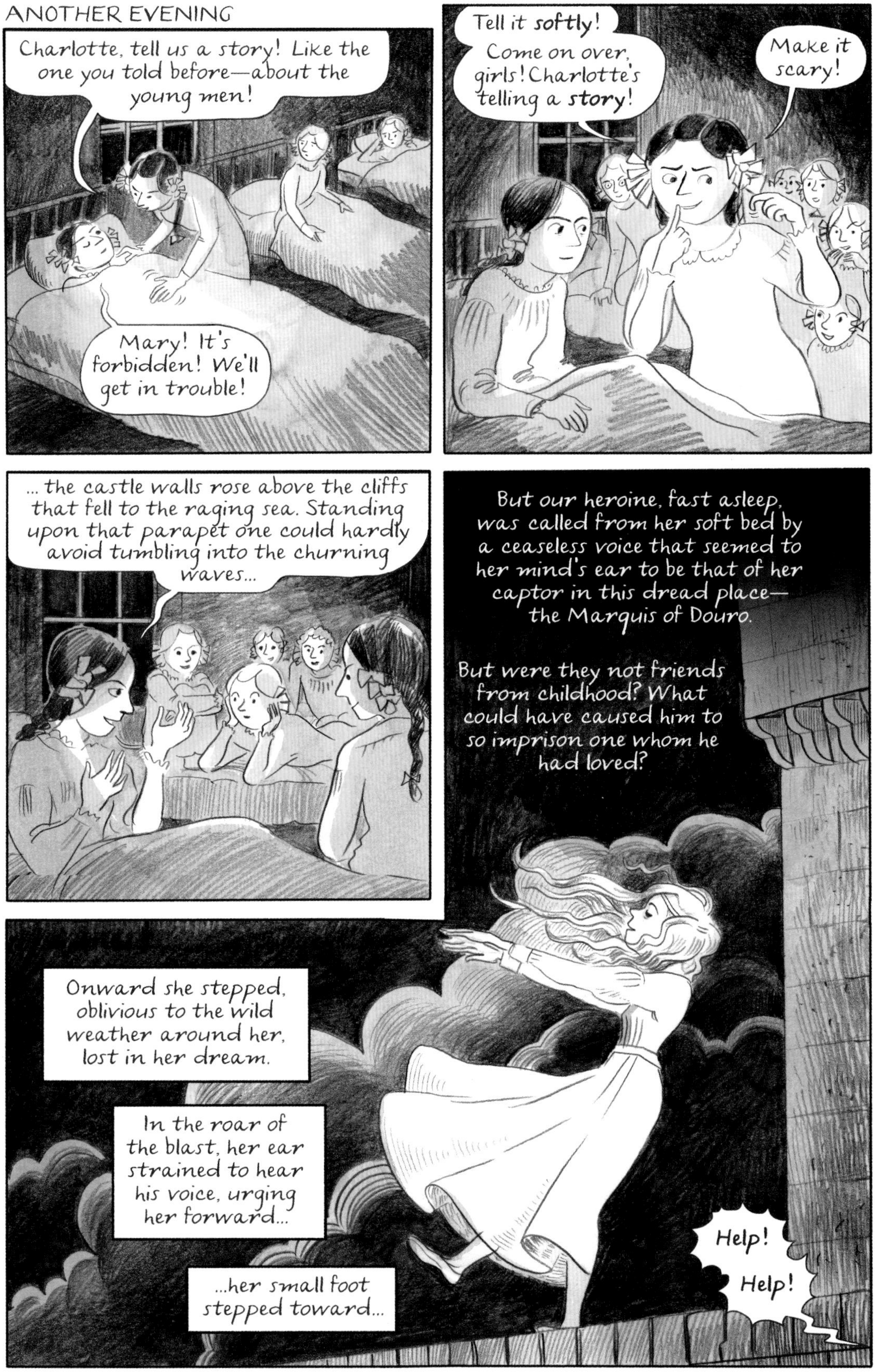
ANOTHER EVENING
Charlotte, tell us a story! Like the one you told before—about the young men!
Mary! It's forbidden! We'll get in trouble!
Tell it softly!
Come on over, girls! Charlotte's telling a story!
Make it scary!
... the castle walls rose above the cliffs that fell to the raging sea. Standing upon that parapet one could hardly avoid tumbling into the churning waves...
But our heroine, fast asleep, was called from her soft bed by a ceaseless voice that seemed to her mind's ear to be that of her captor in this dread place— the Marquis of Douro.
But were they not friends from childhood? What could have caused him to so imprison one whom he had loved?
Onward she stepped, oblivious to the wild weather around her, lost in her dream.
In the roar of the blast, her ear strained to hear his voice, urging her forward...
...her small foot stepped toward...
Help!
Help!

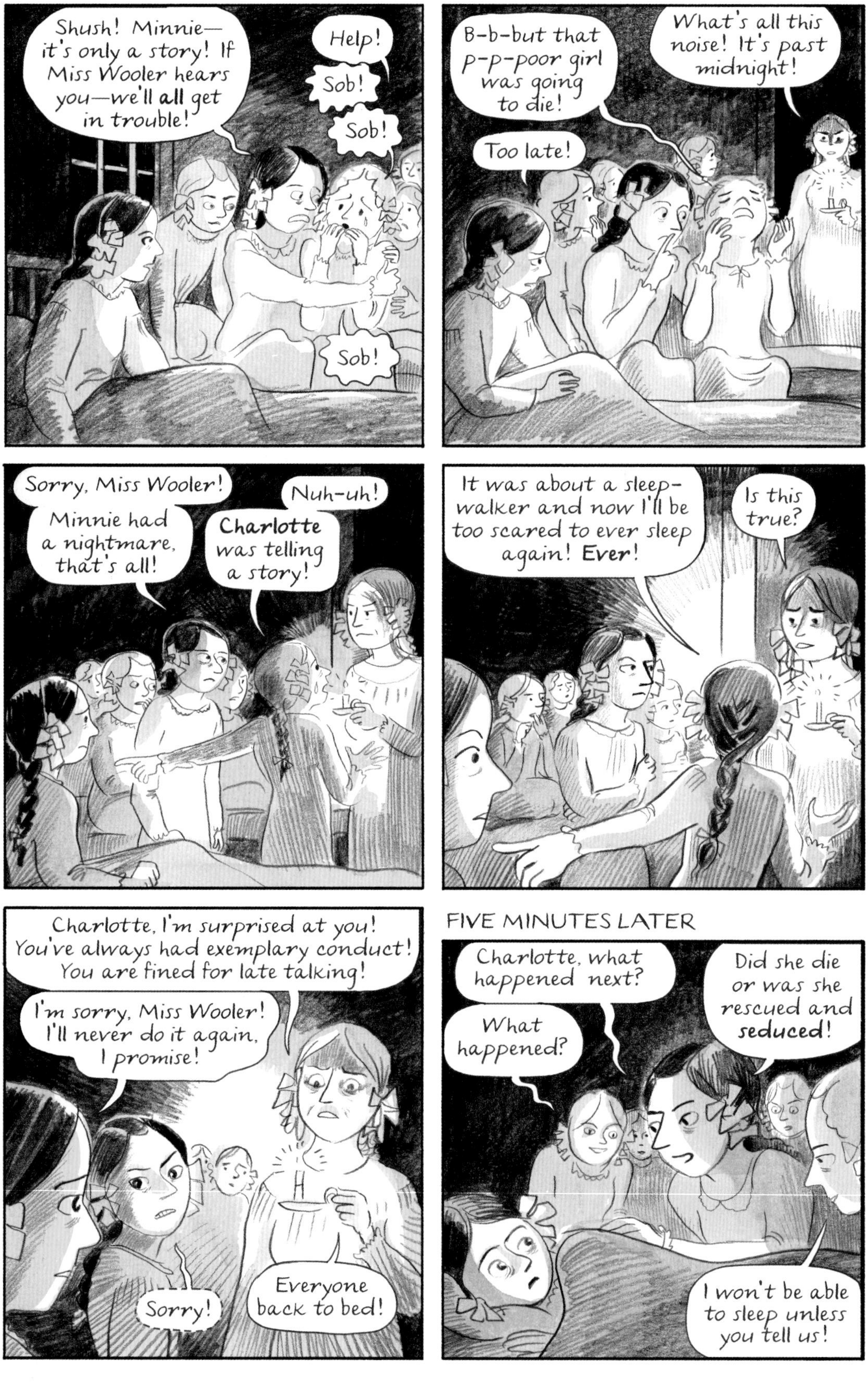
Shush! Minnie—it's only a story! If Miss Wooler hears you—we'll **all** get in trouble!
Help!
Sob!
Sob!
Sob!
B-b-but that p-p-poor girl was going to die!
Too late!
What's all this noise! It's past midnight!
Sorry, Miss Wooler! Minnie had a nightmare, that's all!
Nuh-uh! **Charlotte** was telling a story!
It was about a sleep-walker and now I'll be too scared to ever sleep again! **Ever**!
Is this true?
Charlotte, I'm surprised at you! You've always had exemplary conduct! You are fined for late talking!
I'm sorry, Miss Wooler! I'll never do it again, I promise!
Sorry!
Everyone back to bed!
FIVE MINUTES LATER
Charlotte, what happened next?
What happened?
Did she die or was she rescued and **seduced**!
I won't be able to sleep unless you tell us!

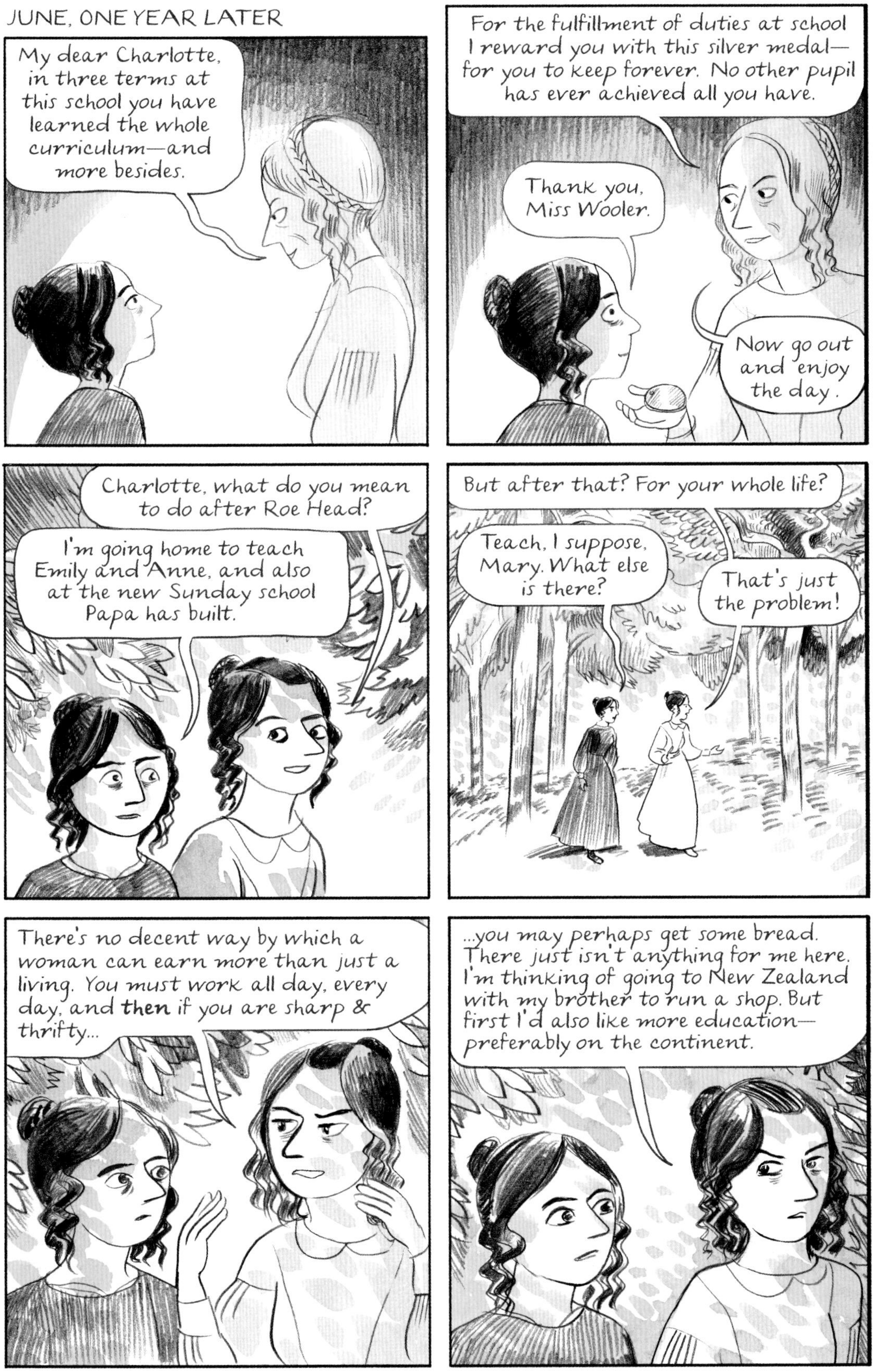
JUNE, ONE YEAR LATER
My dear Charlotte, in three terms at this school you have learned the whole curriculum—and more besides.
For the fulfillment of duties at school I reward you with this silver medal— for you to keep forever. No other pupil has ever achieved all you have.
Thank you, Miss Wooler.
Now go out and enjoy the day.
Charlotte, what do you mean to do after Roe Head?
I'm going home to teach Emily and Anne, and also at the new Sunday school Papa has built.
But after that? For your whole life?
Teach, I suppose, Mary. What else is there?
That's just the problem!
There's no decent way by which a woman can earn more than just a living. You must work all day, every day, and **then** if you are sharp & thrifty...
...you may perhaps get some bread. There just isn't anything for me here. I'm thinking of going to New Zealand with my brother to run a shop. But first I'd also like more education— preferably on the continent.

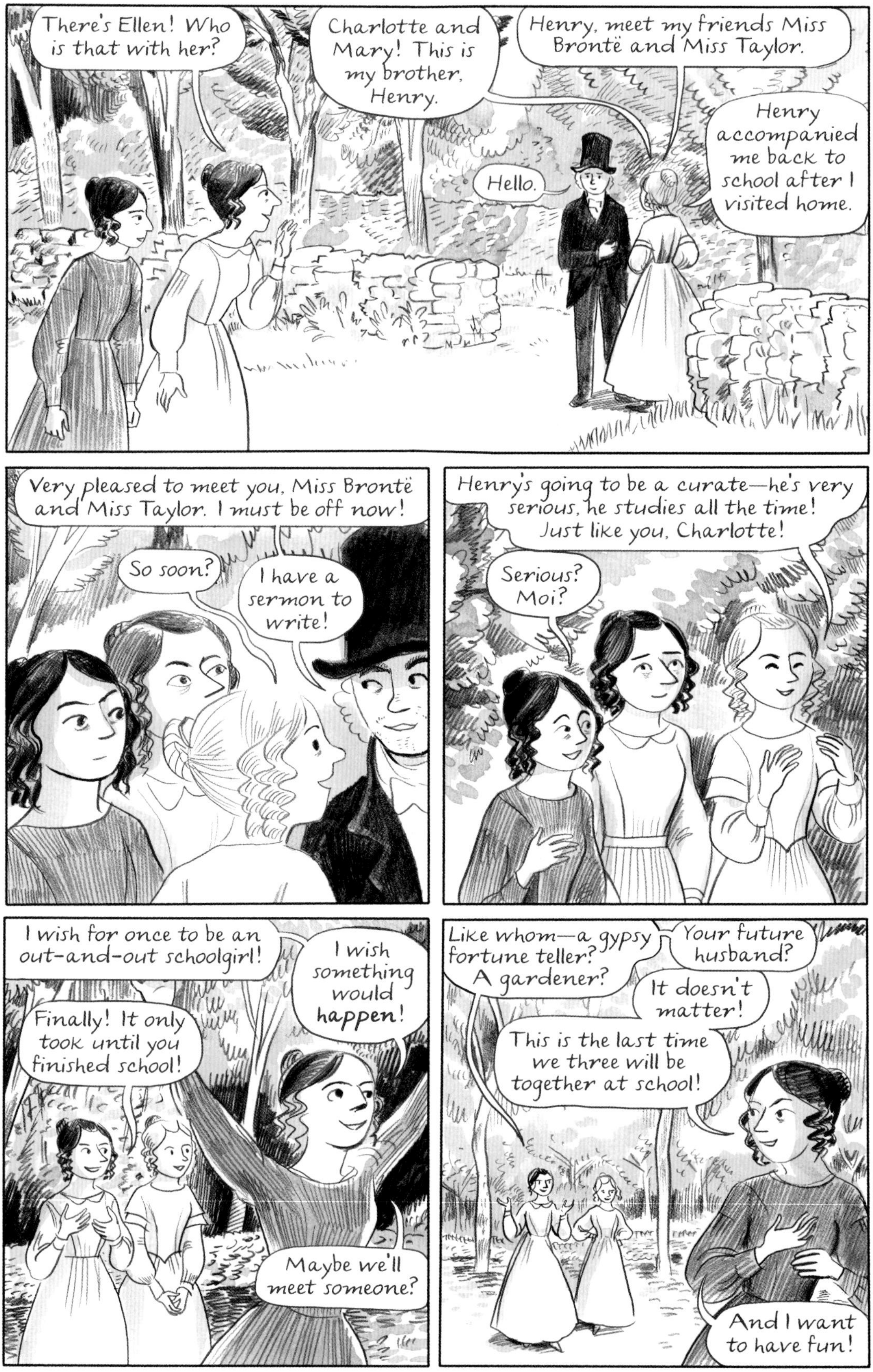
There's Ellen! Who is that with her?
Charlotte and Mary! This is my brother, Henry.
Henry, meet my friends Miss Brontë and Miss Taylor.
Hello.
Henry accompanied me back to school after I visited home.
Very pleased to meet you, Miss Brontë and Miss Taylor. I must be off now!
So soon?
I have a sermon to write!
Henry's going to be a curate—he's very serious, he studies all the time! Just like you, Charlotte!
Serious? Moi?
I wish for once to be an out-and-out schoolgirl!
I wish something would **happen**!
Finally! It only took until you finished school!
Maybe we'll meet someone?
Like whom—a gypsy fortune teller? A gardener?
Your future husband?
It doesn't matter!
This is the last time we three will be together at school!
And I want to have fun!

ONE MONTH LATER, HAWORTH, 21 JULY 1832

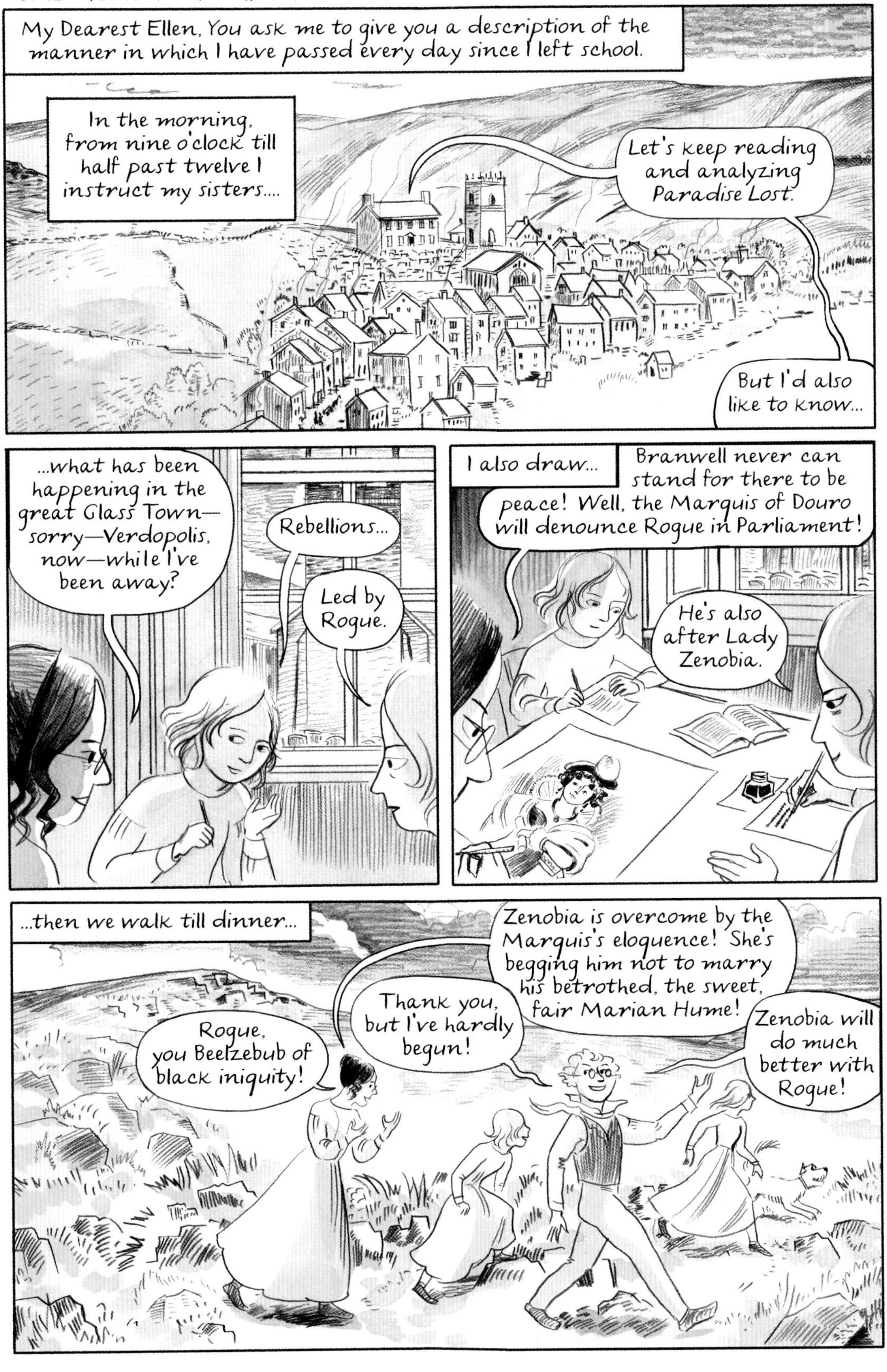

My Dearest Ellen, You ask me to give you a description of the manner in which I have passed every day since I left school.
In the morning, from nine o'clock till half past twelve I instruct my sisters....
Let's keep reading and analyzing Paradise Lost.
But I'd also like to know...
...what has been happening in the great Glass Town—sorry—Verdopolis, now—while I've been away?
Rebellions...
Led by Rogue.
I also draw...
Branwell never can stand for there to be peace! Well, the Marquis of Douro will denounce Rogue in Parliament!
He's also after Lady Zenobia.
...then we walk till dinner...
Zenobia is overcome by the Marquis's eloquence! She's begging him not to marry his betrothed, the sweet, fair Marian Hume!
Rogue, you Beelzebub of black iniquity!
Thank you, but I've hardly begun!
Zenobia will do much better with Rogue!

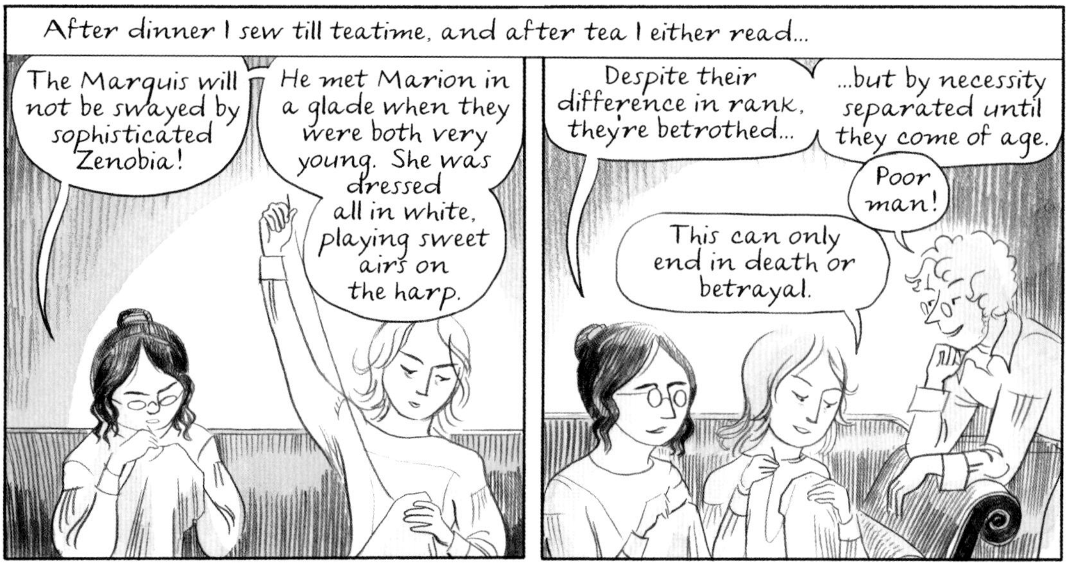
After dinner I sew till teatime, and after tea I either read...
The Marquis will not be swayed by sophisticated Zenobia!
He met Marion in a glade when they were both very young. She was dressed all in white, playing sweet airs on the harp.
Despite their difference in rank, they're betrothed...
...but by necessity separated until they come of age.
Poor man!
This can only end in death or betrayal.

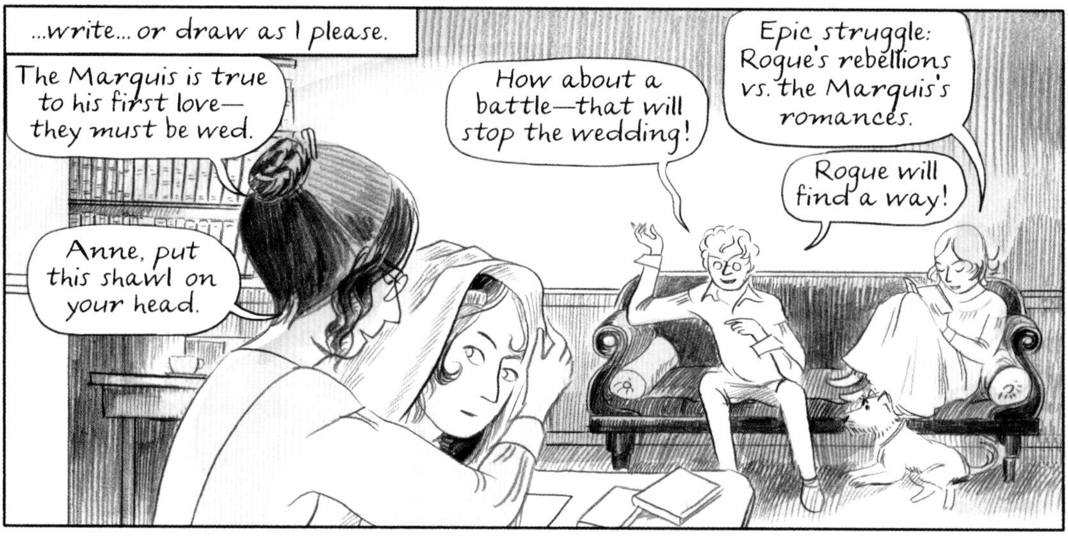
...write... or draw as I please.
The Marquis is true to his first love— they must be wed.
How about a battle—that will stop the wedding!
Epic struggle: Rogue's rebellions vs. the Marquis's romances.
Rogue will find a way!
Anne, put this shawl on your head.

Thus in one delightful, though somewhat monotonous course my life is passed.

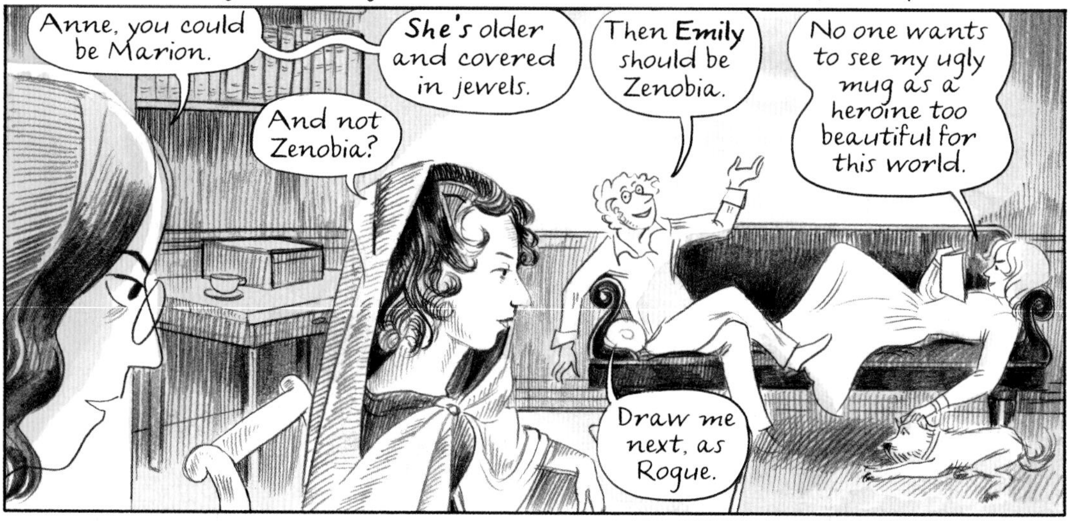
Anne, you could be Marion.
And not Zenobia?
She's older and covered in jewels.
Then **Emily** should be Zenobia.
No one wants to see my ugly mug as a heroine too beautiful for this world.
Draw me next, as Rogue.

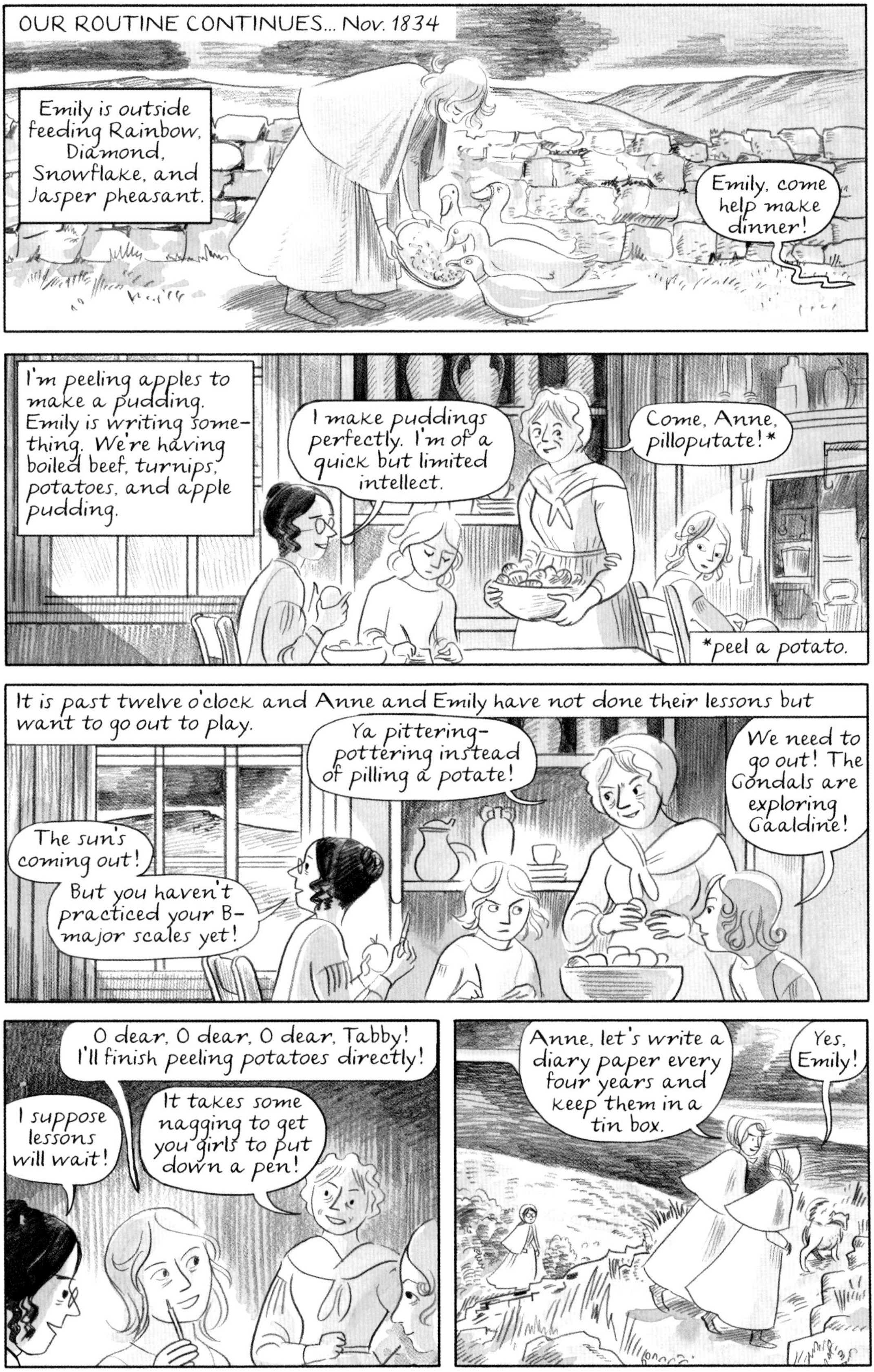
OUR ROUTINE CONTINUES... Nov. 1834
Emily is outside feeding Rainbow, Diamond, Snowflake, and Jasper pheasant.
Emily, come help make dinner!
I'm peeling apples to make a pudding. Emily is writing something. We're having boiled beef, turnips, potatoes, and apple pudding.
I make puddings perfectly. I'm of a quick but limited intellect.
Come, Anne, pilloputate!*
*peel a potato.
It is past twelve o'clock and Anne and Emily have not done their lessons but want to go out to play.
Ya pittering-pottering instead of pilling a potate!
We need to go out! The Gondals are exploring Gaaldine!
The sun's coming out!
But you haven't practiced your B-major scales yet!
O dear, O dear, O dear, Tabby! I'll finish peeling potatoes directly!
I suppose lessons will wait!
It takes some nagging to get you girls to put down a pen!
Anne, let's write a diary paper every four years and keep them in a tin box.
Yes, Emily!

EIGHT MONTHS LATER, JULY 1835, HAWORTH

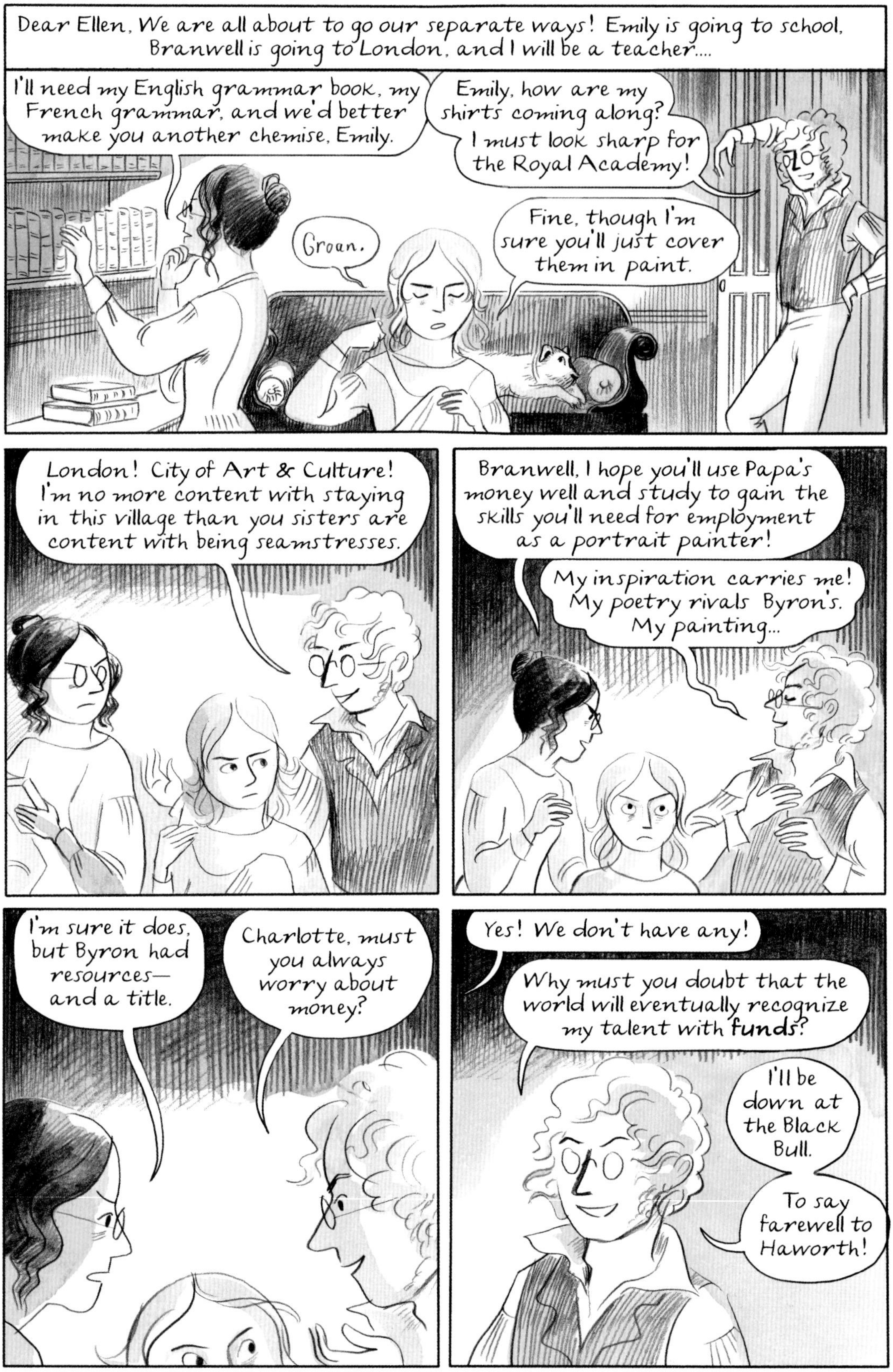
Dear Ellen, We are all about to go our separate ways! Emily is going to school, Branwell is going to London, and I will be a teacher....
I'll need my English grammar book, my French grammar, and we'd better make you another chemise, Emily.
Emily, how are my shirts coming along?
I must look sharp for the Royal Academy!
Groan.
Fine, though I'm sure you'll just cover them in paint.
London! City of Art & Culture! I'm no more content with staying in this village than you sisters are content with being seamstresses.
Branwell, I hope you'll use Papa's money well and study to gain the skills you'll need for employment as a portrait painter!
My inspiration carries me! My poetry rivals Byron's. My painting...
I'm sure it does, but Byron had resources—and a title.
Charlotte, must you always worry about money?
Yes! We don't have any!
Why must you doubt that the world will eventually recognize my talent with **funds**?
I'll be down at the Black Bull.
To say farewell to Haworth!

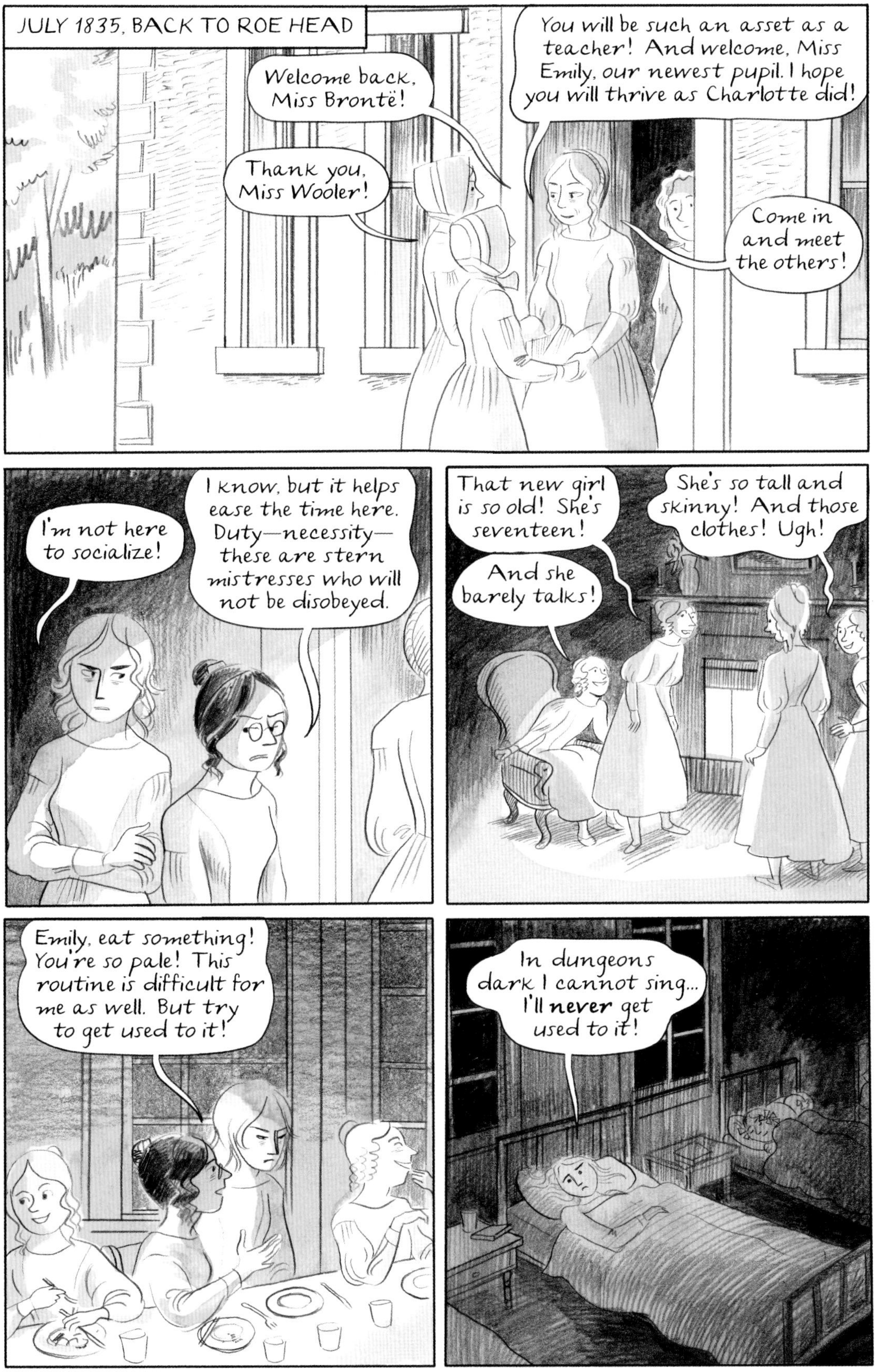
JULY 1835, BACK TO ROE HEAD
Welcome back, Miss Brontë!
Thank you, Miss Wooler!
You will be such an asset as a teacher! And welcome, Miss Emily, our newest pupil. I hope you will thrive as Charlotte did!
Come in and meet the others!
I'm not here to socialize!
I know, but it helps ease the time here. Duty—necessity—these are stern mistresses who will not be disobeyed.
That new girl is so old! She's seventeen!
And she barely talks!
She's so tall and skinny! And those clothes! Ugh!
Emily, eat something! You're so pale! This routine is difficult for me as well. But try to get used to it!
In dungeons dark I cannot sing... I'll **never** get used to it!

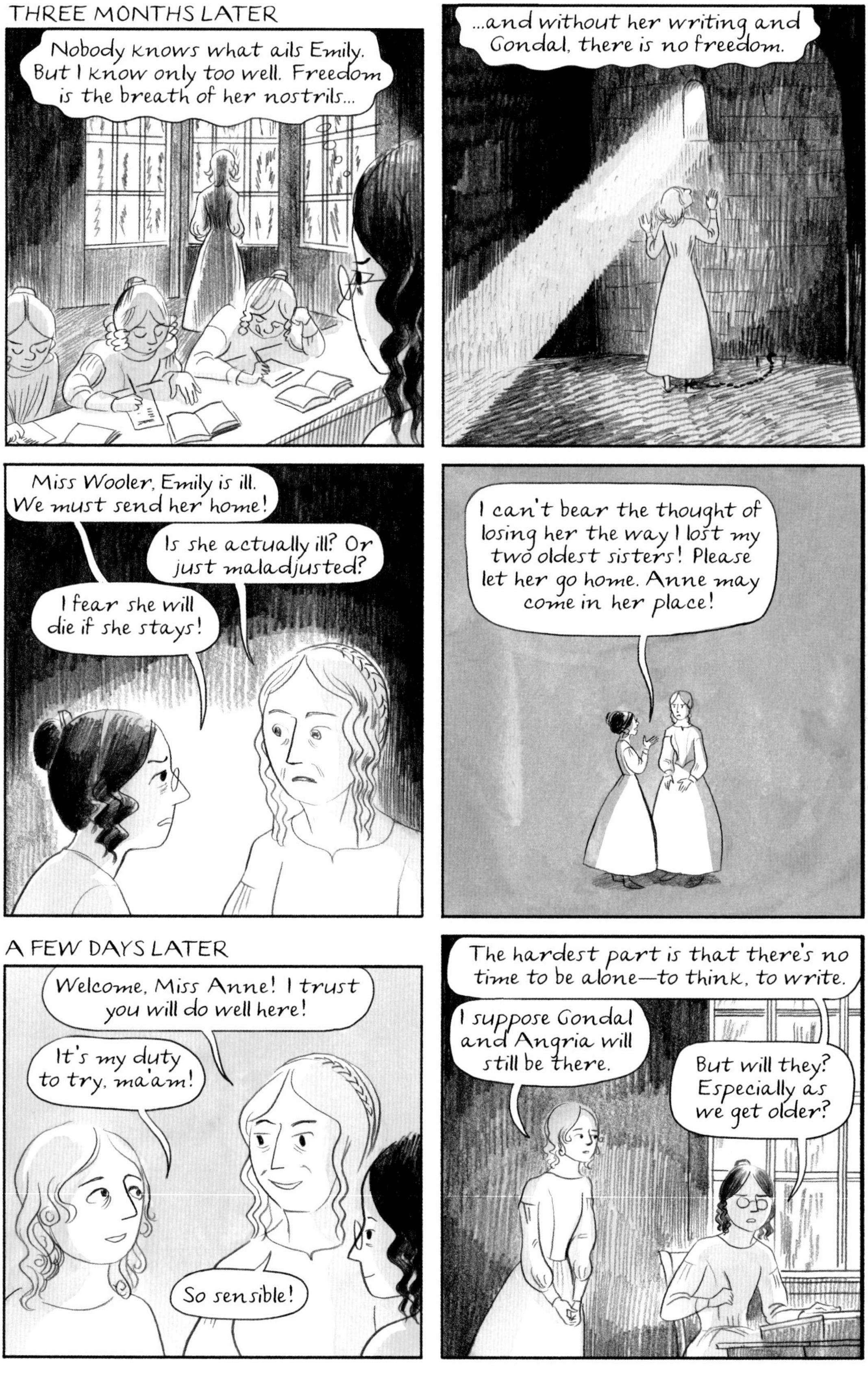
THREE MONTHS LATER
Nobody knows what ails Emily. But I know only too well. Freedom is the breath of her nostrils...
...and without her writing and Gondal, there is no freedom.
Miss Wooler, Emily is ill. We must send her home!
Is she actually ill? Or just maladjusted?
I fear she will die if she stays!
I can't bear the thought of losing her the way I lost my two oldest sisters! Please let her go home. Anne may come in her place!
A FEW DAYS LATER
Welcome, Miss Anne! I trust you will do well here!
It's my duty to try, ma'am!
So sensible!
The hardest part is that there's no time to be alone—to think, to write.
I suppose Gondal and Angria will still be there.
But will they? Especially as we get older?

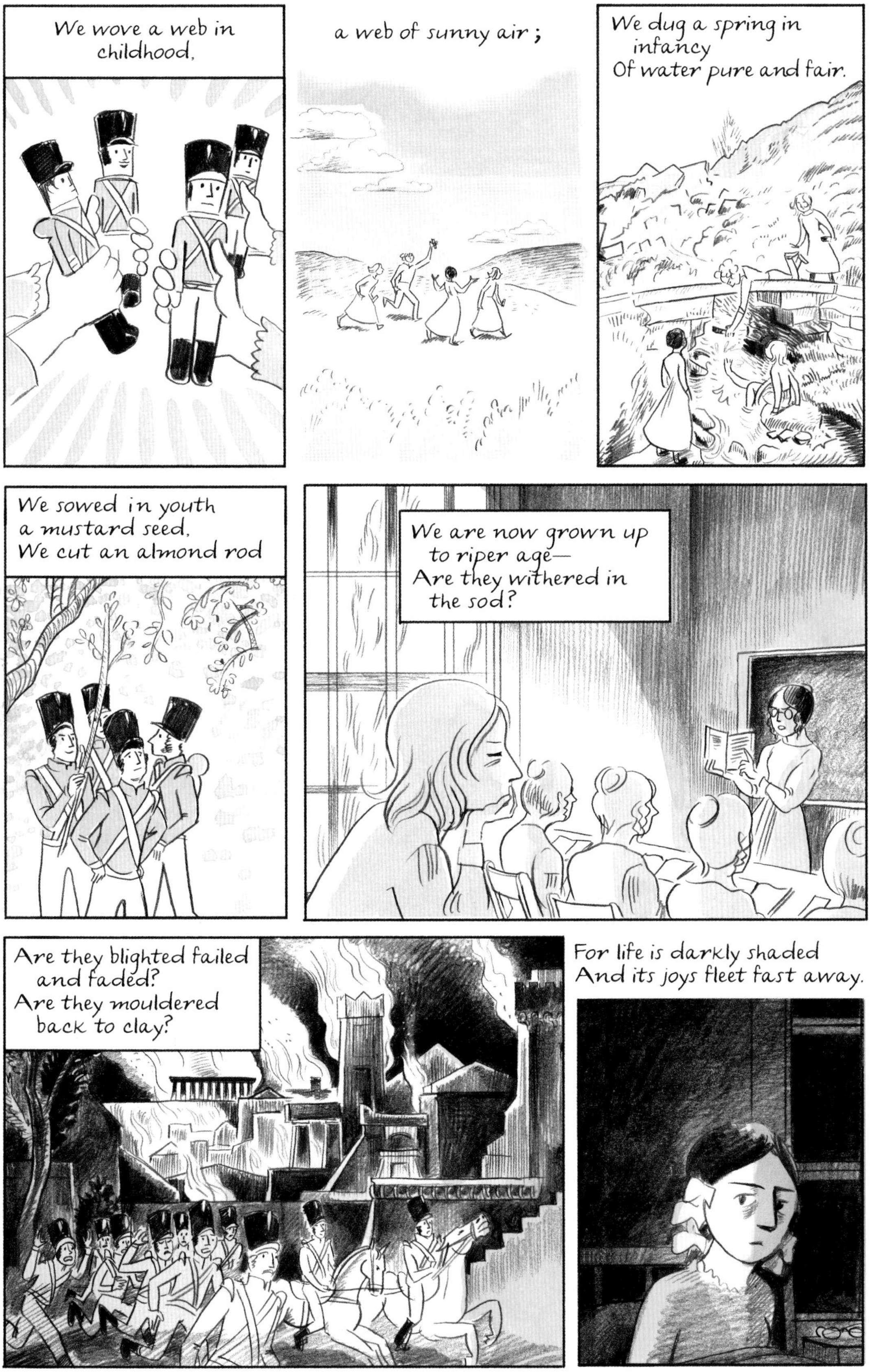
We wove a web in childhood,
a web of sunny air;
We dug a spring in infancy
Of water pure and fair.
We sowed in youth a mustard seed,
We cut an almond rod
We are now grown up to riper age—
Are they withered in the sod?
Are they blighted failed and faded?
Are they mouldered back to clay?
For life is darkly shaded
And its joys fleet fast away.

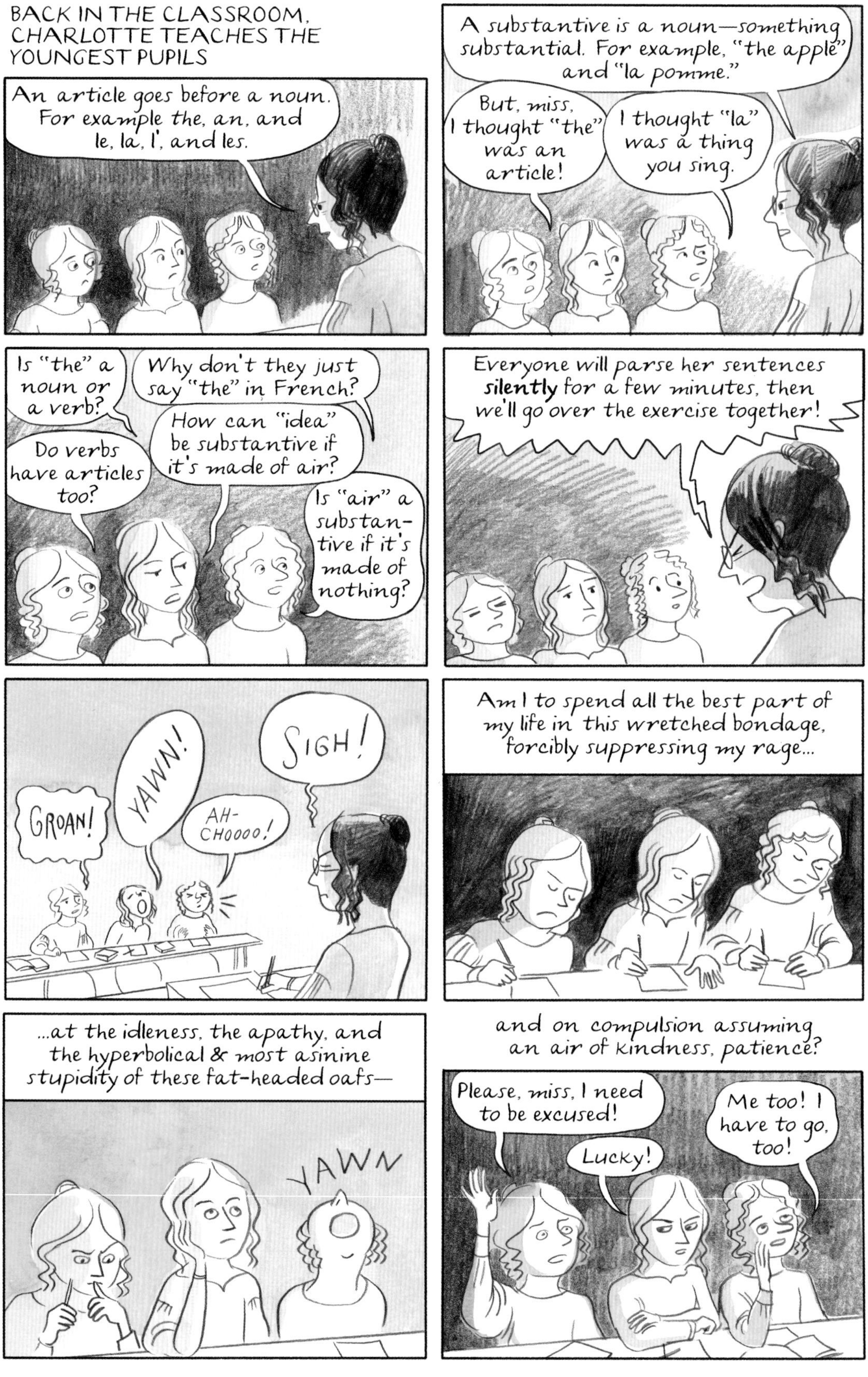
BACK IN THE CLASSROOM, CHARLOTTE TEACHES THE YOUNGEST PUPILS
An article goes before a noun. For example the, an, and le, la, l', and les.
A substantive is a noun—something substantial. For example, "the apple" and "la pomme."
But, miss, I thought "the" was an article!
I thought "la" was a thing you sing.
Is "the" a noun or a verb?
Why don't they just say "the" in French?
How can "idea" be substantive if it's made of air?
Do verbs have articles too?
Is "air" a substantive if it's made of nothing?
Everyone will parse her sentences **silently** for a few minutes, then we'll go over the exercise together!
GROAN!
YAWN!
SIGH!
AH-CHOOOO!
Am I to spend all the best part of my life in this wretched bondage, forcibly suppressing my rage...
...at the idleness, the apathy, and the hyperbolical & most asinine stupidity of these fat-headed oafs—
YAWN
and on compulsion assuming an air of kindness, patience?
Please, miss, I need to be excused!
Lucky!
Me too! I have to go, too!

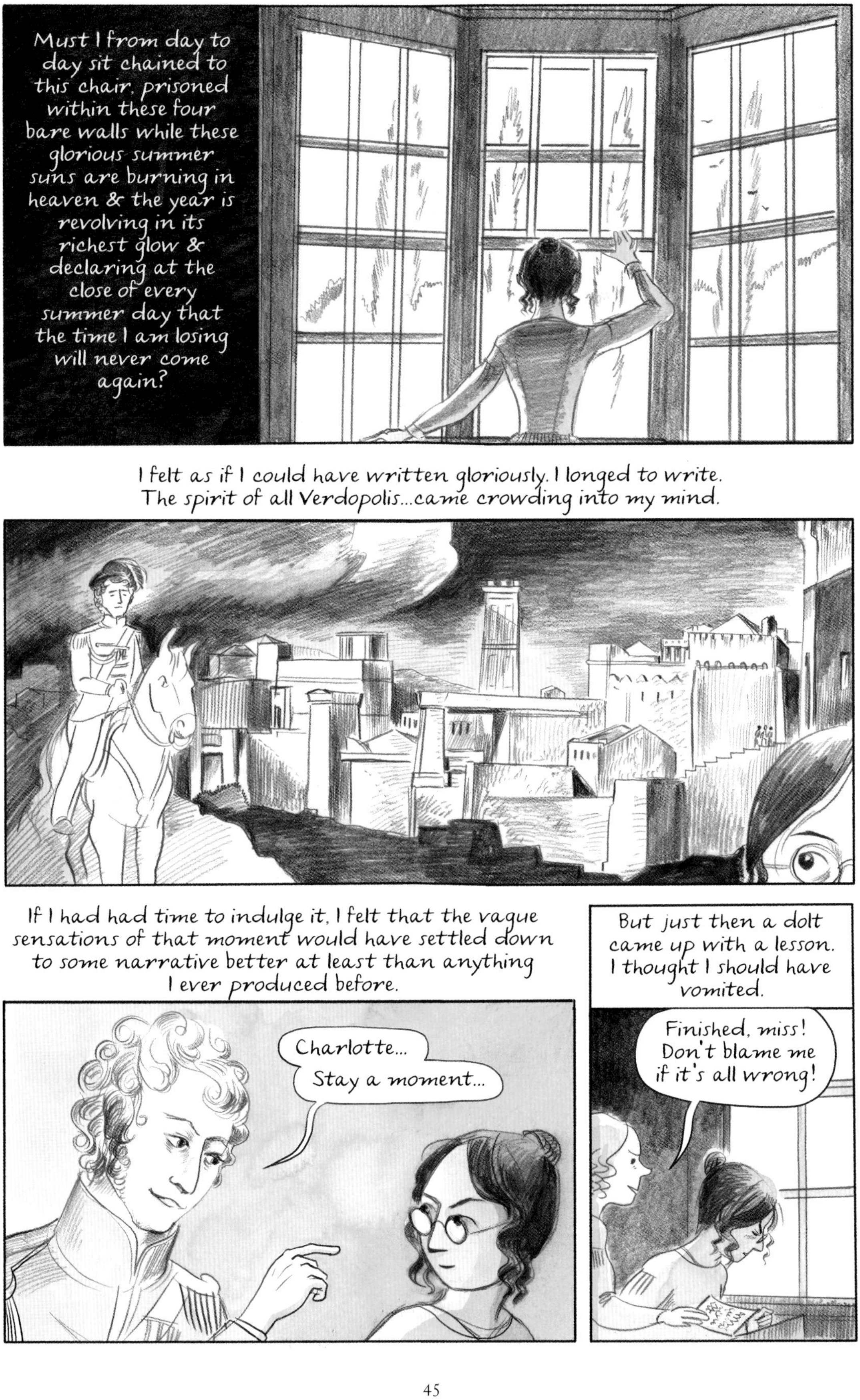
Must I from day to day sit chained to this chair, prisoned within these four bare walls while these glorious summer suns are burning in heaven & the year is revolving in its richest glow & declaring at the close of every summer day that the time I am losing will never come again?
I felt as if I could have written gloriously. I longed to write. The spirit of all Verdopolis...came crowding into my mind.
If I had had time to indulge it, I felt that the vague sensations of that moment would have settled down to some narrative better at least than anything I ever produced before.
Charlotte... Stay a moment...
But just then a dolt came up with a lesson. I thought I should have vomited.
Finished, miss! Don't blame me if it's all wrong!

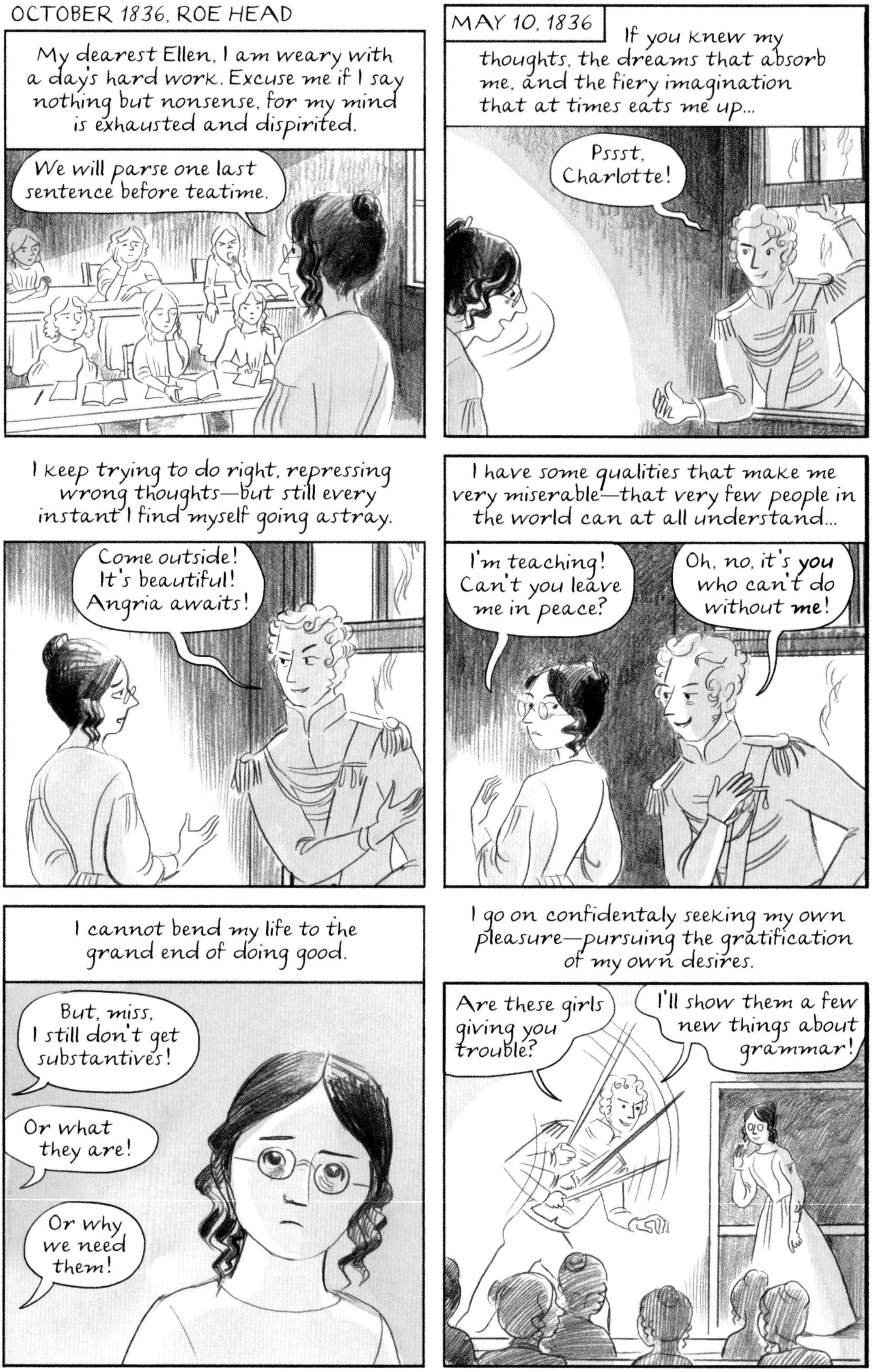
OCTOBER 1836, ROE HEAD
My dearest Ellen, I am weary with a day's hard work. Excuse me if I say nothing but nonsense, for my mind is exhausted and dispirited.
We will parse one last sentence before teatime.
MAY 10, 1836
If you knew my thoughts, the dreams that absorb me, and the fiery imagination that at times eats me up...
Pssst, Charlotte!
I keep trying to do right, repressing wrong thoughts—but still every instant I find myself going astray.
Come outside! It's beautiful! Angria awaits!
I have some qualities that make me very miserable—that very few people in the world can at all understand...
I'm teaching! Can't you leave me in peace?
Oh, no, it's **you** who can't do without **me**!
I cannot bend my life to the grand end of doing good.
But, miss, I still don't get substantives!
Or what they are!
Or why we need them!
I go on confidentaly seeking my own pleasure—pursuing the gratification of my own desires.
Are these girls giving you trouble?
I'll show them a few new things about grammar!

CHRISTMAS VACATION,
DEC. 1836, HAWORTH

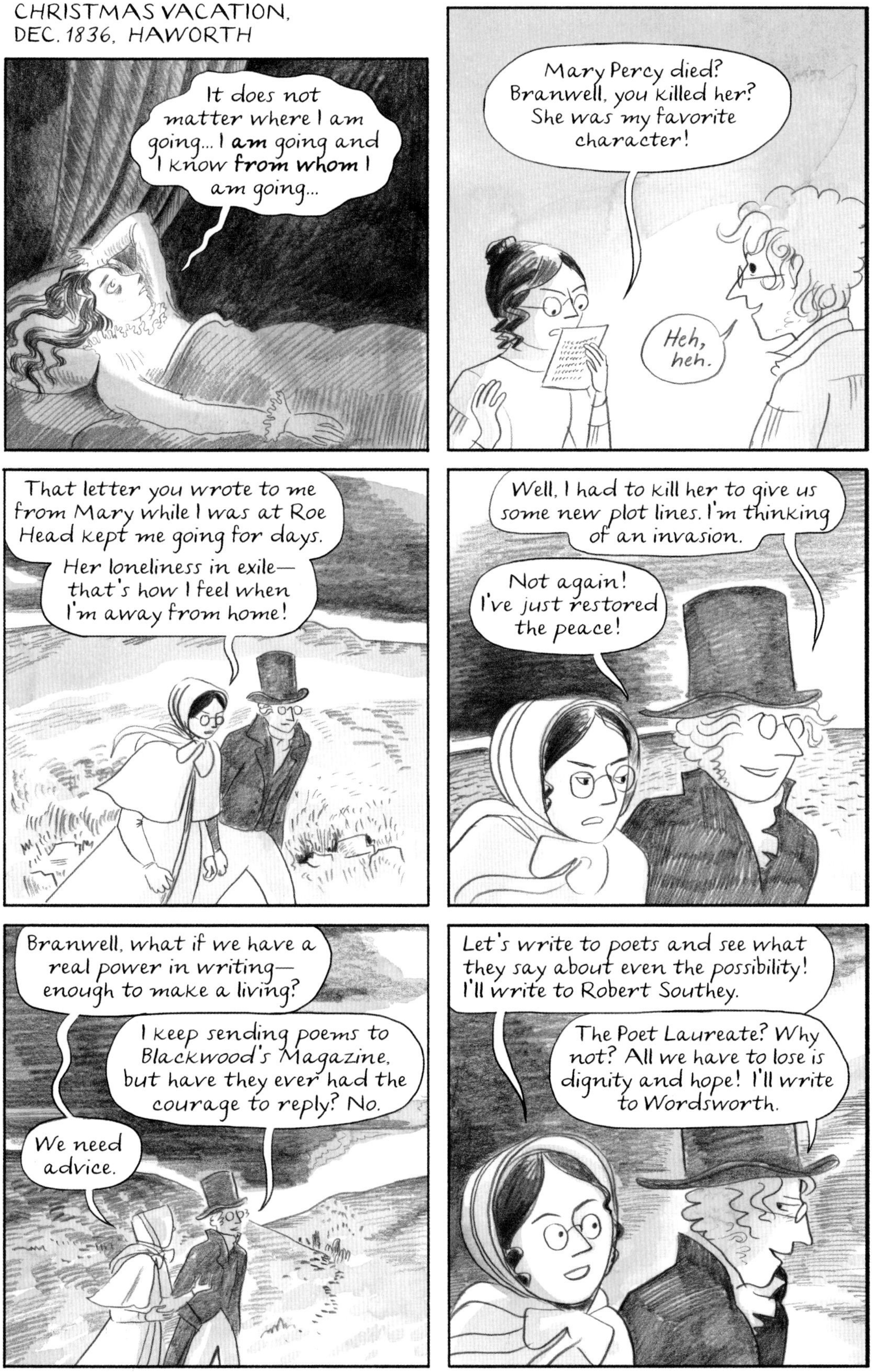
It does not matter where I am going... I **am** going and I know **from whom** I am going...
Mary Percy died? Branwell, you killed her? She was my favorite character!
Heh, heh.
That letter you wrote to me from Mary while I was at Roe Head kept me going for days.
Her loneliness in exile—that's how I feel when I'm away from home!
Well, I had to kill her to give us some new plot lines. I'm thinking of an invasion.
Not again! I've just restored the peace!
Branwell, what if we have a real power in writing—enough to make a living?
I keep sending poems to Blackwood's Magazine, but have they ever had the courage to reply? No.
We need advice.
Let's write to poets and see what they say about even the possibility! I'll write to Robert Southey.
The Poet Laureate? Why not? All we have to lose is dignity and hope! I'll write to Wordsworth.

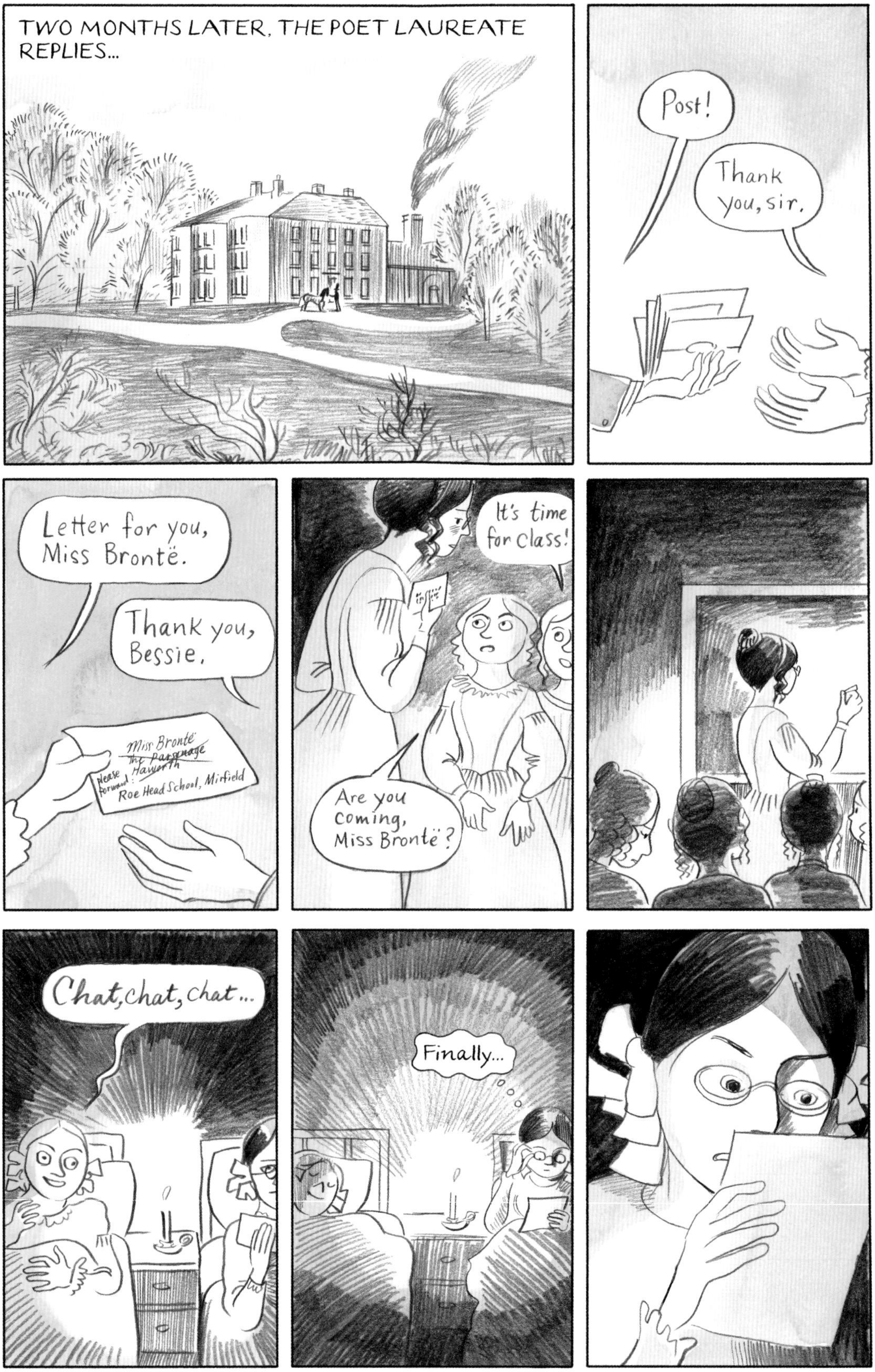
TWO MONTHS LATER, THE POET LAUREATE REPLIES...
Post!
Thank you, sir.
Letter for you, Miss Brontë.
Thank you, Bessie.
Miss Brontë
The Parsonage
Haworth
please forward: Roe Head School, Mirfield
It's time for class!
Are you coming, Miss Brontë?
Chat, chat, chat...
Finally...

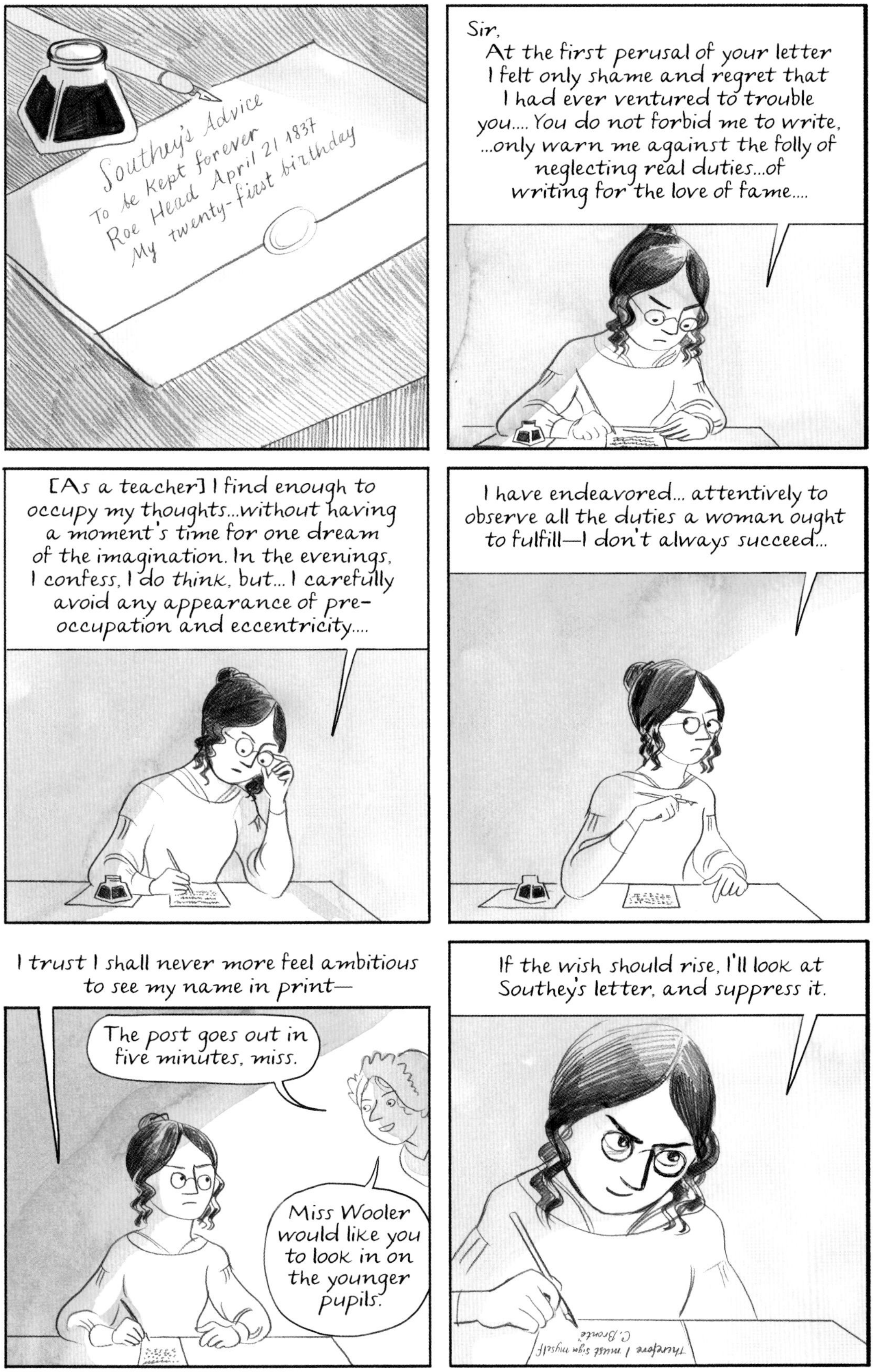
Southey's Advice
To be kept forever
Roe Head April 21 1837
My twenty-first birthday
Sir,
At the first perusal of your letter I felt only shame and regret that I had ever ventured to trouble you.... You do not forbid me to write, ...only warn me against the folly of neglecting real duties...of writing for the love of fame....
[As a teacher] I find enough to occupy my thoughts...without having a moment's time for one dream of the imagination. In the evenings, I confess, I do think, but... I carefully avoid any appearance of pre-occupation and eccentricity....
I have endeavored... attentively to observe all the duties a woman ought to fulfill—I don't always succeed...
I trust I shall never more feel ambitious to see my name in print—
The post goes out in five minutes, miss.
Miss Wooler would like you to look in on the younger pupils.
If the wish should rise, I'll look at Southey's letter, and suppress it.
therefore I must sign myself
C. Brontë

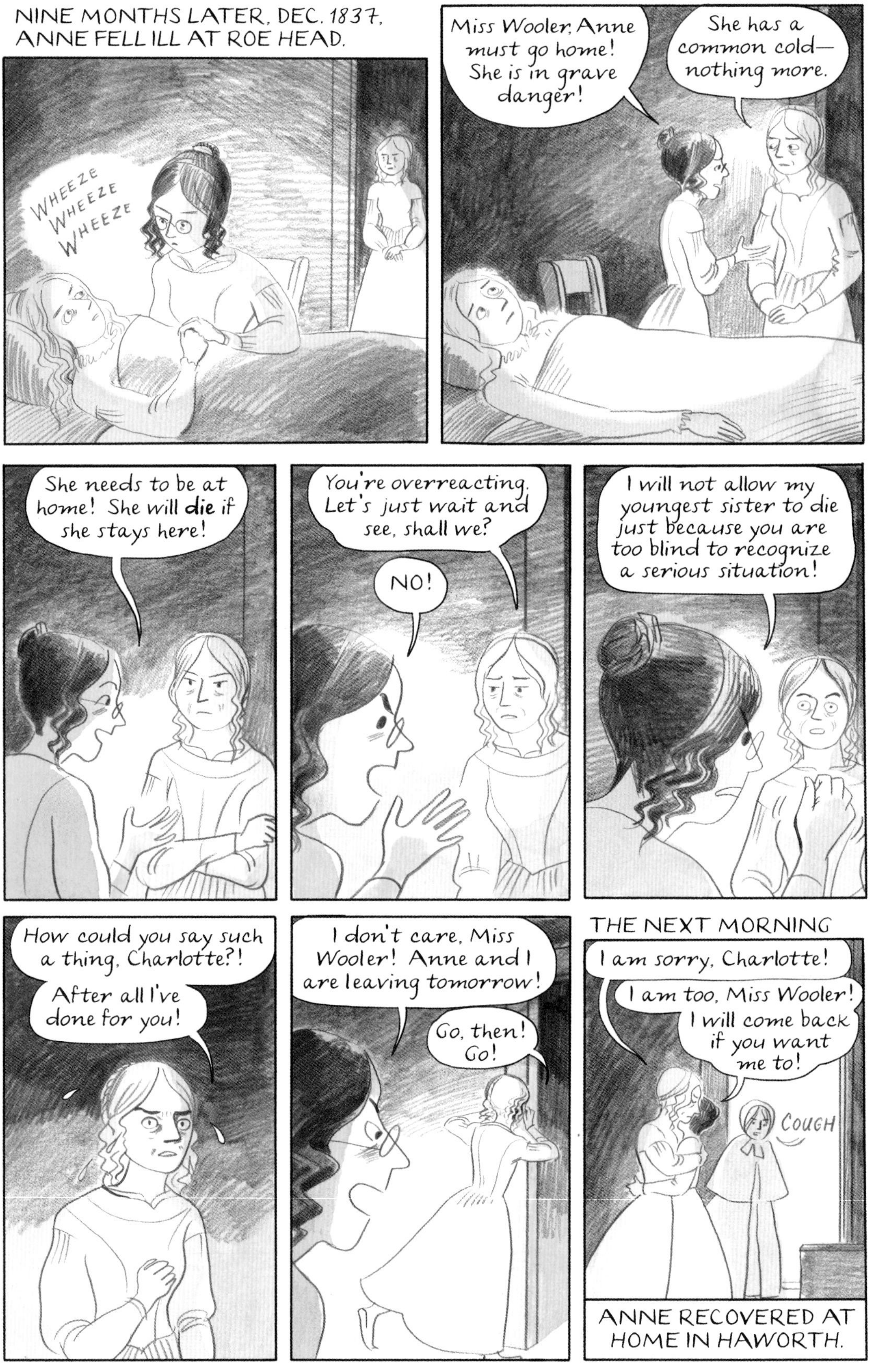
NINE MONTHS LATER, DEC. 1837, ANNE FELL ILL AT ROE HEAD.
WHEEZE WHEEZE WHEEZE
Miss Wooler, Anne must go home! She is in grave danger!
She has a common cold—nothing more.
She needs to be at home! She will **die** if she stays here!
You're overreacting. Let's just wait and see, shall we?
NO!
I will not allow my youngest sister to die just because you are too blind to recognize a serious situation!
How could you say such a thing, Charlotte?!
After all I've done for you!
I don't care, Miss Wooler! Anne and I are leaving tomorrow!
Go, then! Go!
THE NEXT MORNING
I am sorry, Charlotte!
I am too, Miss Wooler! I will come back if you want me to!
COUGH
ANNE RECOVERED AT HOME IN HAWORTH.

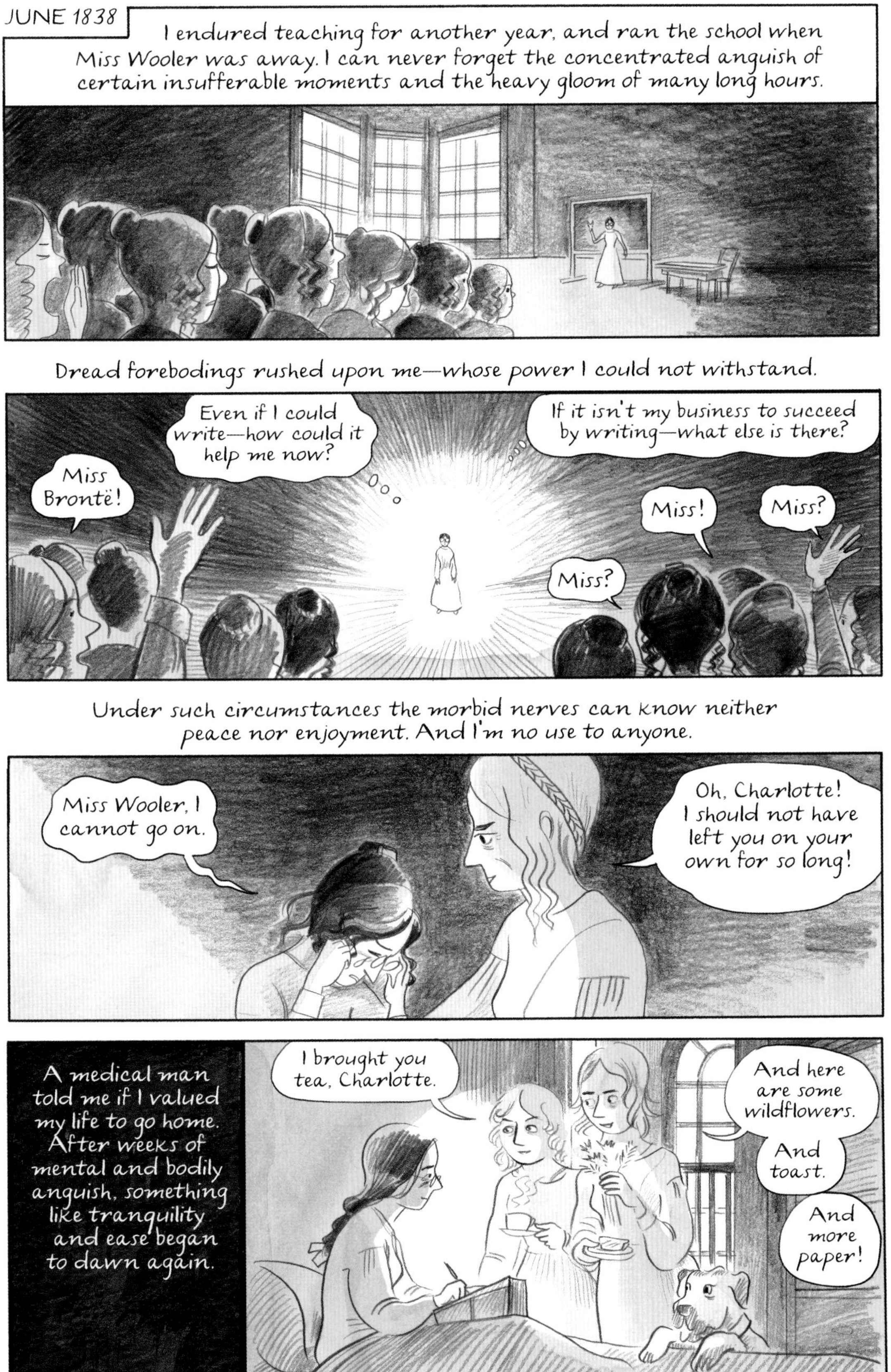
JUNE 1838
I endured teaching for another year, and ran the school when Miss Wooler was away. I can never forget the concentrated anguish of certain insufferable moments and the heavy gloom of many long hours.
Dread forebodings rushed upon me—whose power I could not withstand.
Miss Brontë!
Even if I could write—how could it help me now?
If it isn't my business to succeed by writing—what else is there?
Miss!
Miss?
Miss?
Under such circumstances the morbid nerves can know neither peace nor enjoyment. And I'm no use to anyone.
Miss Wooler, I cannot go on.
Oh, Charlotte! I should not have left you on your own for so long!
A medical man told me if I valued my life to go home. After weeks of mental and bodily anguish, something like tranquility and ease began to dawn again.
I brought you tea, Charlotte.
And here are some wildflowers.
And toast.
And more paper!

SEPTEMBER 1838 EMILY'S TURN

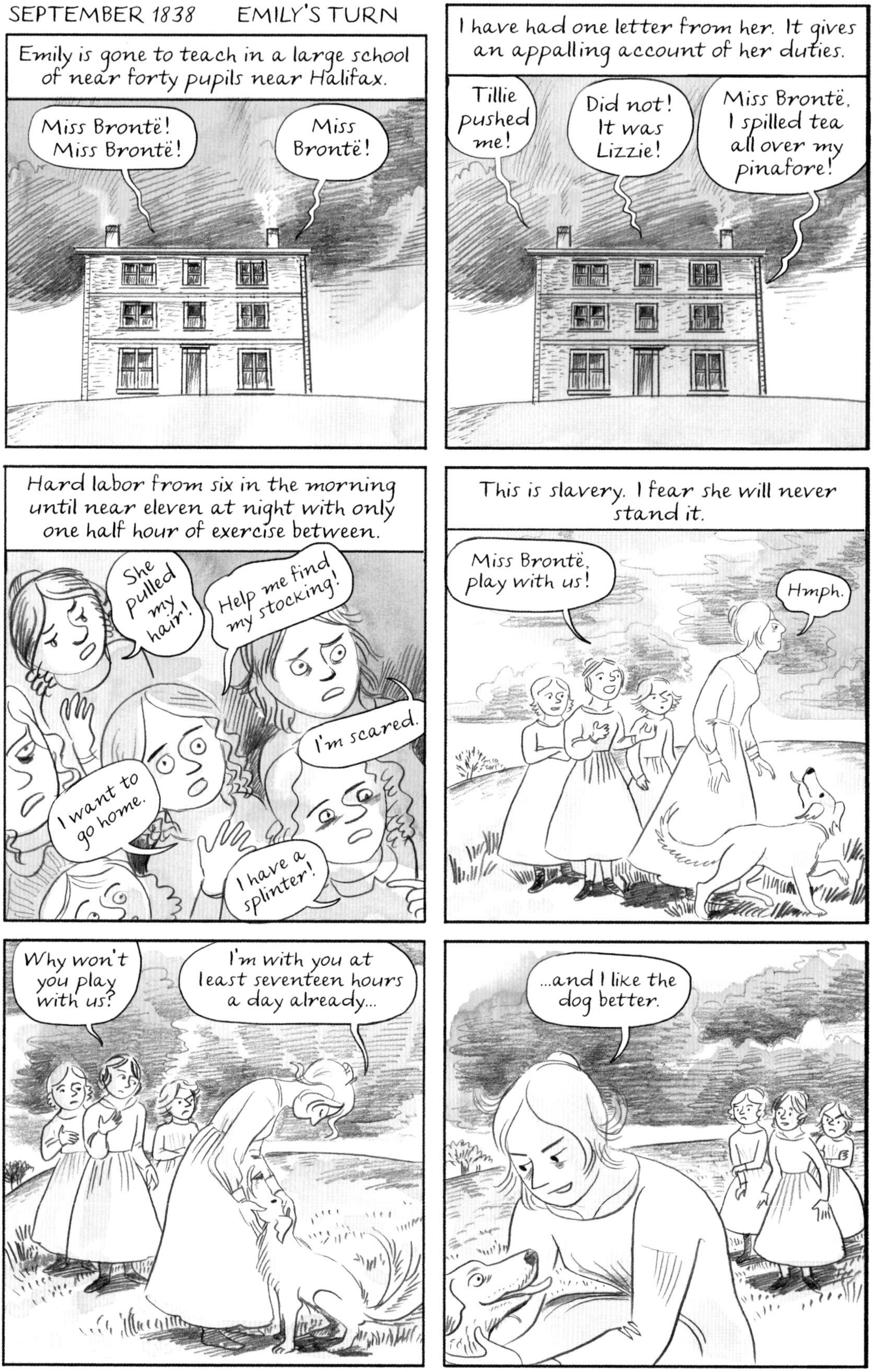
Emily is gone to teach in a large school of near forty pupils near Halifax.
Miss Brontë! Miss Brontë!
Miss Brontë!
I have had one letter from her. It gives an appalling account of her duties.
Tillie pushed me!
Did not! It was Lizzie!
Miss Brontë, I spilled tea all over my pinafore!
Hard labor from six in the morning until near eleven at night with only one half hour of exercise between.
She pulled my hair!
Help me find my stocking!
I'm scared.
I want to go home.
I have a splinter!
This is slavery. I fear she will never stand it.
Miss Brontë, play with us!
Hmph.
Why won't you play with us?
I'm with you at least seventeen hours a day already...
...and I like the dog better.

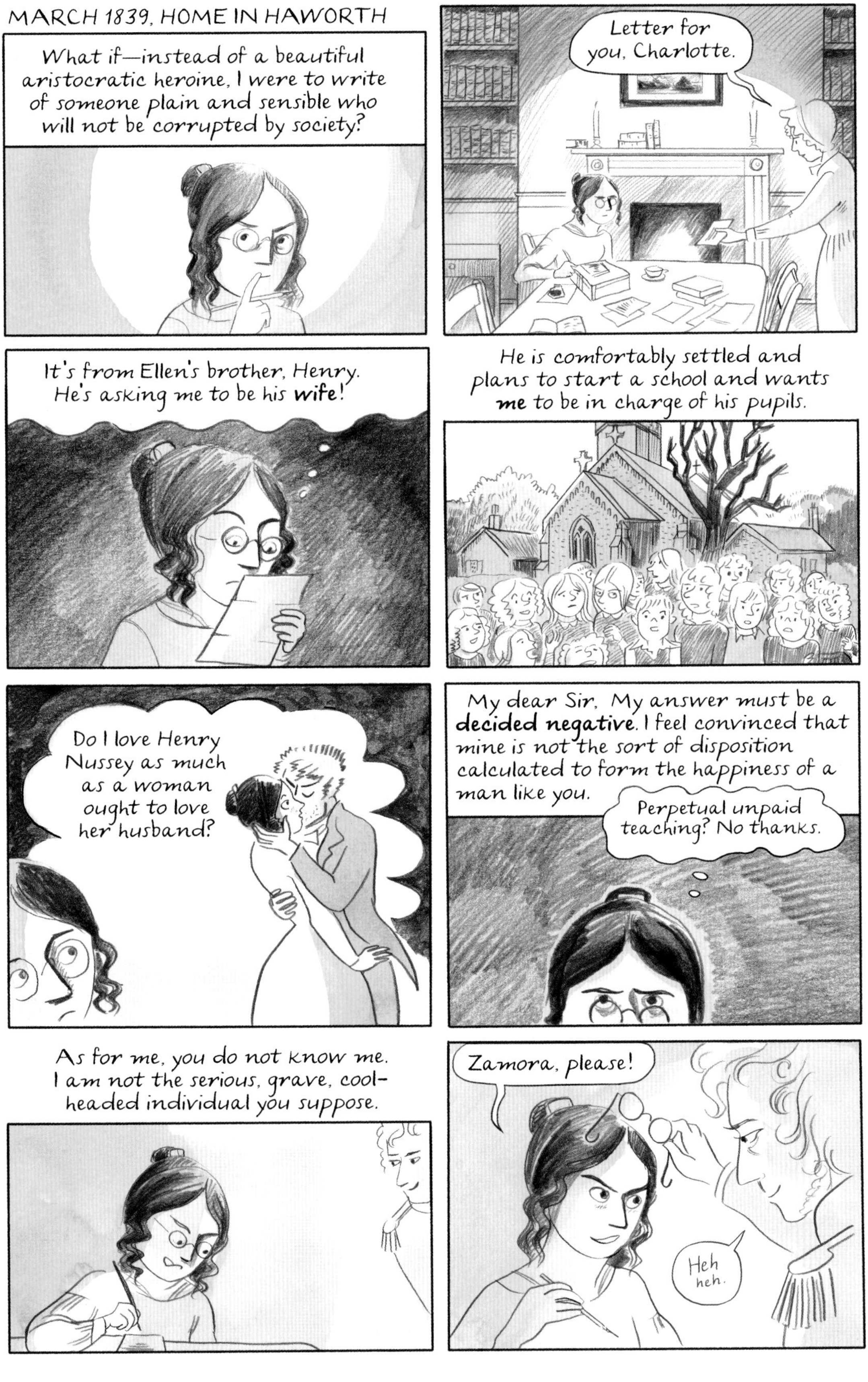
MARCH 1839, HOME IN HAWORTH
What if—instead of a beautiful aristocratic heroine, I were to write of someone plain and sensible who will not be corrupted by society?
Letter for you, Charlotte.
It's from Ellen's brother, Henry. He's asking me to be his **wife**!
He is comfortably settled and plans to start a school and wants **me** to be in charge of his pupils.
Do I love Henry Nussey as much as a woman ought to love her husband?
My dear Sir, My answer must be a **decided negative**. I feel convinced that mine is not the sort of disposition calculated to form the happiness of a man like you.
Perpetual unpaid teaching? No thanks.
As for me, you do not know me. I am not the serious, grave, cool-headed individual you suppose.
Zamora, please!
Heh heh.

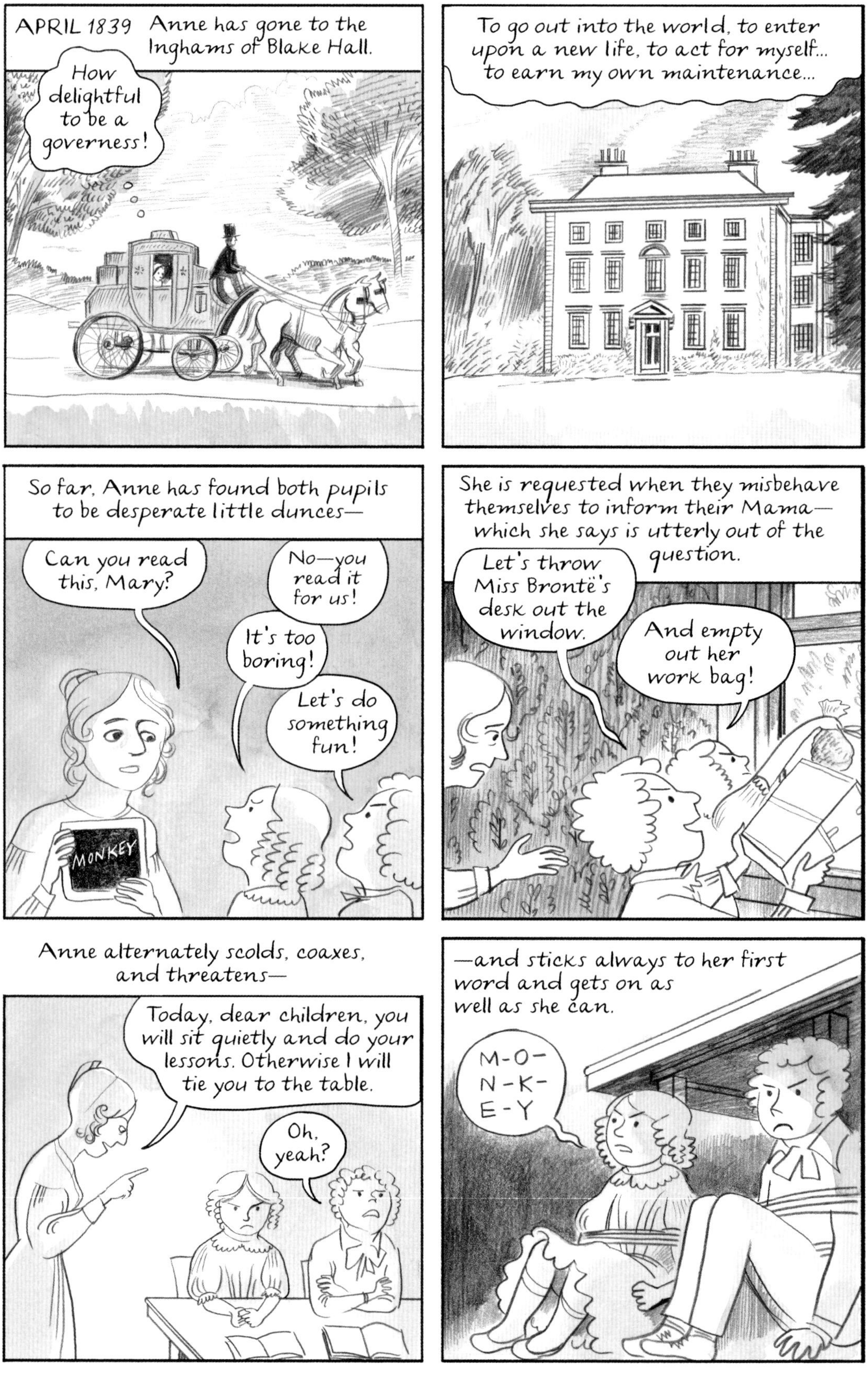
APRIL 1839 Anne has gone to the Inghams of Blake Hall.
How delightful to be a governess!
To go out into the world, to enter upon a new life, to act for myself... to earn my own maintenance...
So far, Anne has found both pupils to be desperate little dunces—
Can you read this, Mary?
No—you read it for us!
It's too boring!
Let's do something fun!
MONKEY
She is requested when they misbehave themselves to inform their Mama—which she says is utterly out of the question.
Let's throw Miss Brontë's desk out the window.
And empty out her work bag!
Anne alternately scolds, coaxes, and threatens—
Today, dear children, you will sit quietly and do your lessons. Otherwise I will tie you to the table.
Oh, yeah?
—and sticks always to her first word and gets on as well as she can.
M-O-N-K-E-Y

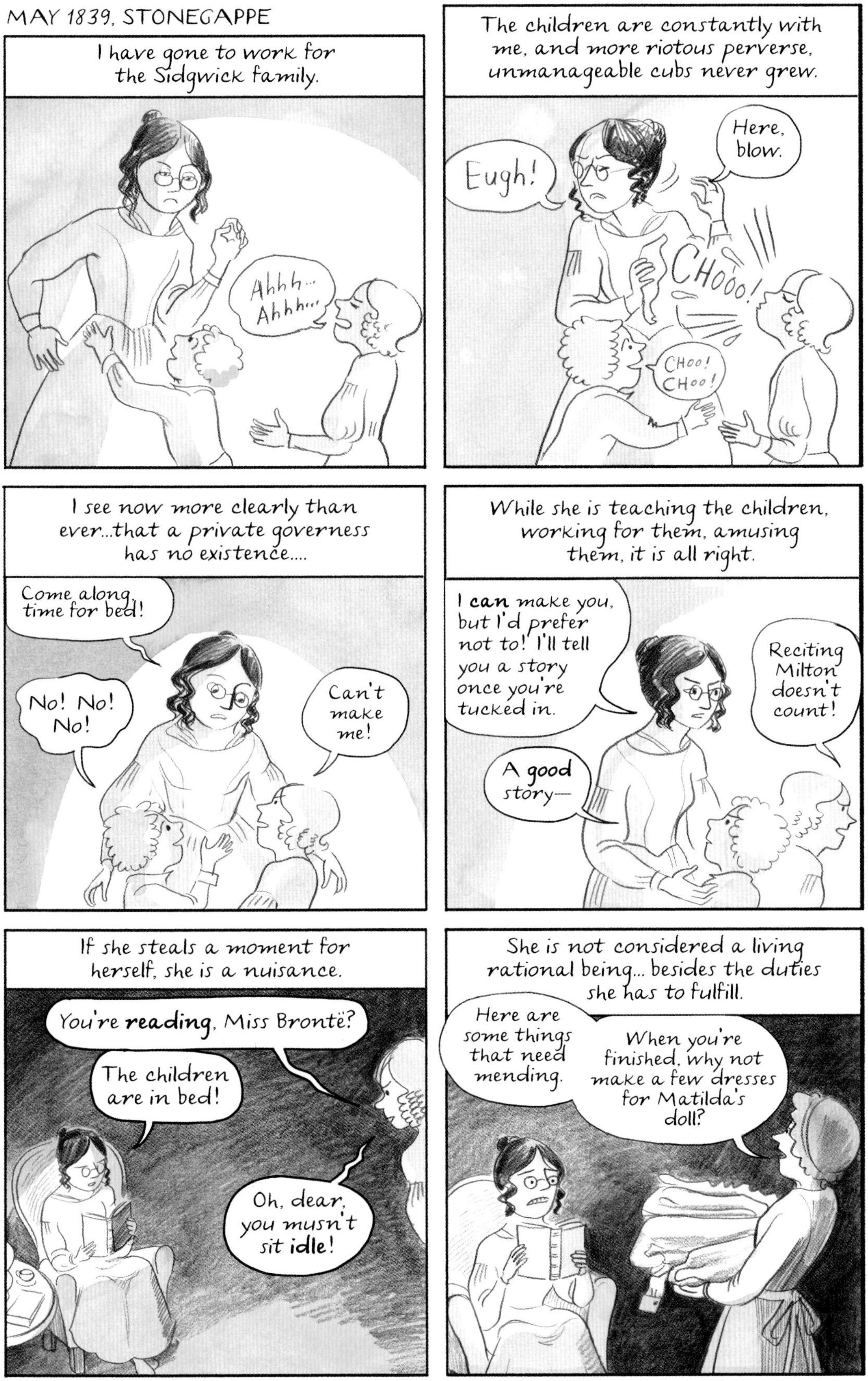
MAY 1839, STONEGAPPE
I have gone to work for the Sidgwick family.
Ahhh... Ahhh...
The children are constantly with me, and more riotous perverse, unmanageable cubs never grew.
Eugh!
Here, blow.
CHOOO!
CHOO! CHOO!
I see now more clearly than ever...that a private governess has no existence....
Come along, time for bed!
No! No! No!
Can't make me!
While she is teaching the children, working for them, amusing them, it is all right.
I **can** make you, but I'd prefer not to! I'll tell you a story once you're tucked in.
Reciting Milton doesn't count!
A **good** story—
If she steals a moment for herself, she is a nuisance.
You're **reading**, Miss Brontë?
The children are in bed!
Oh, dear, you musn't sit **idle**!
She is not considered a living rational being... besides the duties she has to fulfill.
Here are some things that need mending.
When you're finished, why not make a few dresses for Matilda's doll?

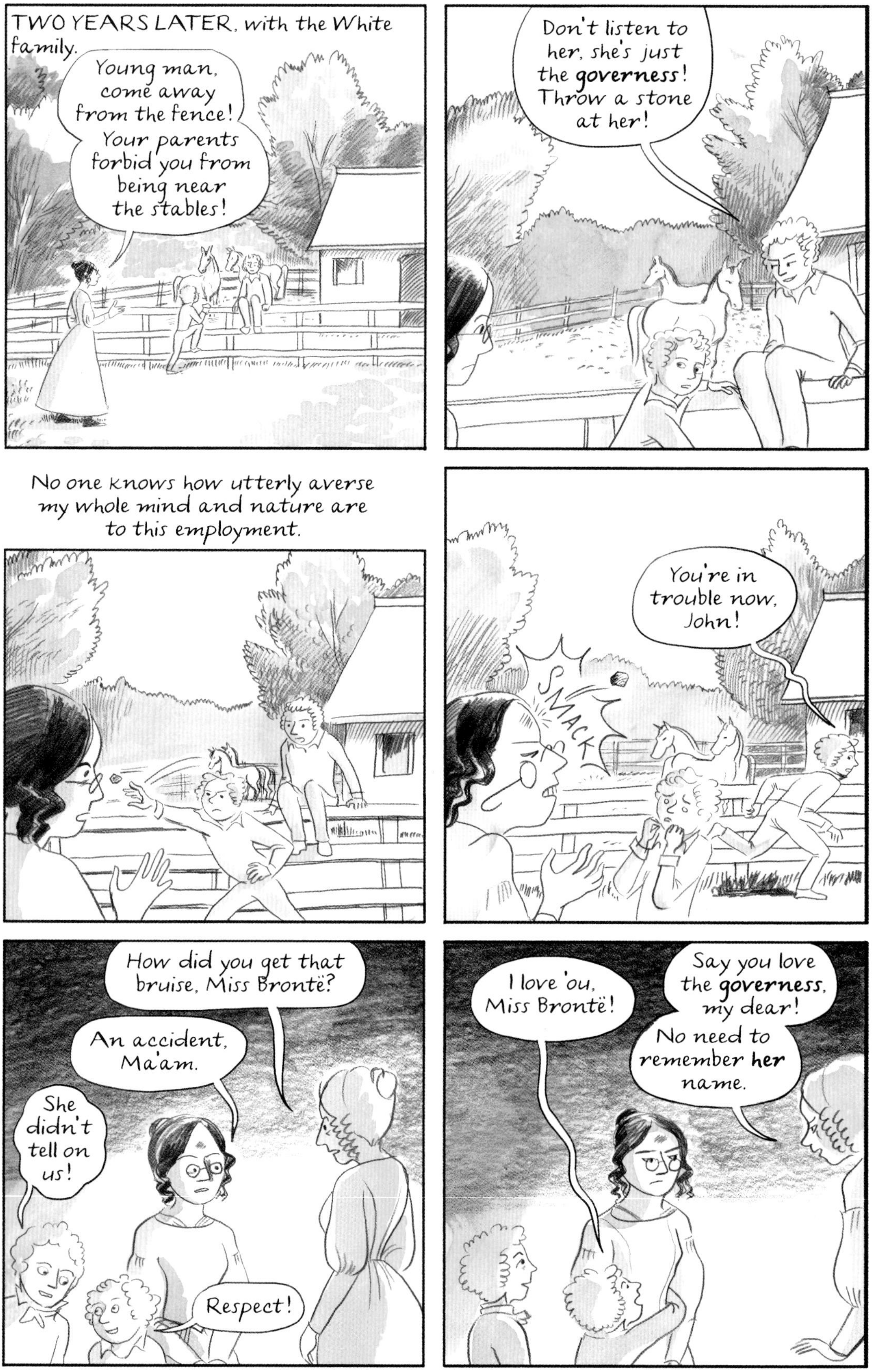
TWO YEARS LATER, with the White family.
Young man, come away from the fence! Your parents forbid you from being near the stables!
Don't listen to her, she's just the **governess**! Throw a stone at her!
No one knows how utterly averse my whole mind and nature are to this employment.
You're in trouble now, John!
SMACK
How did you get that bruise, Miss Brontë?
An accident, Ma'am.
She didn't tell on us!
Respect!
I love 'ou, Miss Brontë!
Say you love the **governess**, my dear!
No need to remember **her** name.

JULY 1841, SUMMER VACATION, HAWORTH

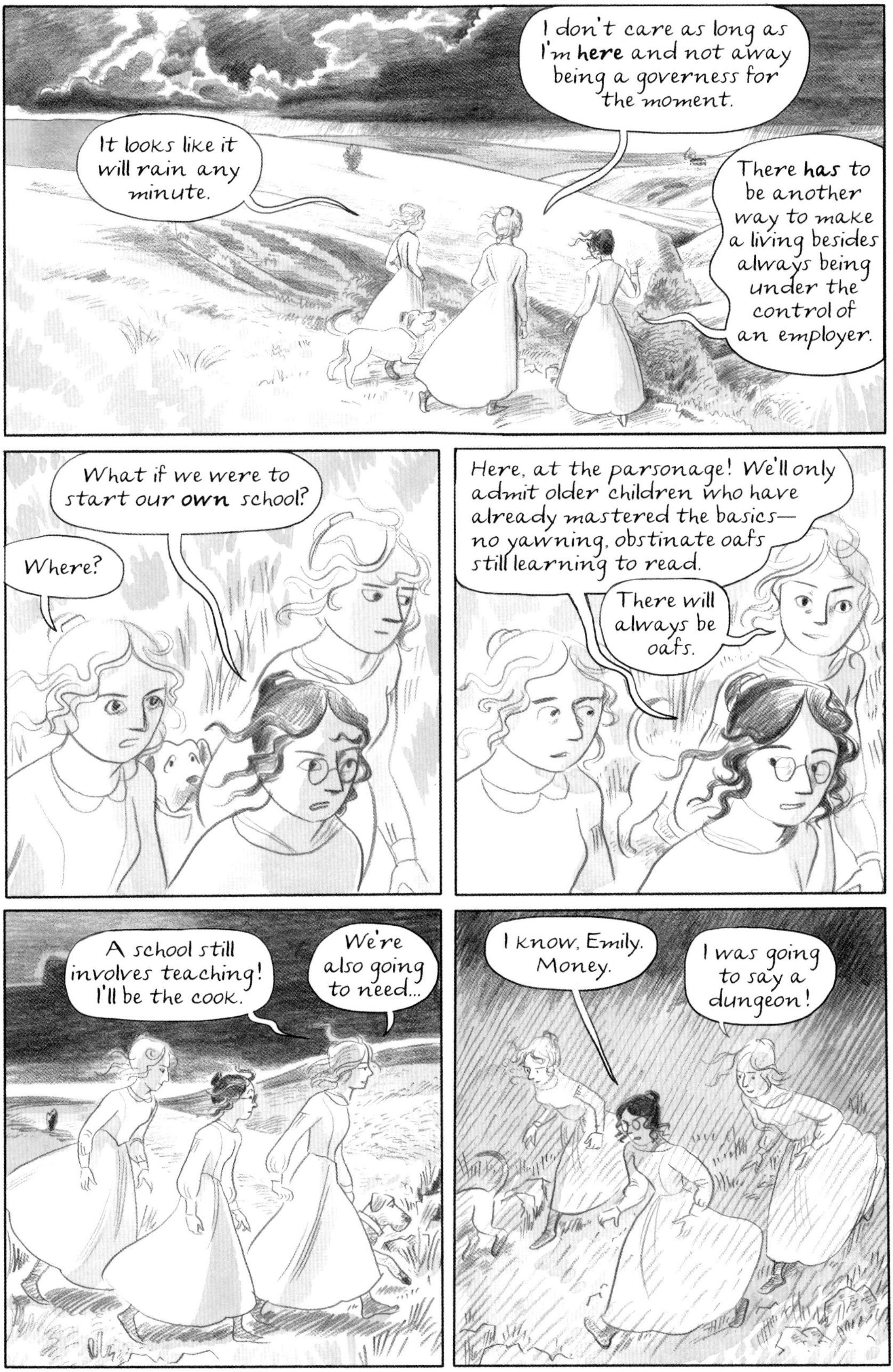

It looks like it will rain any minute.
I don't care as long as I'm **here** and not away being a governess for the moment.
There **has** to be another way to make a living besides always being under the control of an employer.
What if we were to start our **own** school?
Where?
Here, at the parsonage! We'll only admit older children who have already mastered the basics— no yawning, obstinate oafs still learning to read.
There will always be oafs.
A school still involves teaching! I'll be the cook.
We're also going to need...
I know, Emily. Money.
I was going to say a dungeon!

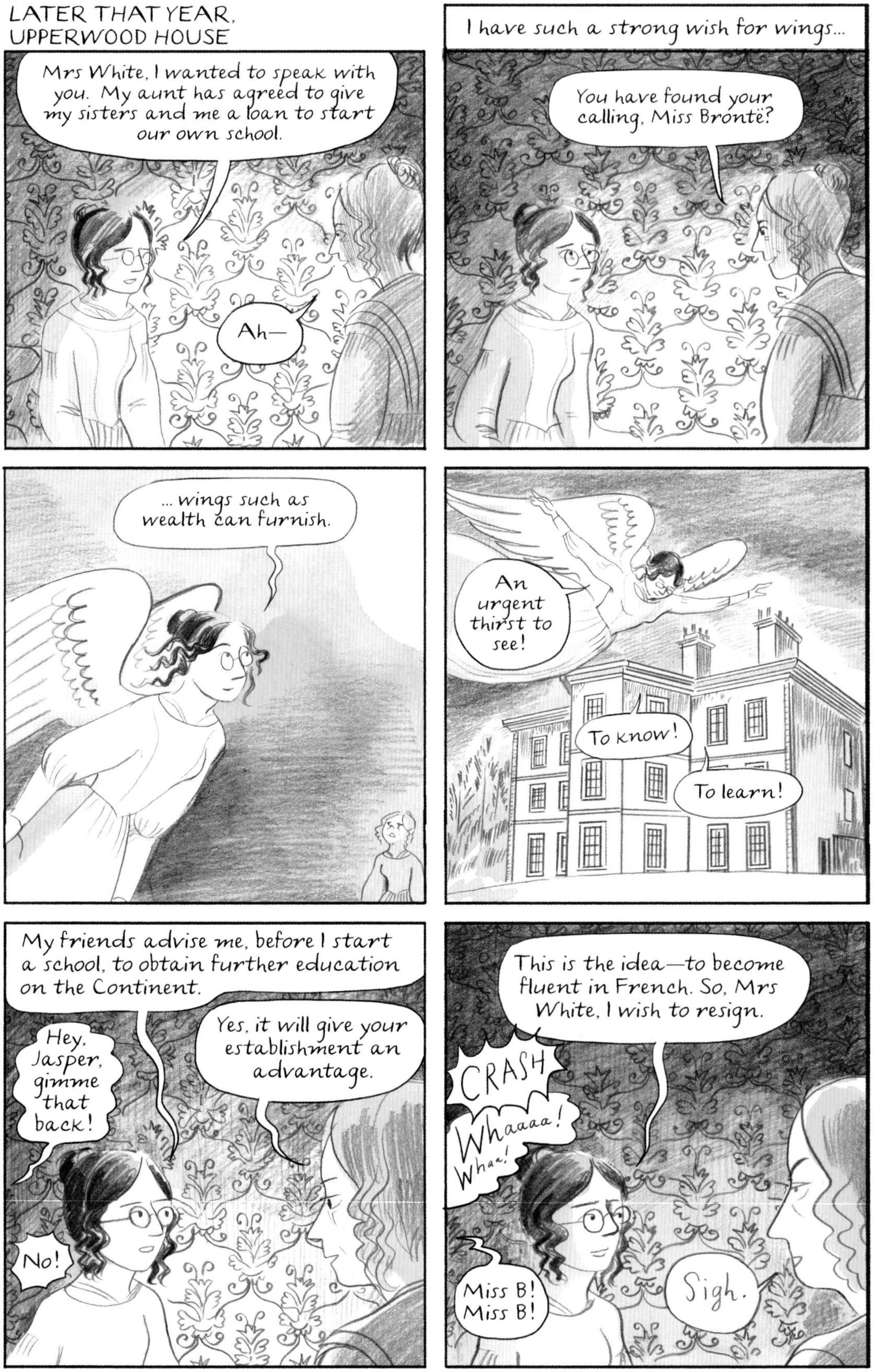

LATER THAT YEAR, UPPERWOOD HOUSE
Mrs White, I wanted to speak with you. My aunt has agreed to give my sisters and me a loan to start our own school.
Ah—
I have such a strong wish for wings...
You have found your calling, Miss Brontë?
...wings such as wealth can furnish.
An urgent thirst to see!
To know!
To learn!
My friends advise me, before I start a school, to obtain further education on the Continent.
Hey, Jasper, gimme that back!
Yes, it will give your establishment an advantage.
No!
This is the idea—to become fluent in French. So, Mrs White, I wish to resign.
CRASH
Whaaaa! Whaa!
Miss B! Miss B!
Sigh.

THE STOPOVER IN LONDON,
8th–11th FEBRUARY

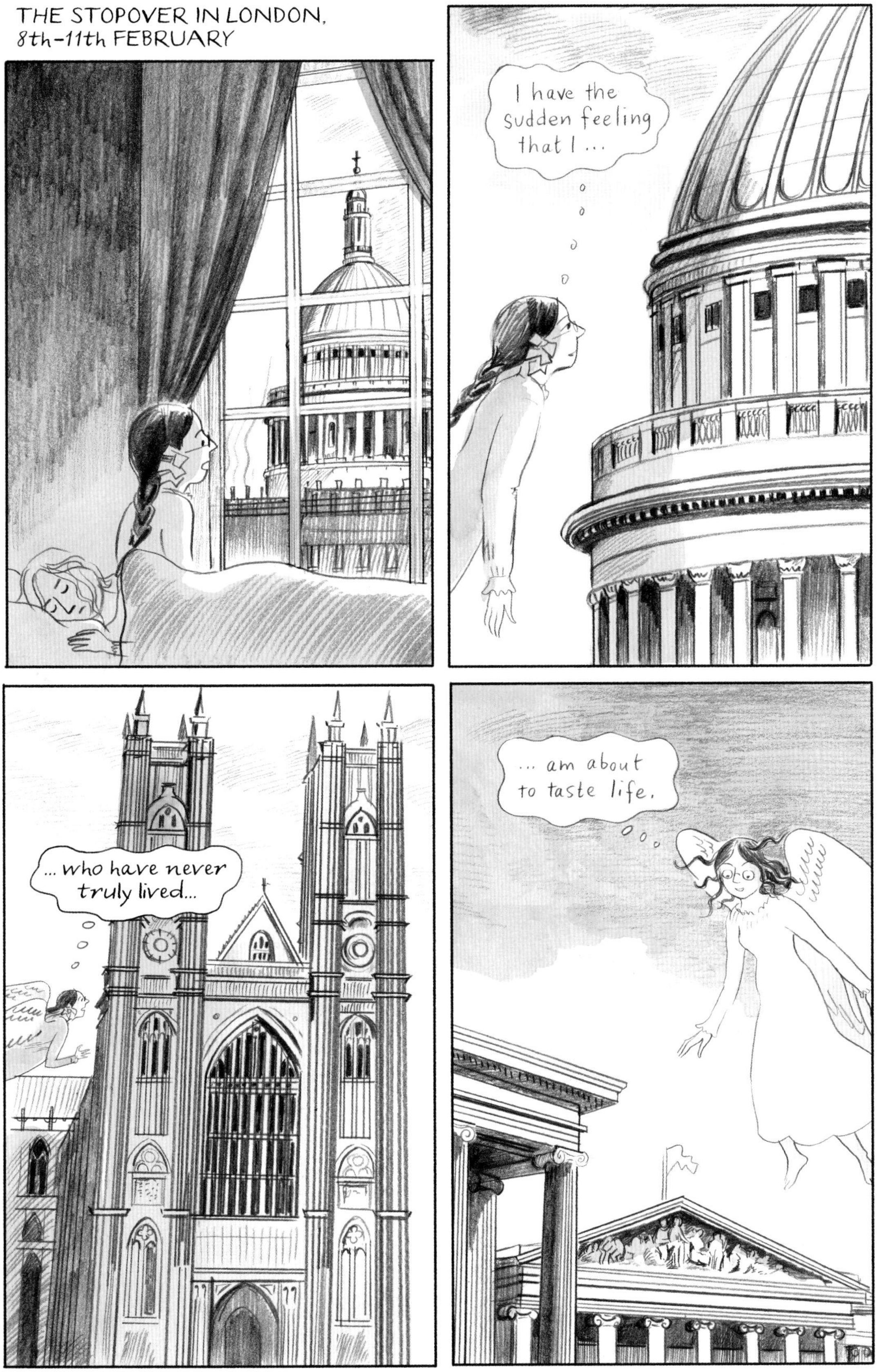
I have the sudden feeling that I ...
... who have never truly lived...
... am about to taste life.

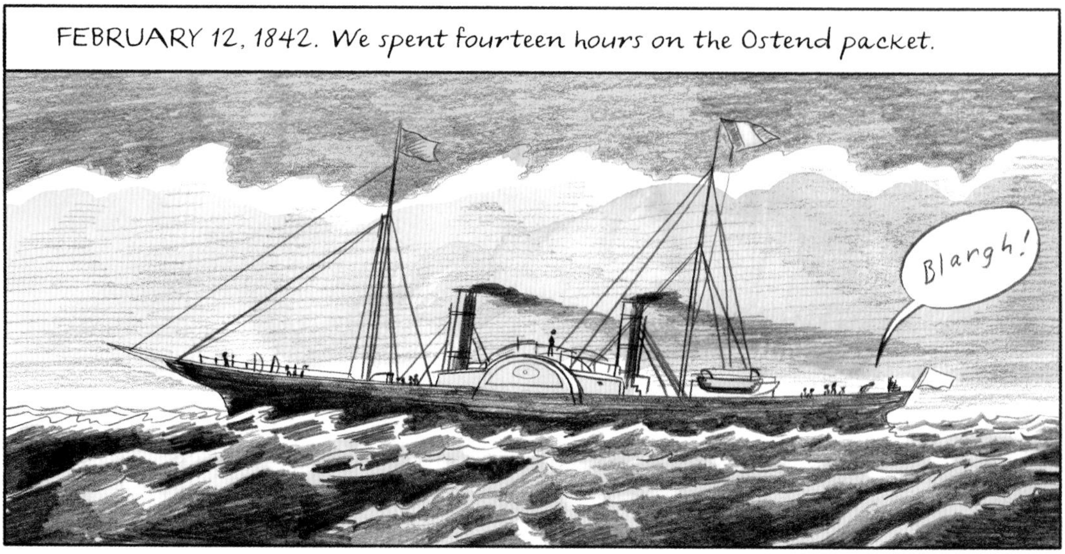
FEBRUARY 12, 1842. We spent fourteen hours on the Ostend packet.
Blargh!

After a night in Ostend, we travelled 70 miles to Brussels by public stagecoach.

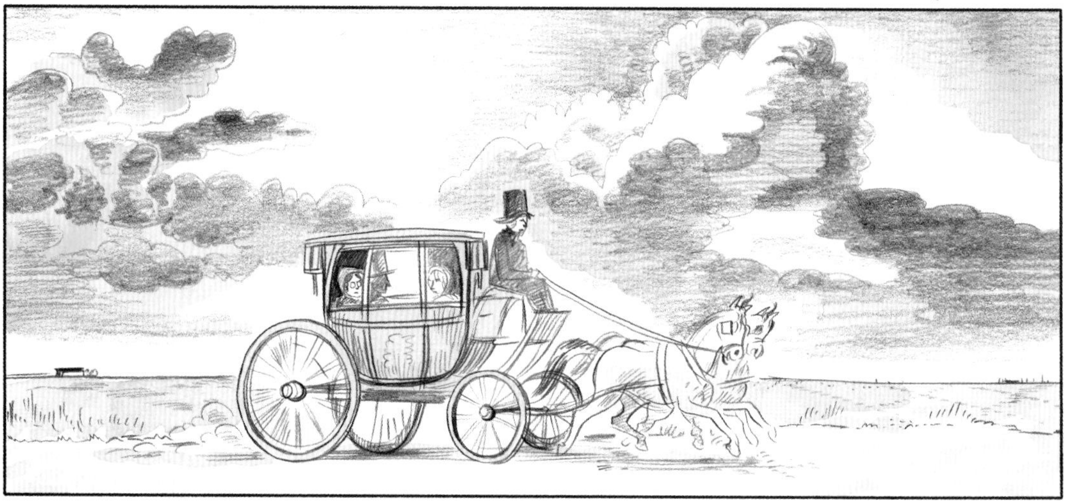

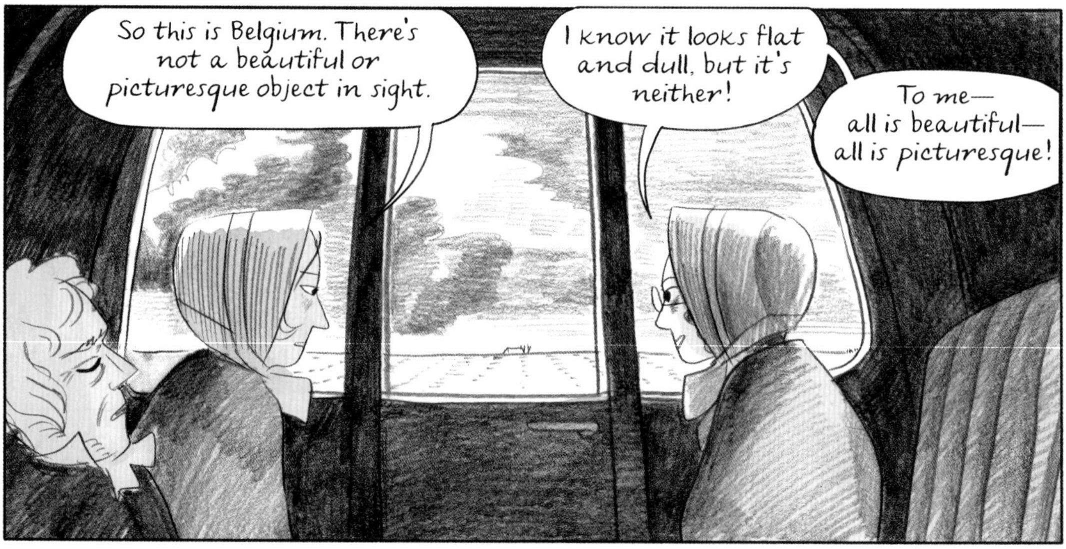
So this is Belgium. There's not a beautiful or picturesque object in sight.
I know it looks flat and dull, but it's neither!
To me— all is beautiful— all is picturesque!

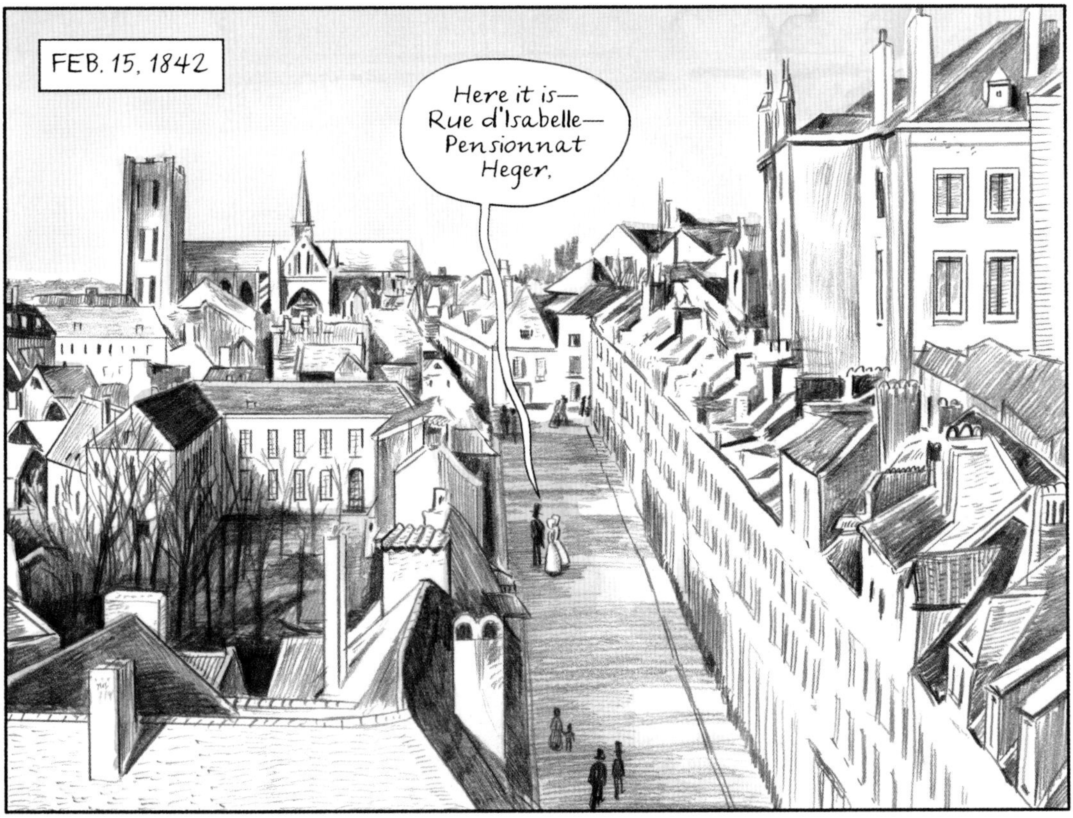
FEB. 15, 1842
Here it is— Rue d'Isabelle— Pensionnat Heger.

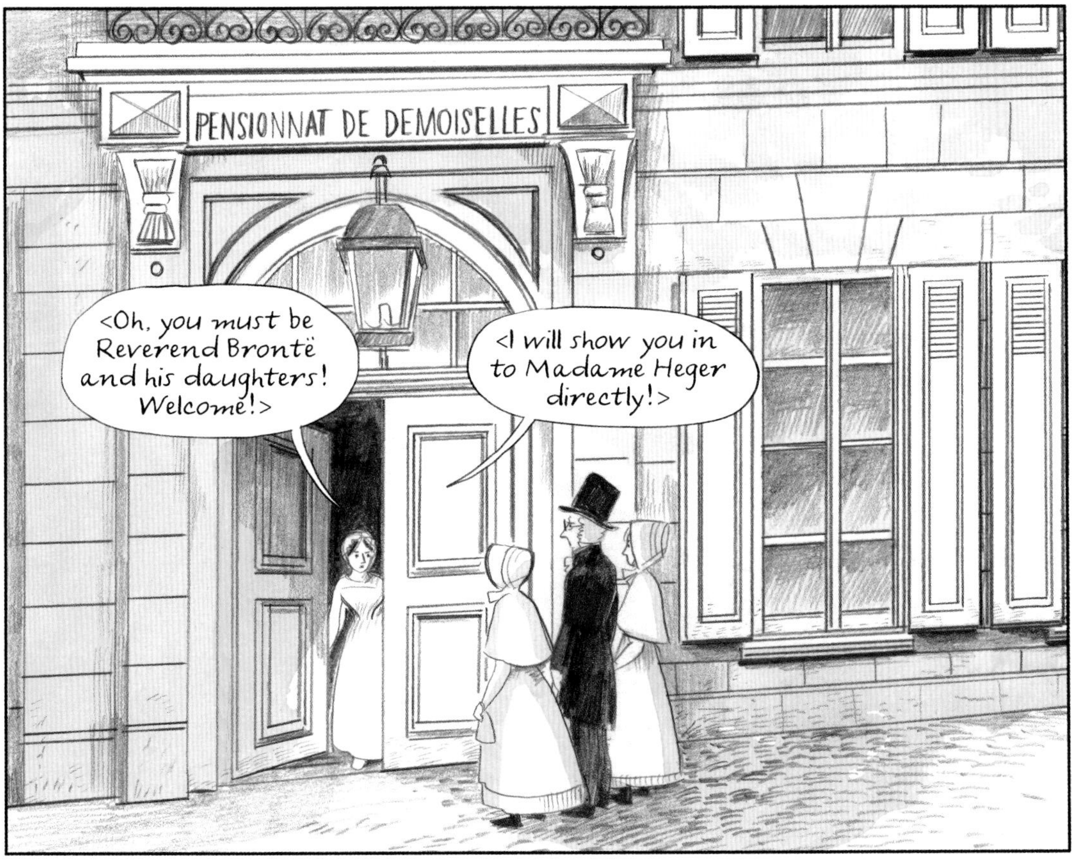
PENSIONNAT DE DEMOISELLES
<Oh, you must be Reverend Brontë and his daughters! Welcome!>
<I will show you in to Madame Heger directly!>

Dear Ellen, I am twenty-six years old and at that ripe time in life I am a schoolgirl—a complete schoolgirl...

Bonjour, Monsieur.

<Here is our professor of French literature, Monsieur Heger, my husband.>

...and on the whole very happy.

<Because you still have much to learn in our language, I shall give you private lessons, Mesdemoiselles Brontë.>

It felt very strange at first to submit to authority instead of exercising it—

<We will begin with a dictation of a notable work of literature. I will read, you will write.>

I returned to it with the same avidity that a cow that has long been kept on dry hay returns to fresh grass— don't laugh at my simile!

<"The Poor Girl" by Alexandre Soumet. I fled from painful slumber / Unattended by any happy dreams...>

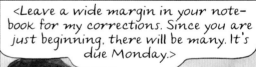

<Now for your homework: You must write an essay in response to this poem—on the model of excellence I have given—but in your own words.>

<Leave a wide margin in your note-book for my corrections. Since you are just beginning, there will be many. It's due Monday.>

Yes, Monsieur!

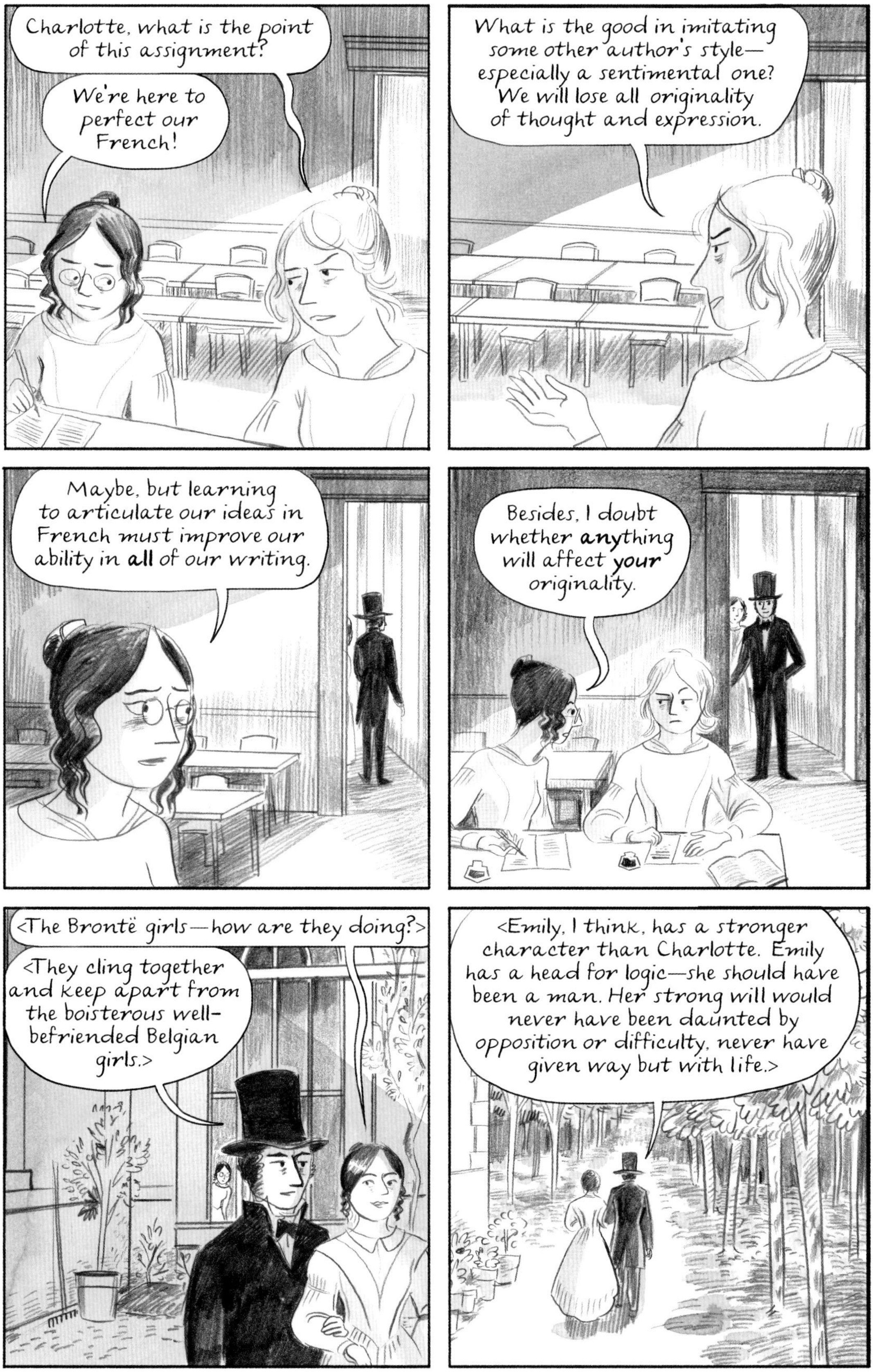
Charlotte, what is the point of this assignment?
We're here to perfect our French!
What is the good in imitating some other author's style—especially a sentimental one? We will lose all originality of thought and expression.
Maybe, but learning to articulate our ideas in French must improve our ability in **all** of our writing.
Besides, I doubt whether **any**thing will affect **your** originality.
<The Brontë girls—how are they doing?>
<They cling together and keep apart from the boisterous well-befriended Belgian girls.>
<Emily, I think, has a stronger character than Charlotte. Emily has a head for logic—she should have been a man. Her strong will would never have been daunted by opposition or difficulty, never have given way but with life.>

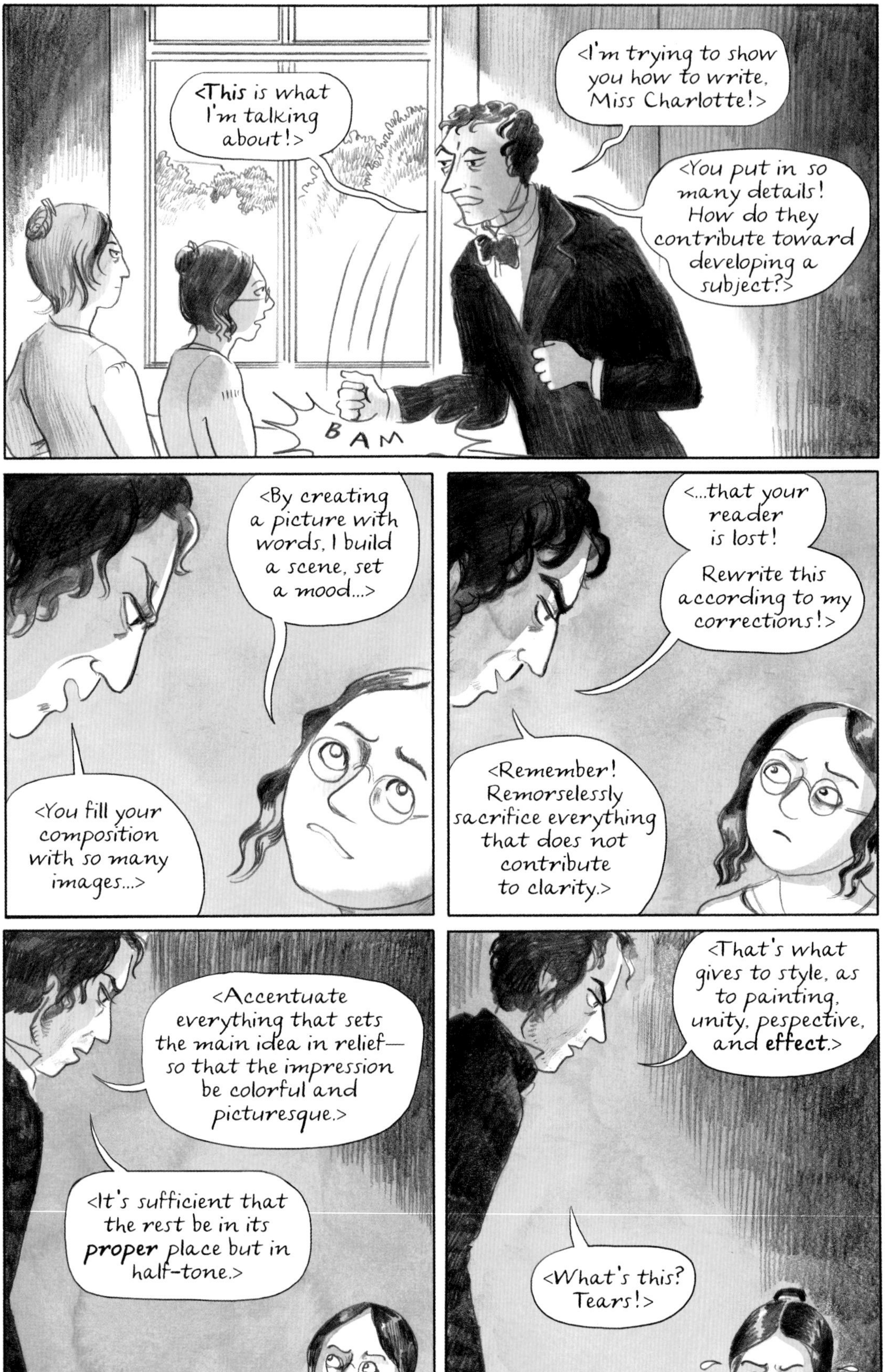
<This is what I'm talking about!>
BAM
<I'm trying to show you how to write, Miss Charlotte!>
<You put in so many details! How do they contribute toward developing a subject?>
<By creating a picture with words, I build a scene, set a mood...>
<You fill your composition with so many images...>
<...that your reader is lost!
Rewrite this according to my corrections!>
<Remember! Remorselessly sacrifice everything that does not contribute to clarity.>
<Accentuate everything that sets the main idea in relief—so that the impression be colorful and picturesque.>
<It's sufficient that the rest be in its **proper** place but in half-tone.>
<That's what gives to style, as to painting, unity, pespective, and **effect**.>
<What's this? Tears!>

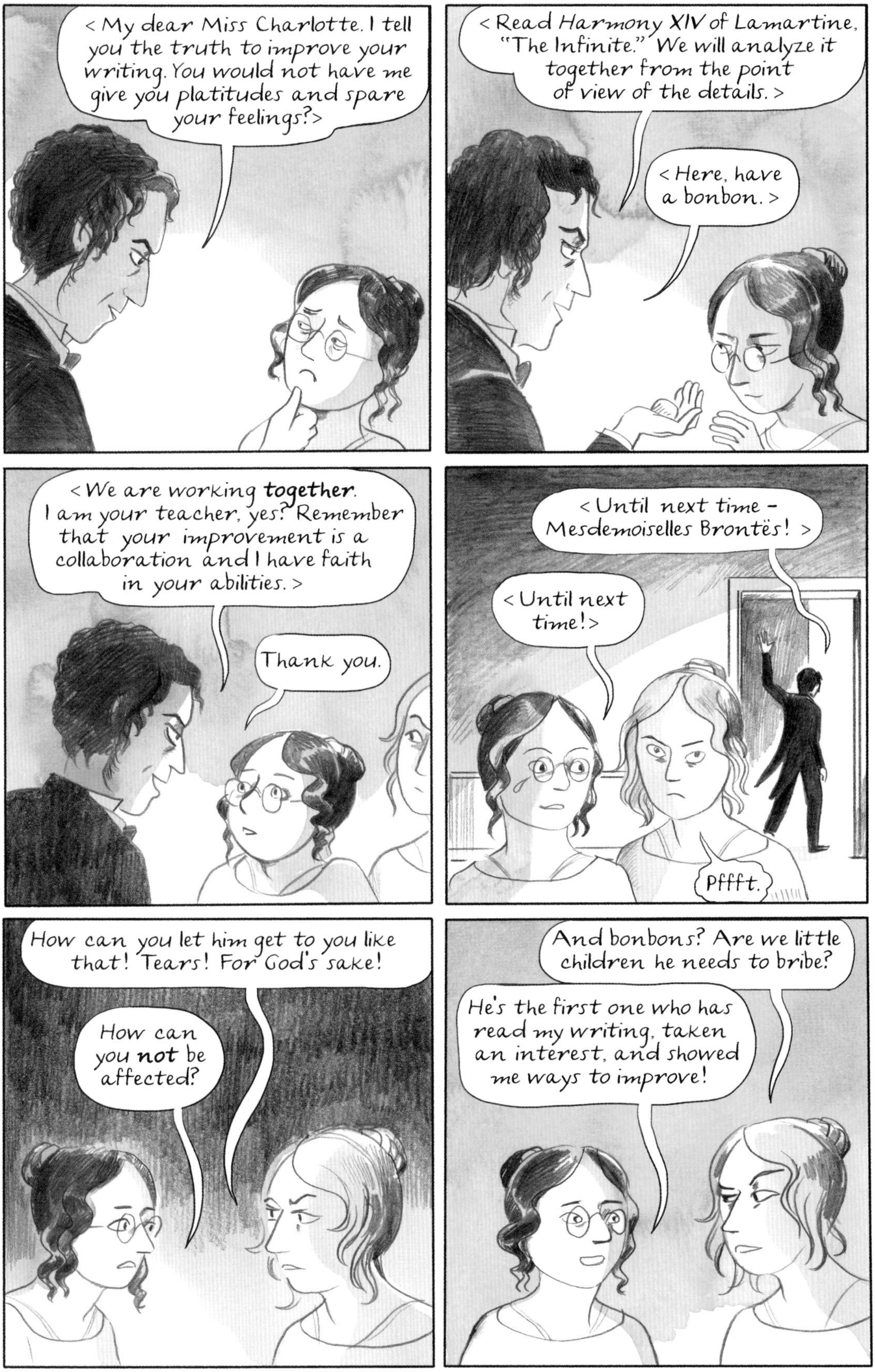
< My dear Miss Charlotte. I tell you the truth to improve your writing. You would not have me give you platitudes and spare your feelings?>
< Read *Harmony* **XIV** of Lamartine, "The Infinite." We will analyze it together from the point of view of the details. >
< Here, have a bonbon. >
< We are working **together**. I am your teacher, yes? Remember that your improvement is a collaboration and I have faith in your abilities. >
Thank you.
< Until next time - Mesdemoiselles Brontës! >
< Until next time!>
Pffft.
How can you let him get to you like that! Tears! For God's sake!
How can you **not** be affected?
And bonbons? Are we little children he needs to bribe?
He's the first one who has read my writing, taken an interest, and showed me ways to improve!

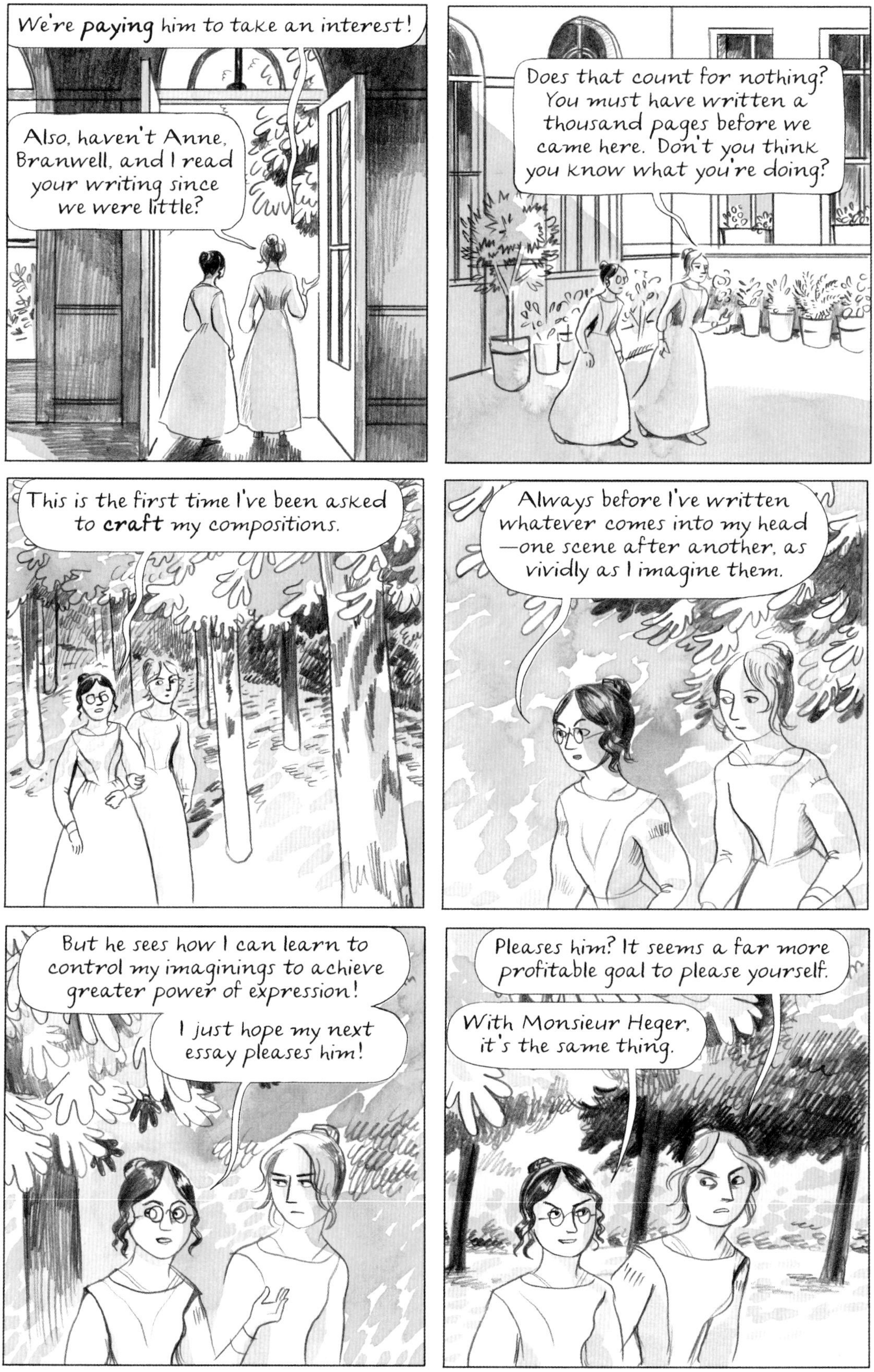
We're **paying** him to take an interest!
Also, haven't Anne, Branwell, and I read your writing since we were little?
Does that count for nothing? You must have written a thousand pages before we came here. Don't you think you know what you're doing?
This is the first time I've been asked to **craft** my compositions.
Always before I've written whatever comes into my head —one scene after another, as vividly as I imagine them.
But he sees how I can learn to control my imaginings to achieve greater power of expression!
I just hope my next essay pleases him!
Pleases him? It seems a far more profitable goal to please yourself.
With Monsieur Heger, it's the same thing.

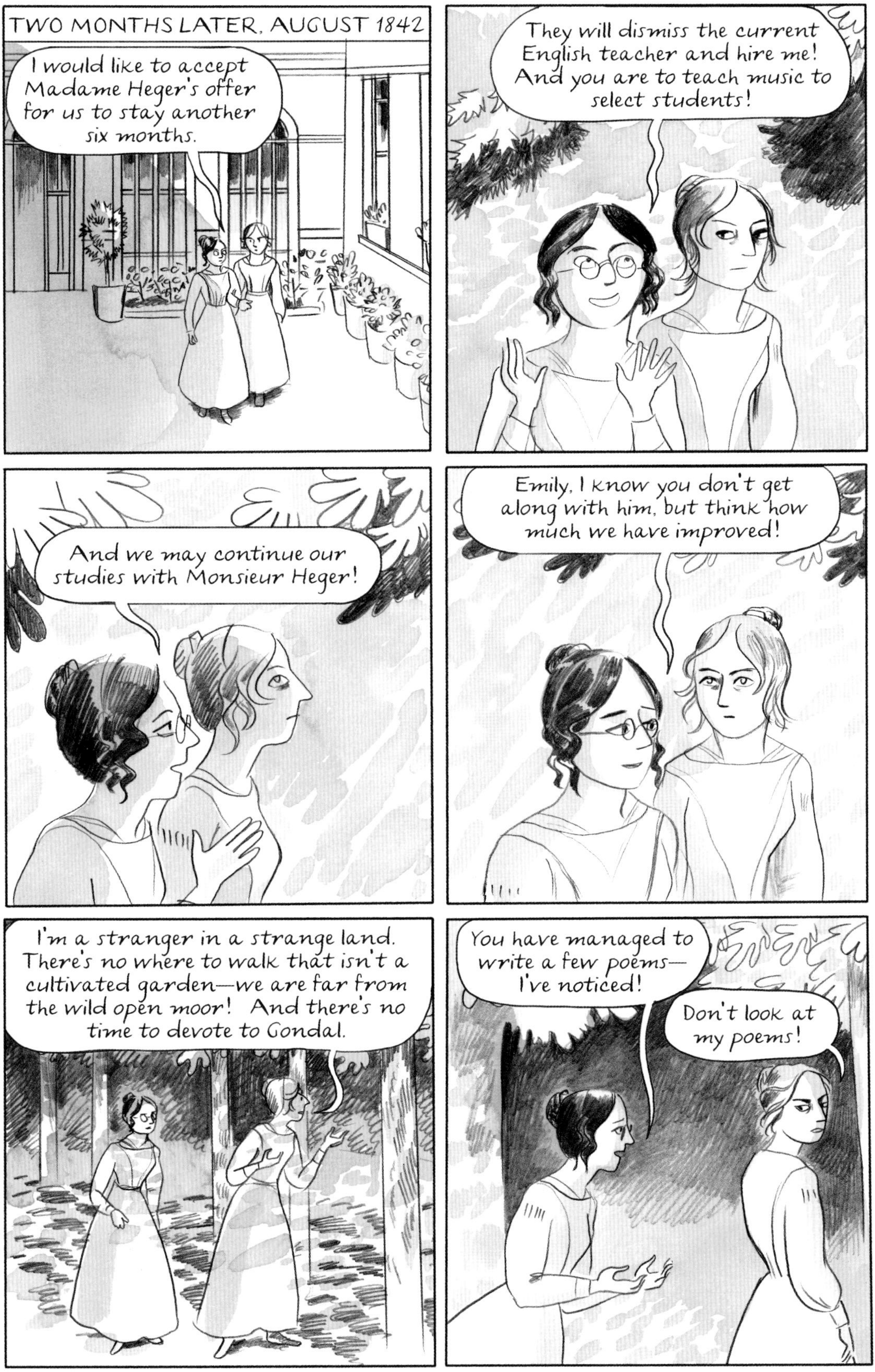
TWO MONTHS LATER, AUGUST 1842
I would like to accept Madame Heger's offer for us to stay another six months.
They will dismiss the current English teacher and hire me! And you are to teach music to select students!
And we may continue our studies with Monsieur Heger!
Emily, I know you don't get along with him, but think how much we have improved!
I'm a stranger in a strange land. There's no where to walk that isn't a cultivated garden—we are far from the wild open moor! And there's no time to devote to Gondal.
You have managed to write a few poems—I've noticed!
Don't look at my poems!

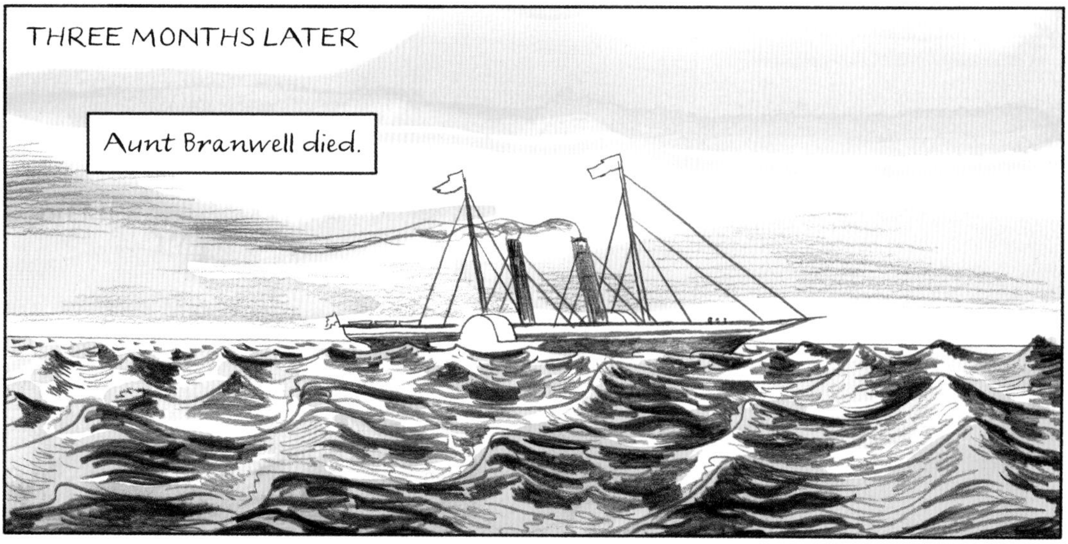
THREE MONTHS LATER
Aunt Branwell died.

Emily and I returned to Haworth as soon as we could, but not in time for the funeral. Anne came home from Thorp Green. Branwell was with our aunt when she died.

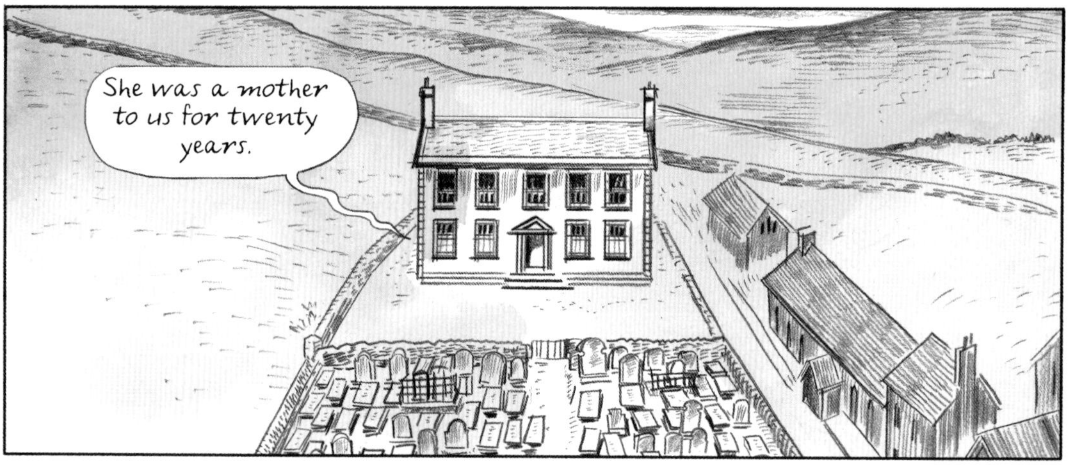
She was a mother to us for twenty years.

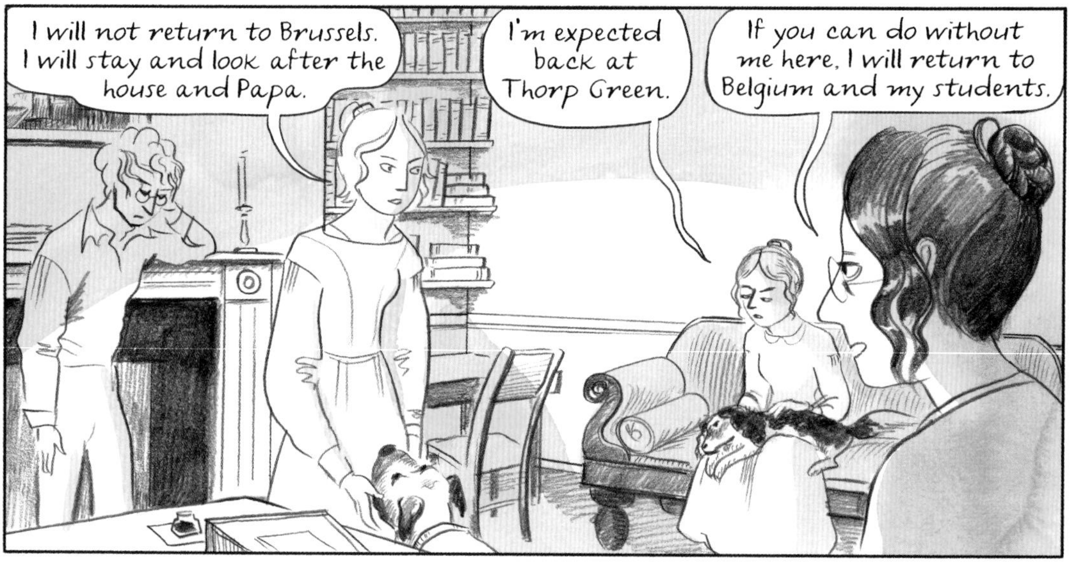
I will not return to Brussels. I will stay and look after the house and Papa.
I'm expected back at Thorp Green.
If you can do without me here, I will return to Belgium and my students.

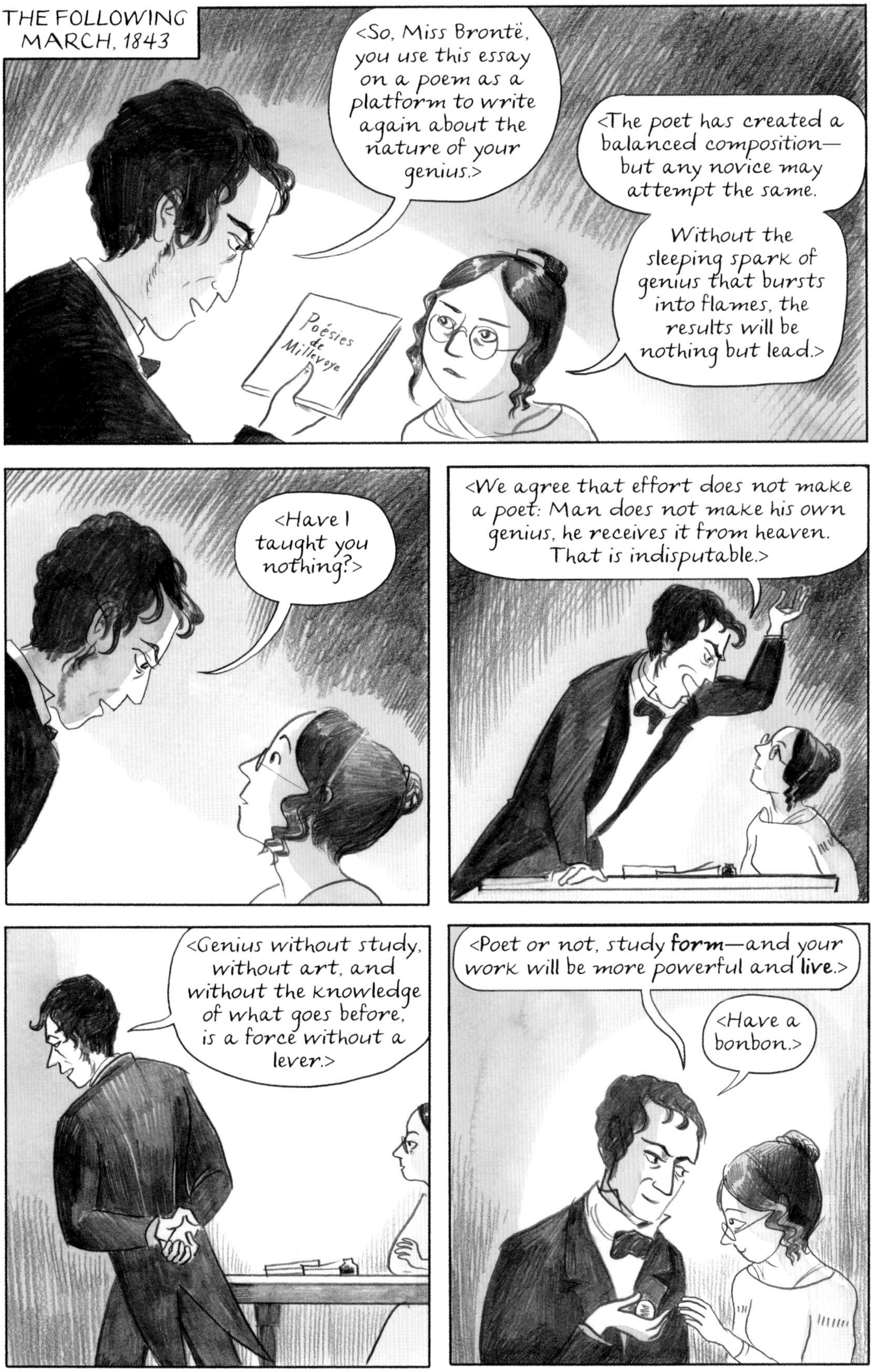
THE FOLLOWING MARCH, 1843
<So, Miss Brontë, you use this essay on a poem as a platform to write again about the nature of your genius.>
Poésies de Millevoye
<The poet has created a balanced composition— but any novice may attempt the same.
Without the sleeping spark of genius that bursts into flames, the results will be nothing but lead.>
<Have I taught you nothing?>
<We agree that effort does not make a poet: Man does not make his own genius, he receives it from heaven. That is indisputable.>
<Genius without study, without art, and without the knowledge of what goes before, is a force without a lever.>
<Poet or not, study **form**—and your work will be more powerful and **live**.>
<Have a bonbon.>

LATER THAT MONTH

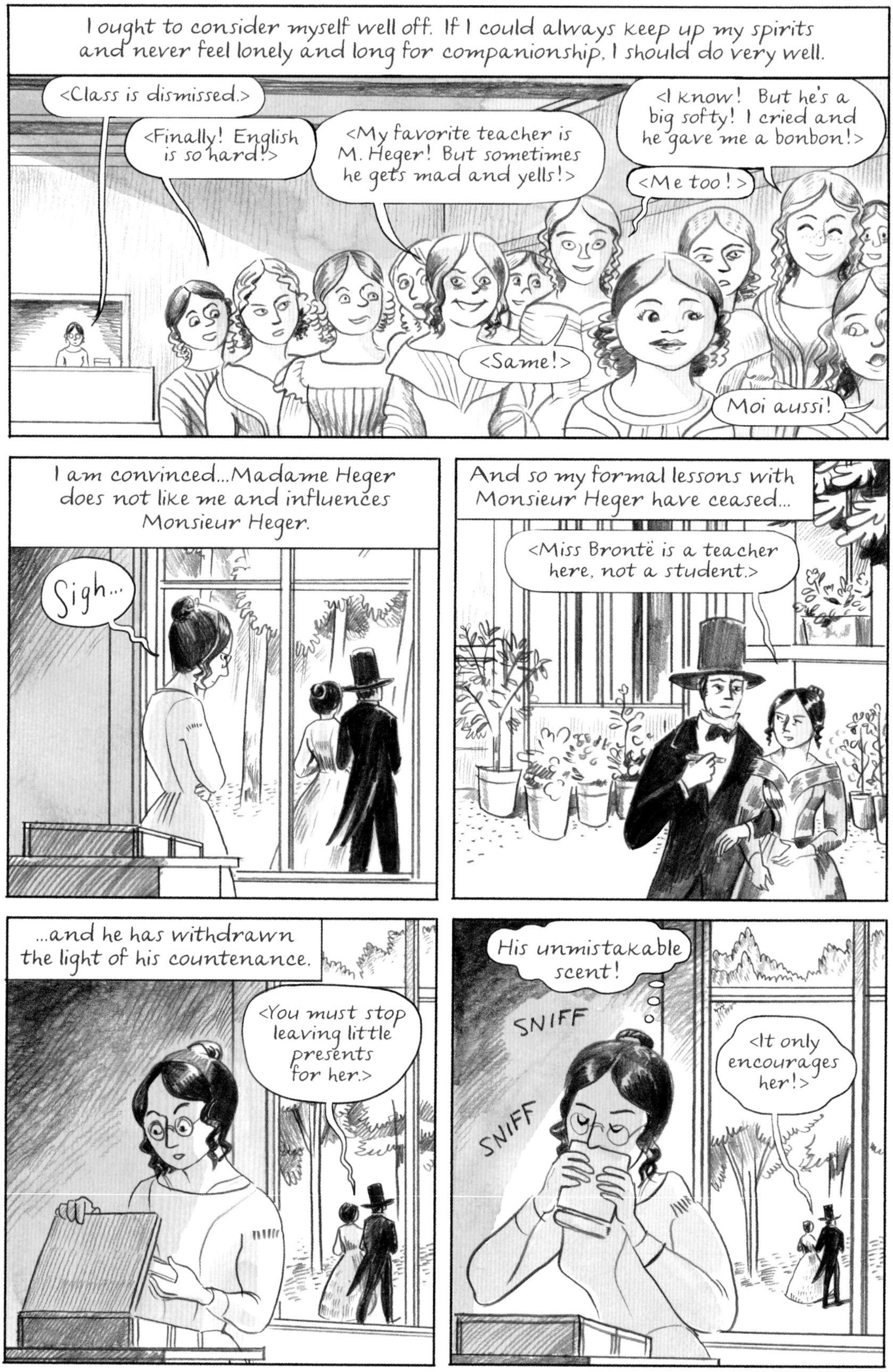
I ought to consider myself well off. If I could always keep up my spirits and never feel lonely and long for companionship, I should do very well.
<Class is dismissed.>
<Finally! English is so hard!>
<My favorite teacher is M. Heger! But sometimes he gets mad and yells!>
<I know! But he's a big softy! I cried and he gave me a bonbon!>
<Me too!>
<Same!>
Moi aussi!
I am convinced...Madame Heger does not like me and influences Monsieur Heger.
Sigh...
And so my formal lessons with Monsieur Heger have ceased...
<Miss Brontë is a teacher here, not a student.>
...and he has withdrawn the light of his countenance.
<You must stop leaving little presents for her.>
His unmistakable scent!
SNIFF
SNIFF
<It only encourages her!>

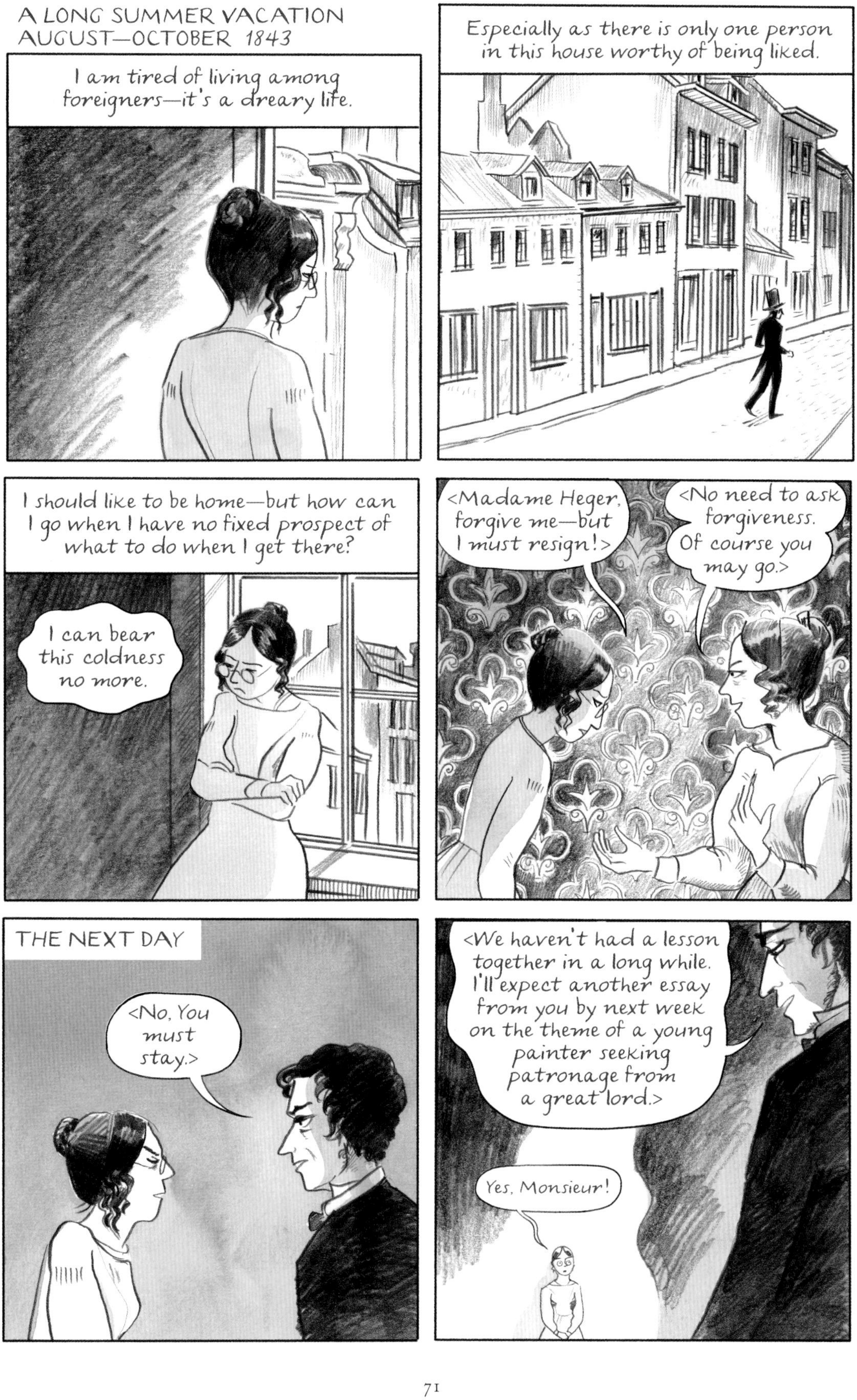
A LONG SUMMER VACATION
AUGUST—OCTOBER 1843
I am tired of living among foreigners—it's a dreary life.
Especially as there is only one person in this house worthy of being liked.
I should like to be home—but how can I go when I have no fixed prospect of what to do when I get there?
I can bear this coldness no more.
<Madame Heger, forgive me—but I must resign!>
<No need to ask forgiveness. Of course you may go.>
THE NEXT DAY
<No, You must stay.>
<We haven't had a lesson together in a long while. I'll expect another essay from you by next week on the theme of a young painter seeking patronage from a great lord.>
Yes, Monsieur!

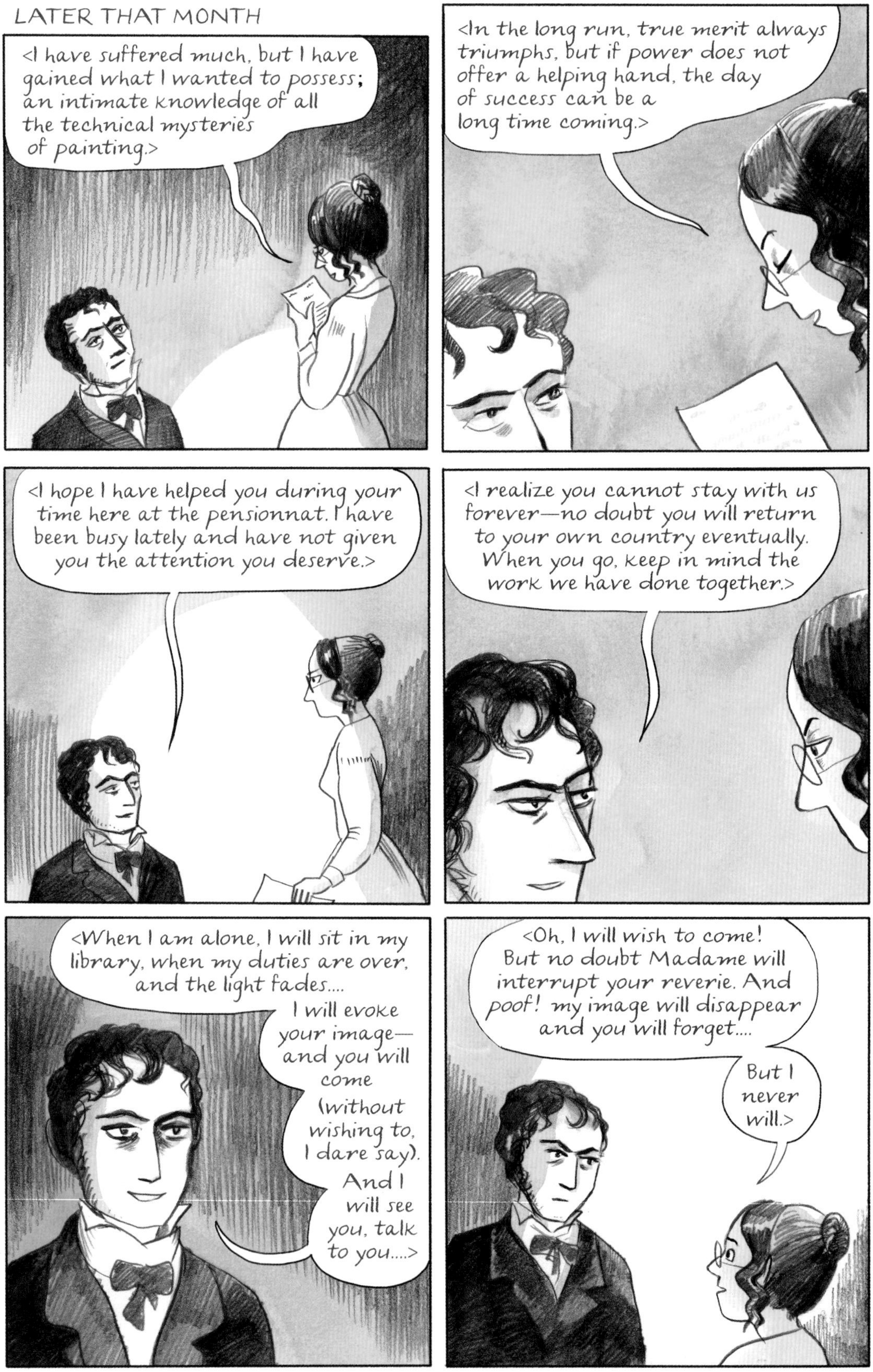
LATER THAT MONTH
<I have suffered much, but I have gained what I wanted to possess; an intimate knowledge of all the technical mysteries of painting.>
<In the long run, true merit always triumphs, but if power does not offer a helping hand, the day of success can be a long time coming.>
<I hope I have helped you during your time here at the pensionnat. I have been busy lately and have not given you the attention you deserve.>
<I realize you cannot stay with us forever—no doubt you will return to your own country eventually. When you go, keep in mind the work we have done together.>
<When I am alone, I will sit in my library, when my duties are over, and the light fades....
I will evoke your image—and you will come (without wishing to, I dare say).
And I will see you, talk to you....>
<Oh, I will wish to come! But no doubt Madame will interrupt your reverie. And *poof!* my image will disappear and you will forget....
But I never will.>

DECEMBER 1843

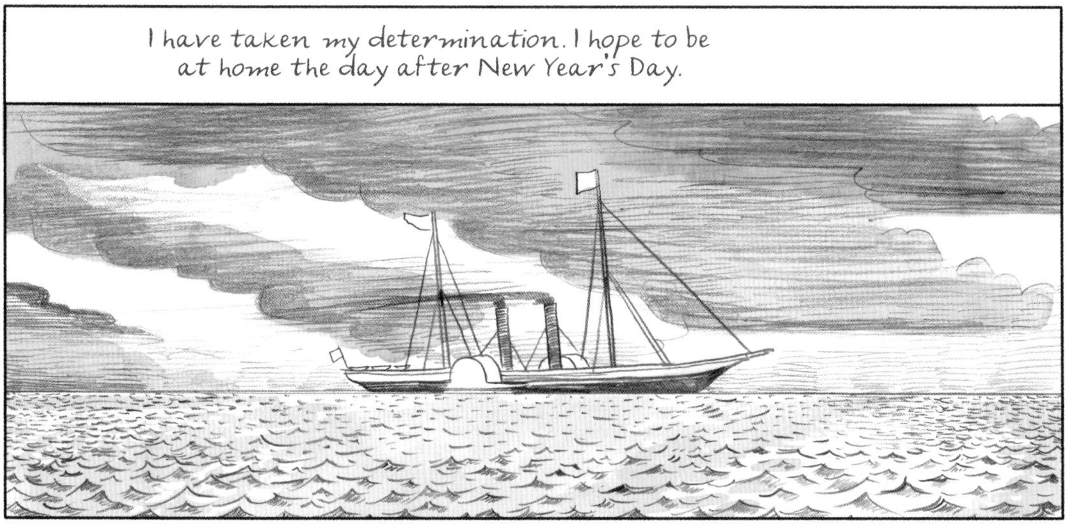
I have taken my determination. I hope to be at home the day after New Year's Day.

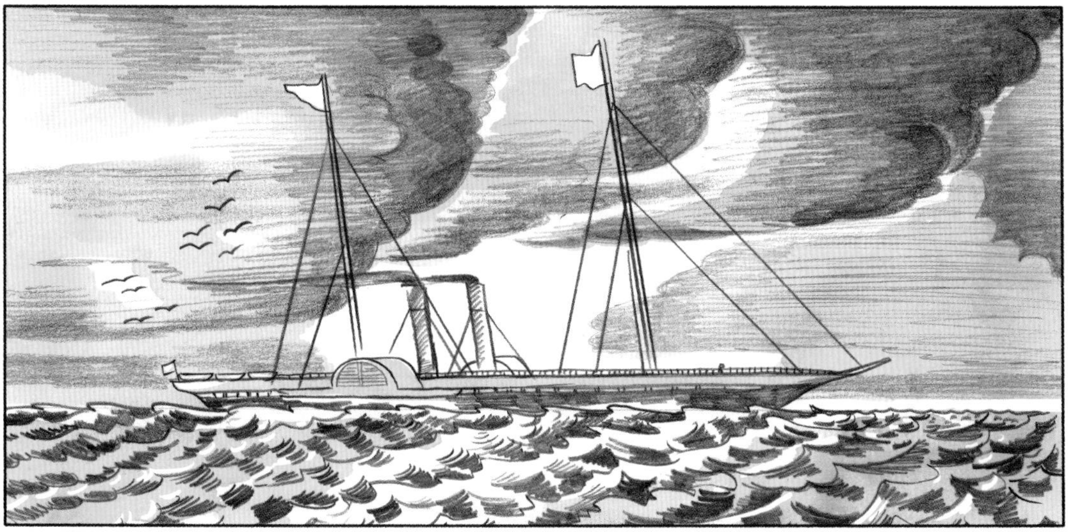

However long I live I shall not forget what the parting with Monsieur Heger cost me.

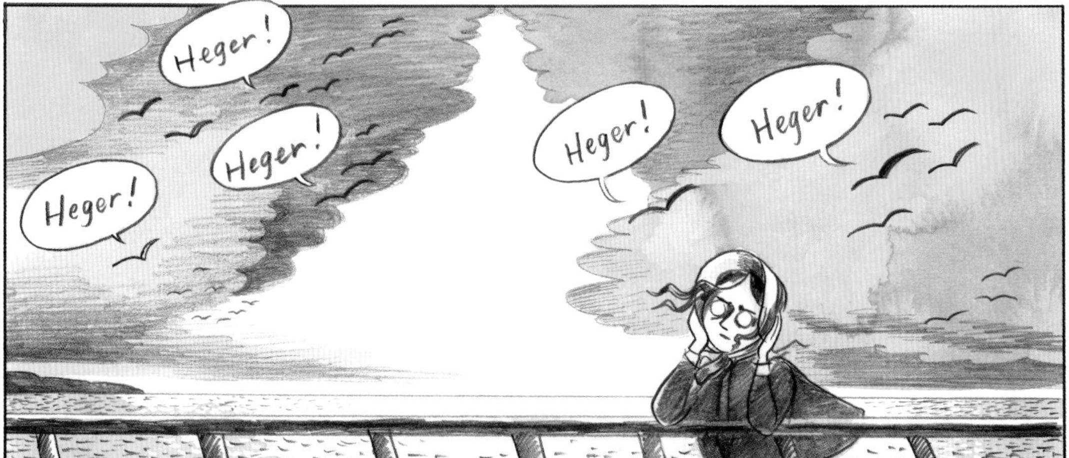
Heger!
Heger!
Heger!
Heger!
Heger!

JULY 1844 I have had notices printed.

The Misses Brontë's Establishment

FOR

THE BOARD AND EDUCATION

OF A LIMITED NUMBER OF

YOUNG LADIES,

THE PARSONAGE, HAWORTH,

NEAR BRADFORD.

Terms	L. s. d.
BOARD AND EDUCATION, including Writing, Arithmetic, History, Grammar, Geography, and Needle Work, per Annum	35. 0 0
French ... German ... Latin ... } ... ... each per Quarter	1 1 0
Music ... Drawing ... } ... ... each per Quarter	1 1 0
Use of piano forte, per Quarter...	0 5 0
Washing, per Quarter, ...	0 15 0

I've sent copies to Ellen Nussey and everyone else we know to distribute.

I'm done with the housework and am going for a walk.

Coming?

No—I'll stay here and write a letter.

<Monsieur, I have a lack of employment until we gain pupils for the school. I would not experience this lethargy if I could write. Once upon a time I used to spend whole days, weeks, complete months in writing—but now—if I could—do you know what I would do?>

<I would write a book and I would dedicate it to my literature master.>

<But it cannot be—a literary career is closed to me.>

Miss Bwontë, you're going to teach us to wead!

POP!

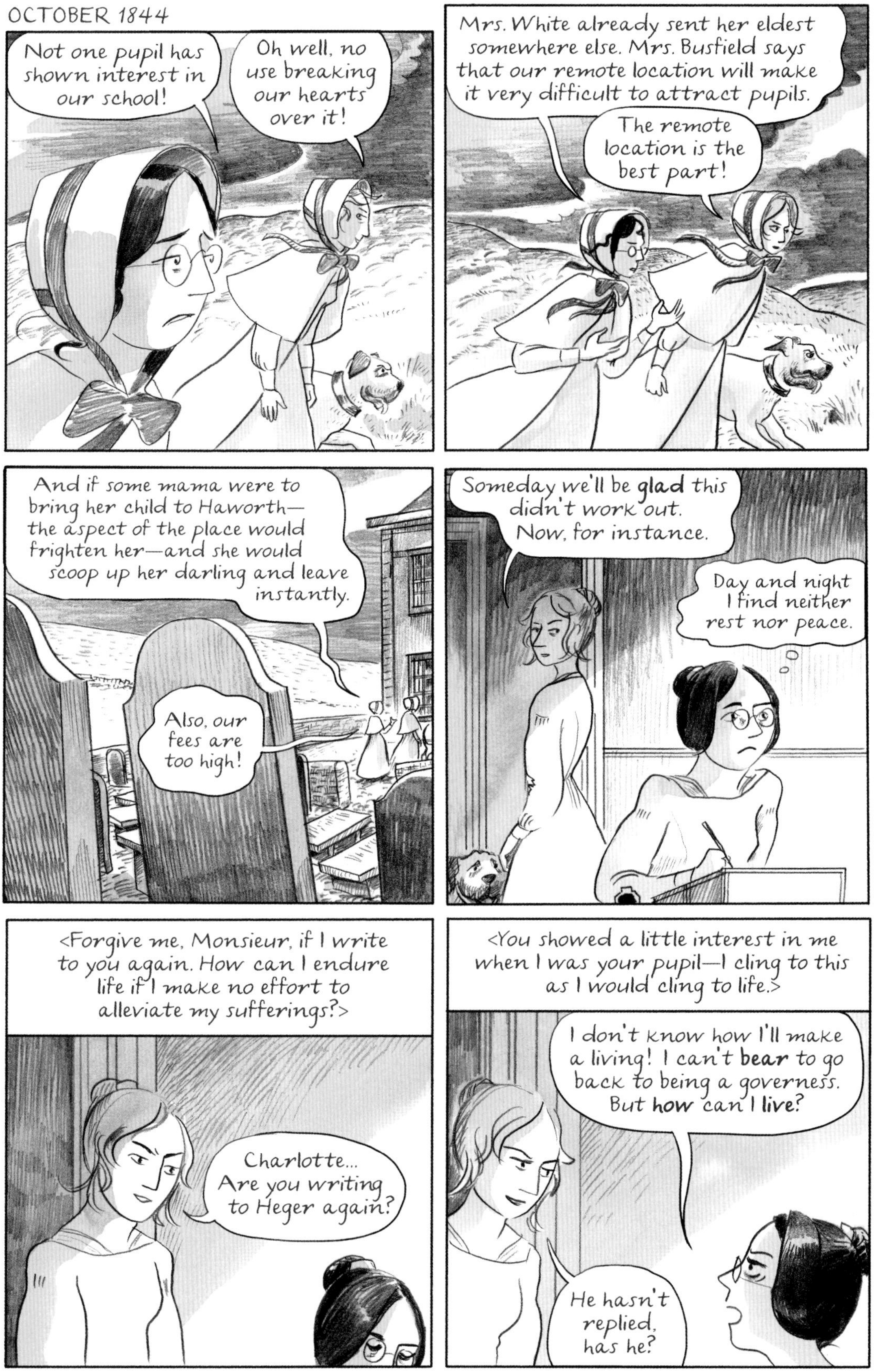
OCTOBER 1844
Not one pupil has shown interest in our school!
Oh well, no use breaking our hearts over it!
Mrs. White already sent her eldest somewhere else. Mrs. Busfield says that our remote location will make it very difficult to attract pupils.
The remote location is the best part!
And if some mama were to bring her child to Haworth—the aspect of the place would frighten her—and she would scoop up her darling and leave instantly.
Also, our fees are too high!
Someday we'll be **glad** this didn't work out. Now, for instance.
Day and night I find neither rest nor peace.
<Forgive me, Monsieur, if I write to you again. How can I endure life if I make no effort to alleviate my sufferings?>
Charlotte... Are you writing to Heger again?
<You showed a little interest in me when I was your pupil—I cling to this as I would cling to life.>
I don't know how I'll make a living! I can't **bear** to go back to being a governess. But **how can I live?**
He hasn't replied, has he?

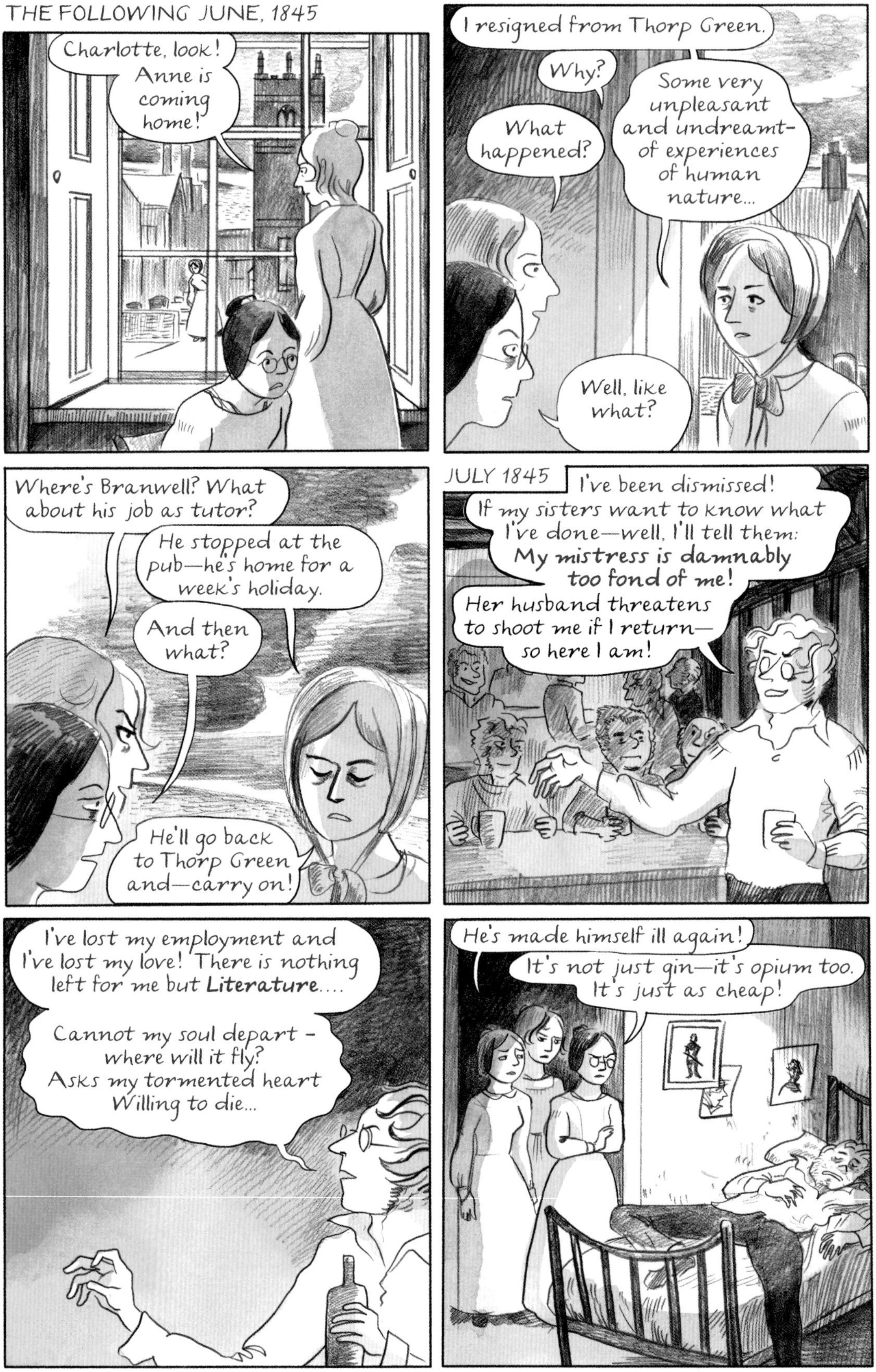
THE FOLLOWING JUNE, 1845
Charlotte, look! Anne is coming home!
I resigned from Thorp Green.
Why?
What happened?
Some very unpleasant and undreamt-of experiences of human nature...
Well, like what?
Where's Branwell? What about his job as tutor?
He stopped at the pub—he's home for a week's holiday.
And then what?
He'll go back to Thorp Green and—carry on!
JULY 1845
I've been dismissed! If my sisters want to know what I've done—well, I'll tell them: My mistress is damnably too fond of me!
Her husband threatens to shoot me if I return—so here I am!
I've lost my employment and I've lost my love! There is nothing left for me but Literature....
Cannot my soul depart - where will it fly? Asks my tormented heart Willing to die...
He's made himself ill again!
It's not just gin—it's opium too. It's just as cheap!

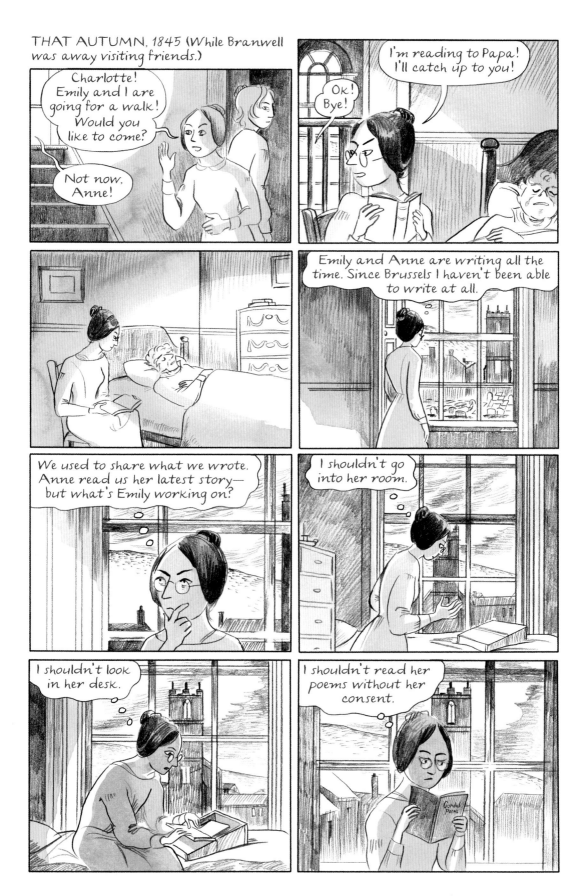

THAT AUTUMN, 1845 (While Branwell was away visiting friends.)

Charlotte! Emily and I are going for a walk! Would you like to come?

Not now, Anne!

I'm reading to Papa! I'll catch up to you!

Ok! Bye!

Emily and Anne are writing all the time. Since Brussels I haven't been able to write at all.

We used to share what we wrote. Anne read us her latest story— but what's Emily working on?

I shouldn't go into her room.

I shouldn't look in her desk.

I shouldn't read her poems without her consent.

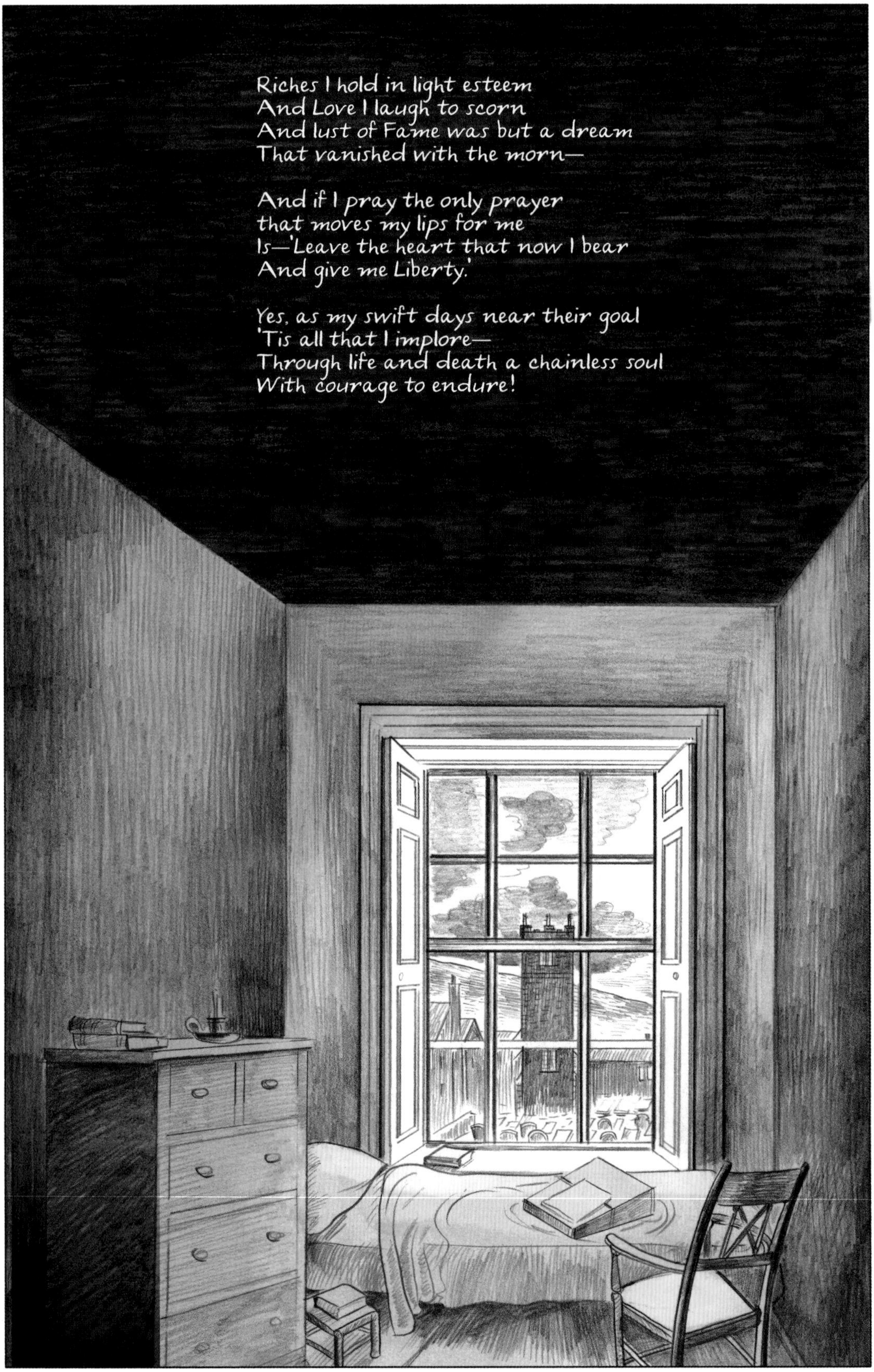
Riches I hold in light esteem
And Love I laugh to scorn
And lust of Fame was but a dream
That vanished with the morn—
And if I pray the only prayer
that moves my lips for me
Is—'Leave the heart that now I bear
And give me Liberty.'
Yes, as my swift days near their goal
'Tis all that I implore—
Through life and death a chainless soul
With courage to endure!

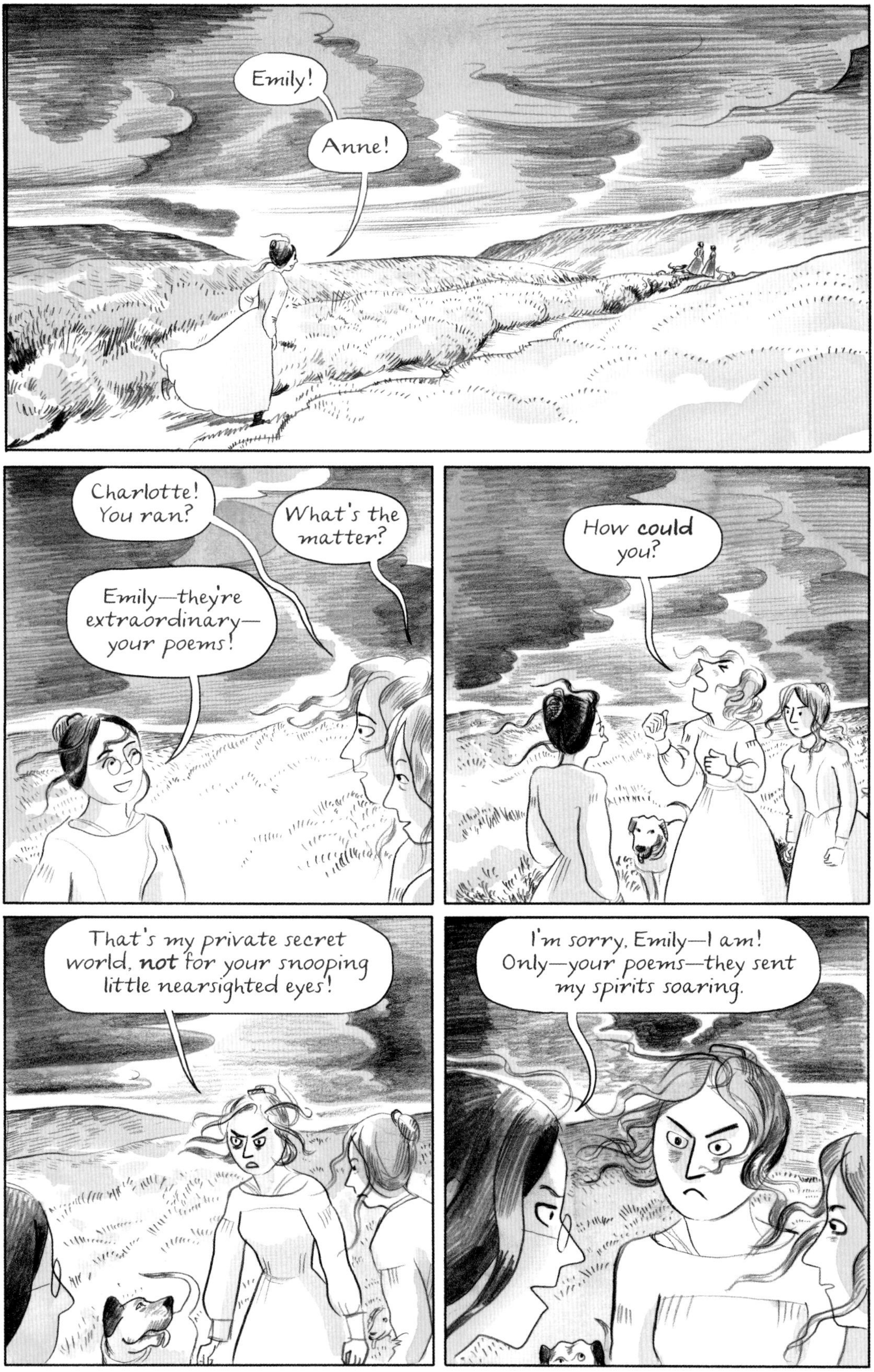
Emily!
Anne!
Charlotte! You ran?
What's the matter?
Emily—they're extraordinary—your poems!
How **could** you?
That's my private secret world, **not** for your snooping little nearsighted eyes!
I'm sorry, Emily—I am! Only—your poems—they sent my spirits soaring.

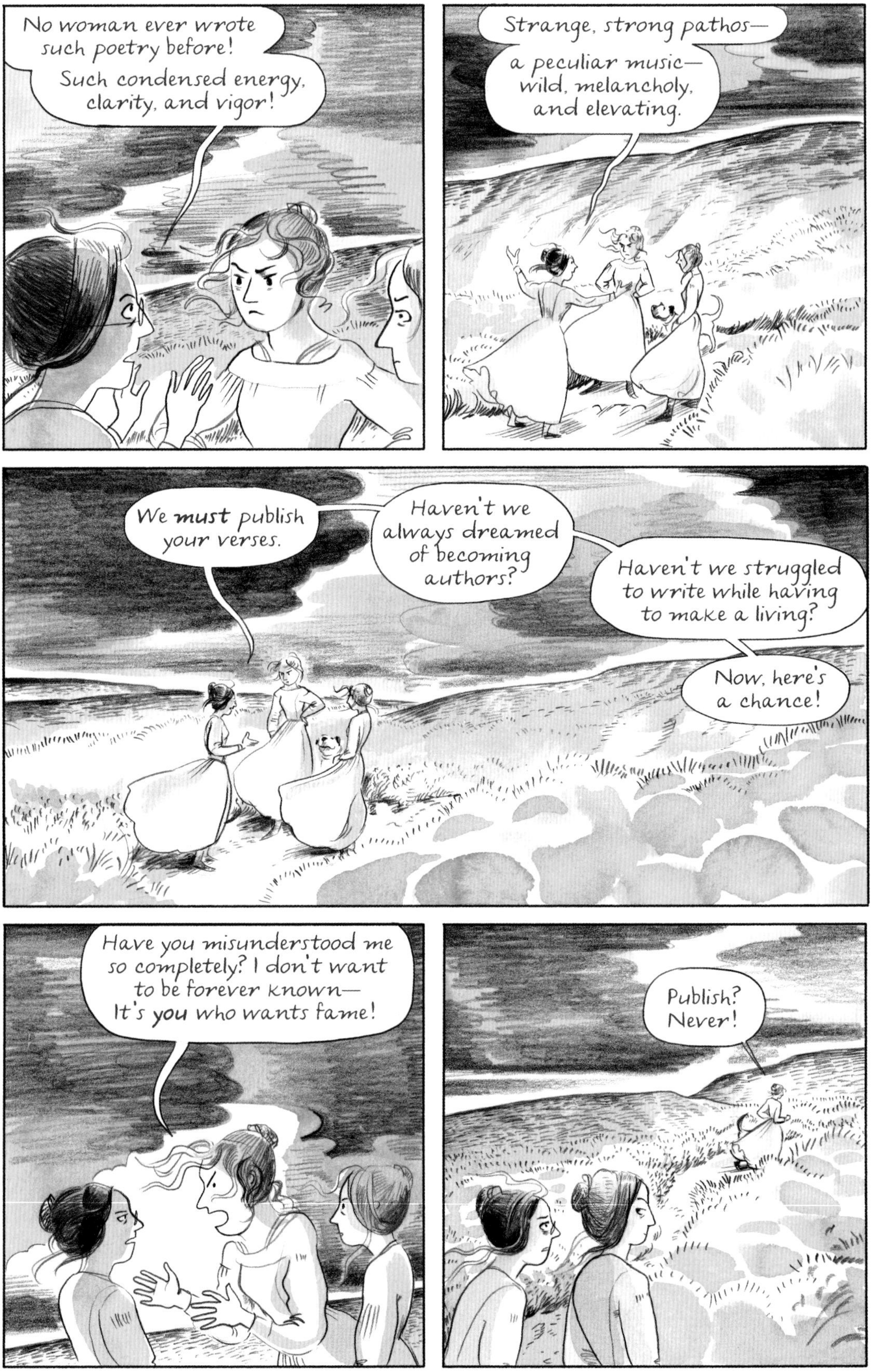
No woman ever wrote such poetry before!
Such condensed energy, clarity, and vigor!
Strange, strong pathos—
a peculiar music—wild, melancholy, and elevating.
We **must** publish your verses.
Haven't we always dreamed of becoming authors?
Haven't we struggled to write while having to make a living?
Now, here's a chance!
Have you misunderstood me so completely? I don't want to be forever known—It's **you** who wants fame!
Publish? Never!

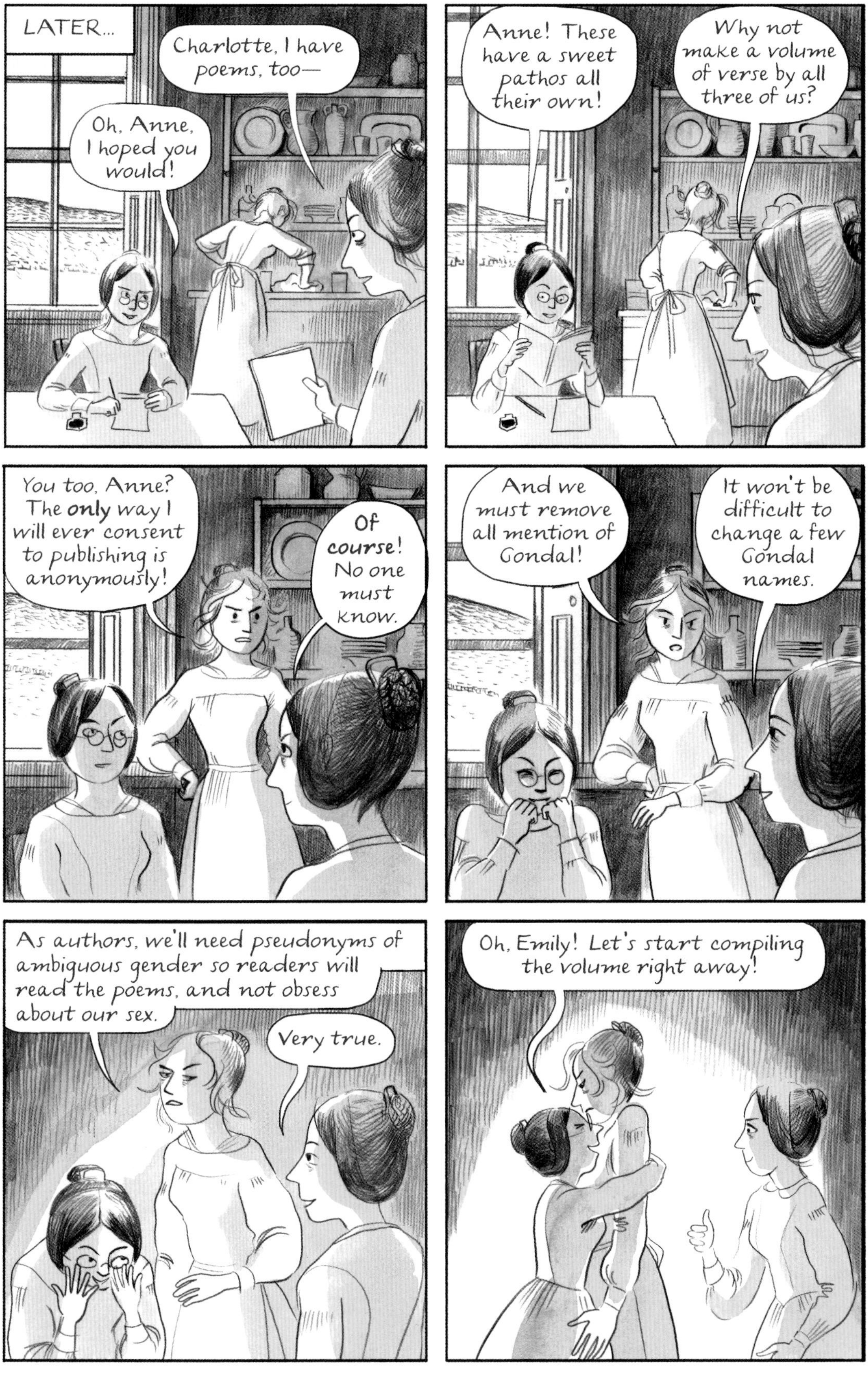
LATER...
Charlotte, I have poems, too—
Oh, Anne, I hoped you would!
Anne! These have a sweet pathos all their own!
Why not make a volume of verse by all three of us?
You too, Anne? The **only** way I will ever consent to publishing is anonymously!
Of **course**! No one must know.
And we must remove all mention of Gondal!
It won't be difficult to change a few Gondal names.
As authors, we'll need pseudonyms of ambiguous gender so readers will read the poems, and not obsess about our sex.
Very true.
Oh, Emily! Let's start compiling the volume right away!

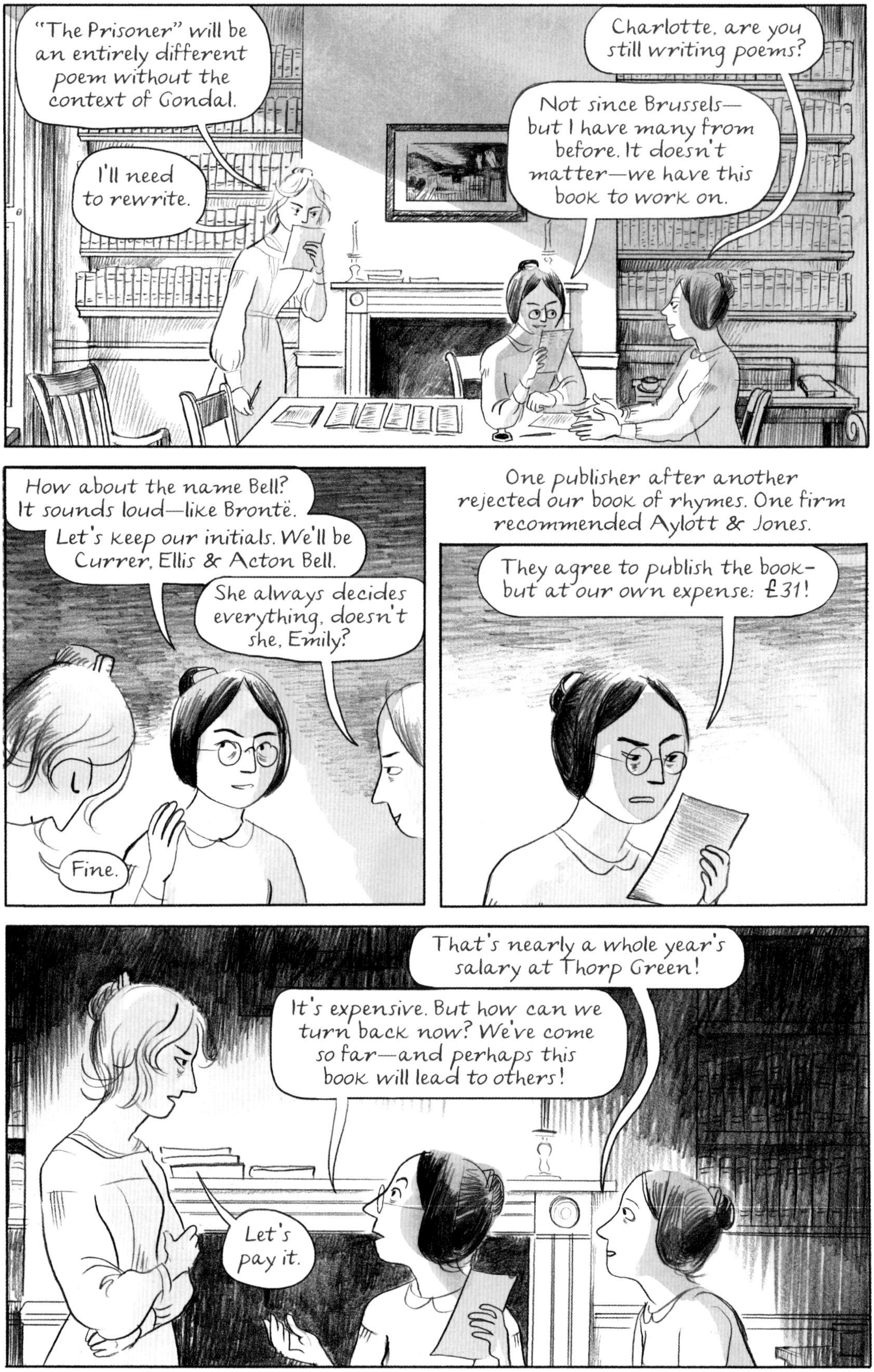
"The Prisoner" will be an entirely different poem without the context of Gondal.
I'll need to rewrite.
Charlotte, are you still writing poems?
Not since Brussels—but I have many from before. It doesn't matter—we have this book to work on.
How about the name Bell? It sounds loud—like Brontë.
Let's keep our initials. We'll be Currer, Ellis & Acton Bell.
She always decides everything, doesn't she, Emily?
Fine.
One publisher after another rejected our book of rhymes. One firm recommended Aylott & Jones.
They agree to publish the book—but at our own expense: £31!
That's nearly a whole year's salary at Thorp Green!
It's expensive. But how can we turn back now? We've come so far—and perhaps this book will lead to others!
Let's pay it.

SPRING 1846

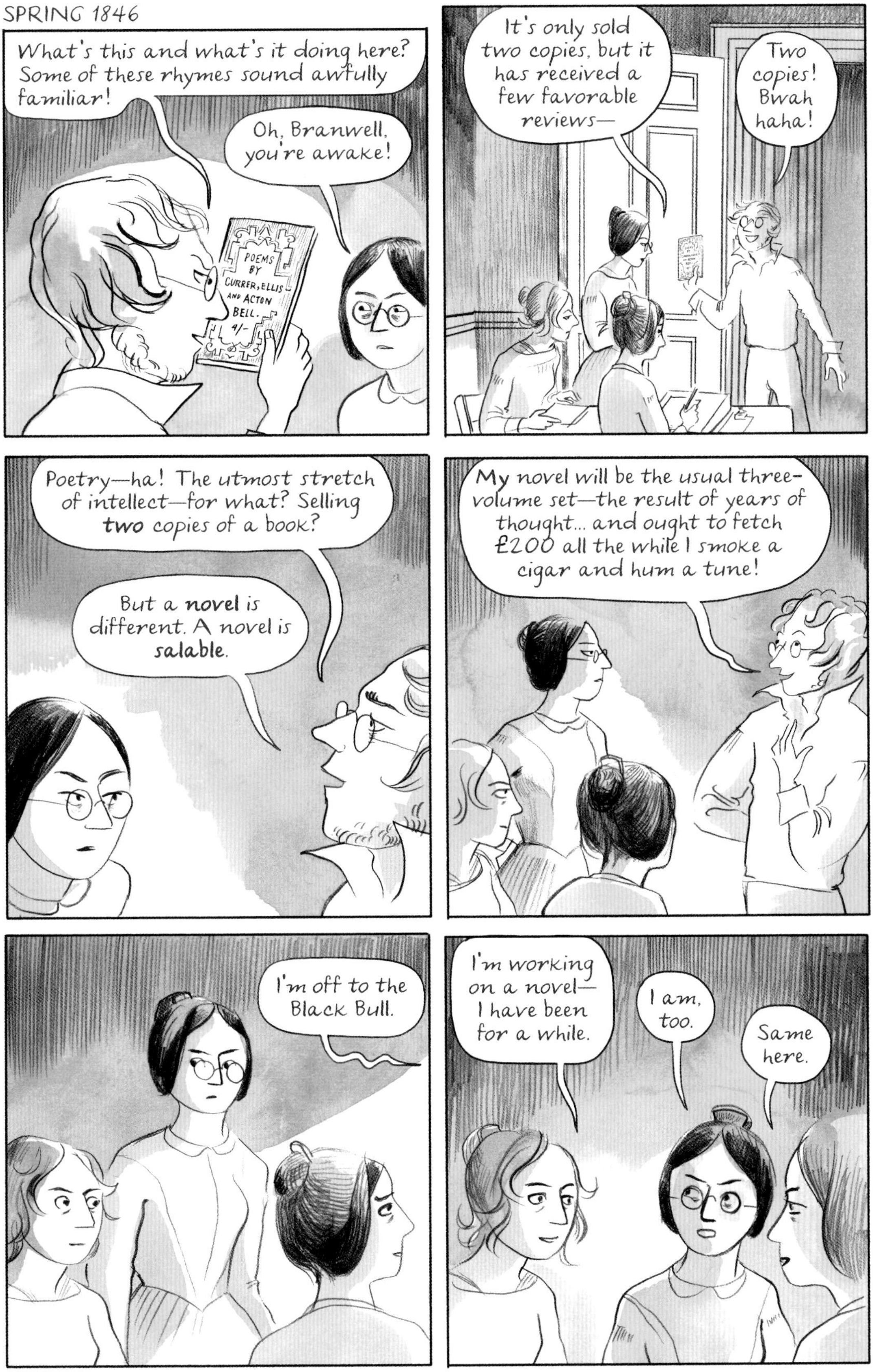

What's this and what's it doing here? Some of these rhymes sound awfully familiar!
POEMS BY CURRER, ELLIS AND ACTON BELL. 4/-
Oh, Branwell, you're awake!
It's only sold two copies, but it has received a few favorable reviews—
Two copies! Bwah haha!
Poetry—ha! The utmost stretch of intellect—for what? Selling **two** copies of a book?
But a **novel** is different. A novel is **salable**.
My novel will be the usual three-volume set—the result of years of thought... and ought to fetch £200 all the while I smoke a cigar and hum a tune!
I'm off to the Black Bull.
I'm working on a novel—I have been for a while.
I am, too.
Same here.

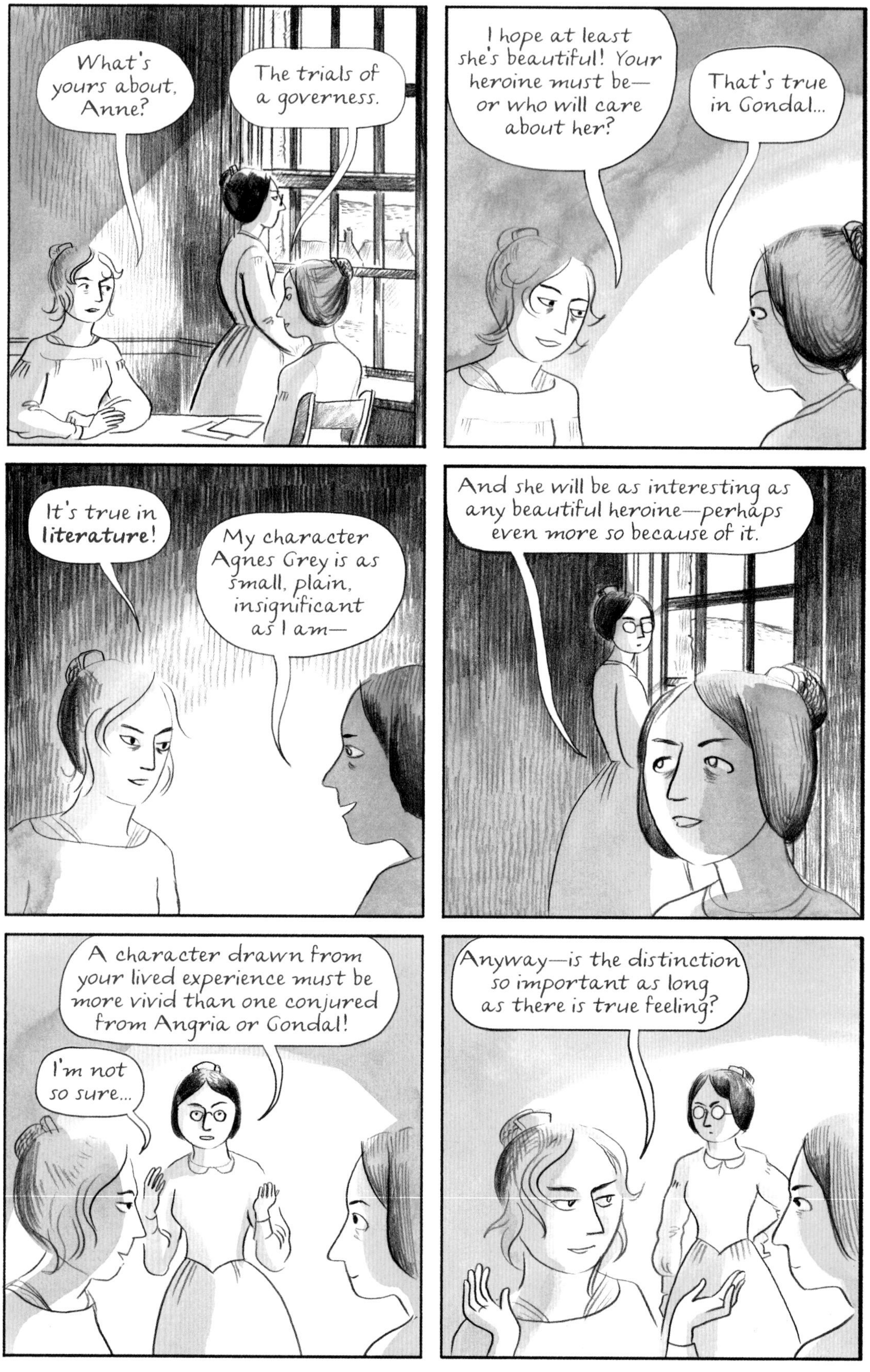
What's yours about, Anne?
The trials of a governess.
I hope at least she's beautiful! Your heroine must be— or who will care about her?
That's true in Gondal...
It's true in **literature**!
My character Agnes Grey is as small, plain, insignificant as I am—
And she will be as interesting as any beautiful heroine—perhaps even more so because of it.
A character drawn from your lived experience must be more vivid than one conjured from Angria or Gondal!
I'm not so sure...
Anyway—is the distinction so important as long as there is true feeling?

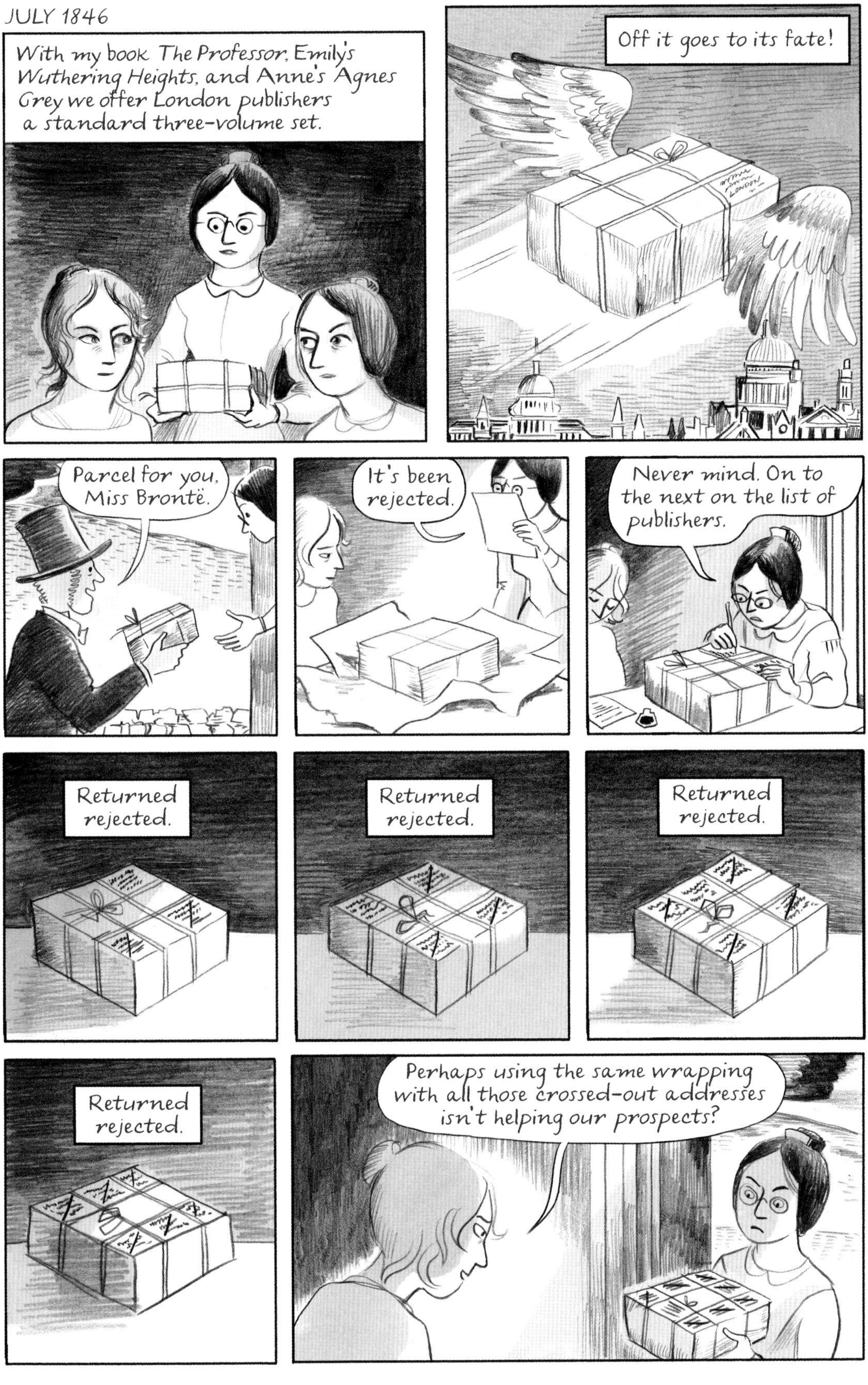
JULY 1846
With my book The Professor, Emily's Wuthering Heights, and Anne's Agnes Grey we offer London publishers a standard three-volume set.
Off it goes to its fate!
LONDON
Parcel for you, Miss Brontë.
It's been rejected.
Never mind. On to the next on the list of publishers.
Returned rejected.
Returned rejected.
Returned rejected.
Returned rejected.
Perhaps using the same wrapping with all those crossed-out addresses isn't helping our prospects?

THE FOLLOWING MONTH

I am in Manchester with Papa. The eye surgery he so desparately needed was successful. Emily and Anne are looking after Branwell at the parsonage.

Do you need anything, Papa?

Papa is confined in a dark room for a month, bandages over his eyes, with a nurse attending him night and day.

No, Charlotte, dear, but this proximity to mortality—and this time of inactivity...

...calls to mind memories of your dear mother and sisters... only 10 and 11 years old when they died. That horrible school... I think of them every day....

So do I, Papa.

There is no chance I'll hear from Heger **here**. So, there's time...to write.

Jane Eyre
by Currer Bell

Chap. 1st

There was no possibility of taking a walk that day. We had been wandering indeed in the leafless shrubbery an hour in the mourning, but since dinner (Mrs Reed when there was no company. dined early) the cold Winter wind had brought with it clouds so somber, a rain so penetrating that further out-door exercise was now out of the question.

I was glad of

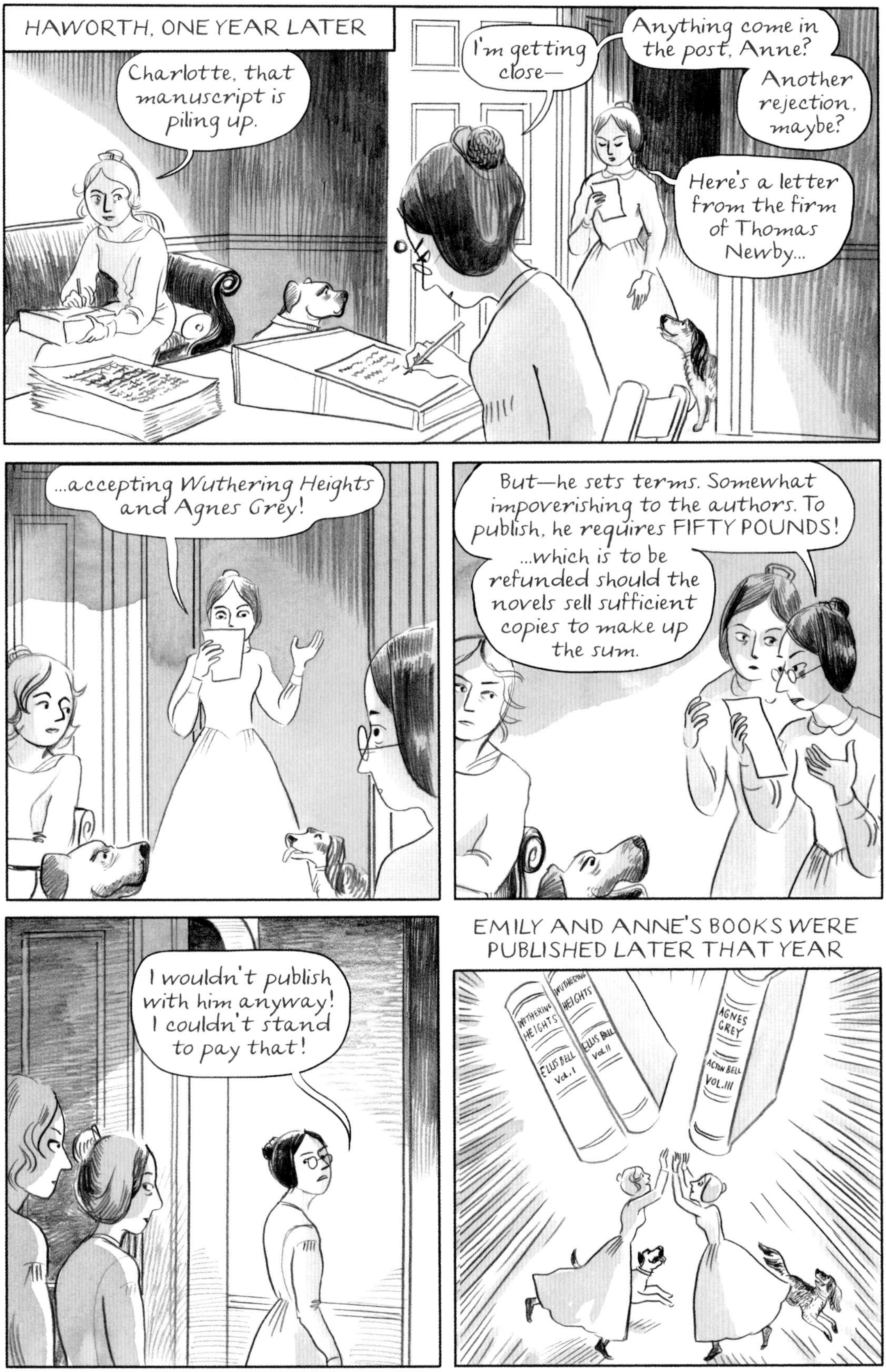

HAWORTH, ONE YEAR LATER
Charlotte, that manuscript is piling up.
I'm getting close—
Anything come in the post, Anne?
Another rejection, maybe?
Here's a letter from the firm of Thomas Newby...
...accepting Wuthering Heights and Agnes Grey!
But—he sets terms. Somewhat impoverishing to the authors. To publish, he requires FIFTY POUNDS!
...which is to be refunded should the novels sell sufficient copies to make up the sum.
I wouldn't publish with him anyway! I couldn't stand to pay that!
EMILY AND ANNE'S BOOKS WERE PUBLISHED LATER THAT YEAR
WUTHERING HEIGHTS ELLIS BELL Vol. I
WUTHERING HEIGHTS ELLIS BELL Vol. II
AGNES GREY ACTON BELL VOL. III

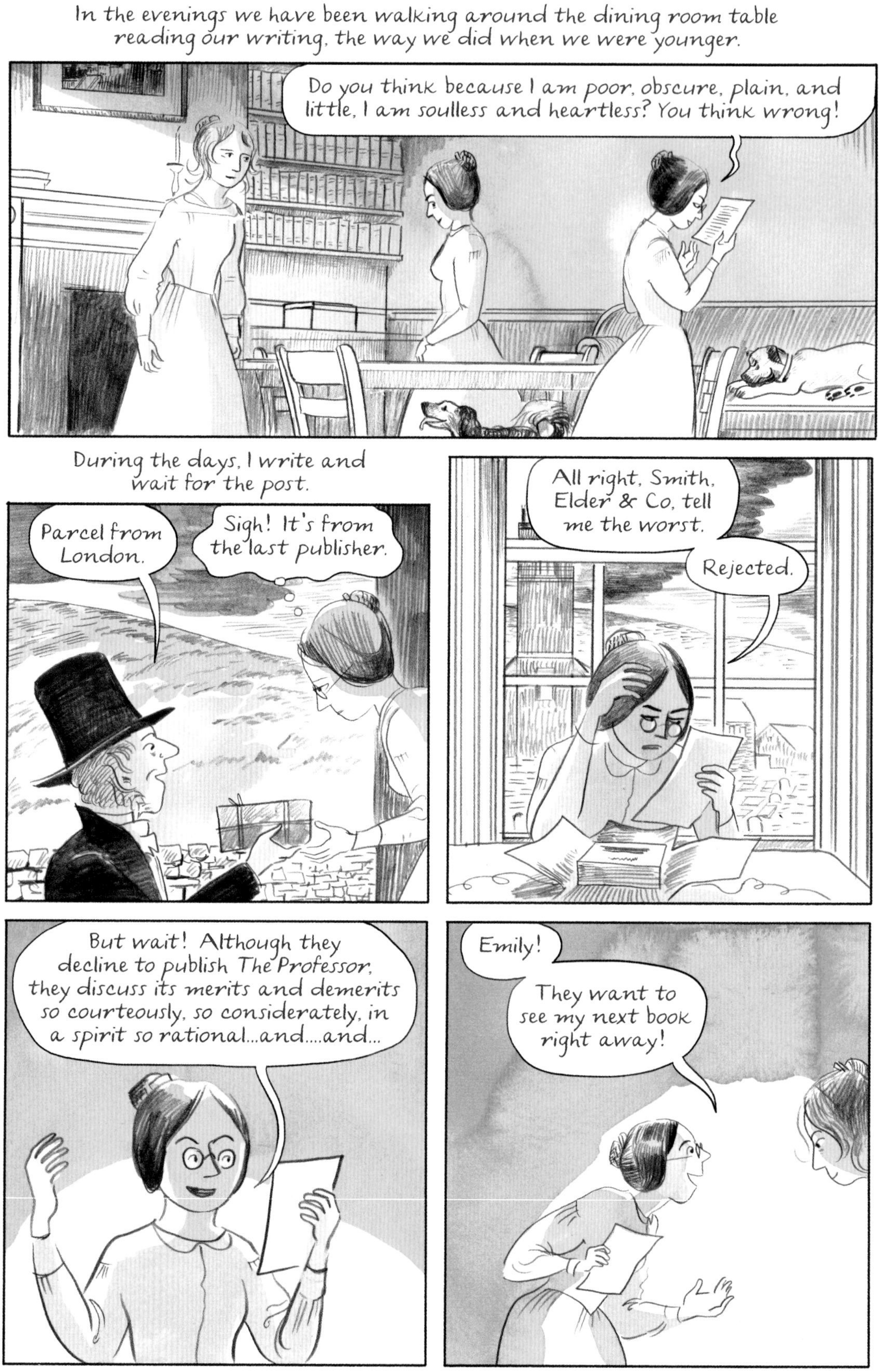
In the evenings we have been walking around the dining room table reading our writing, the way we did when we were younger.
Do you think because I am poor, obscure, plain, and little, I am soulless and heartless? You think wrong!
During the days, I write and wait for the post.
Parcel from London.
Sigh! It's from the last publisher.
All right, Smith, Elder & Co, tell me the worst.
Rejected.
But wait! Although they decline to publish The Professor, they discuss its merits and demerits so courteously, so considerately, in a spirit so rational...and....and...
Emily!
They want to see my next book right away!

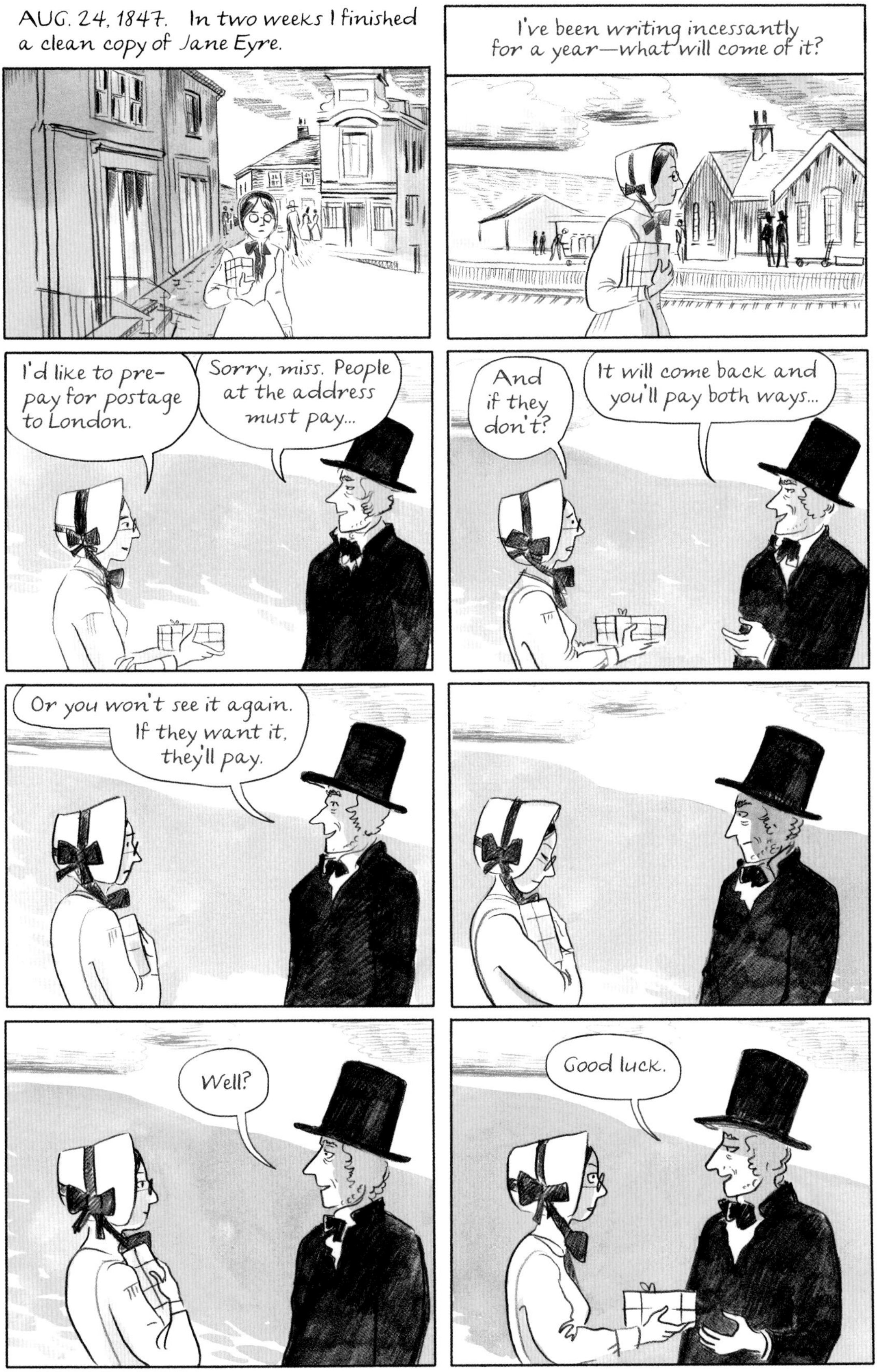
AUG. 24, 1847. In two weeks I finished a clean copy of *Jane Eyre*.
I've been writing incessantly for a year—what will come of it?
I'd like to pre-pay for postage to London.
Sorry, miss. People at the address must pay...
And if they don't?
It will come back and you'll pay both ways...
Or you won't see it again. If they want it, they'll pay.
Well?
Good luck.

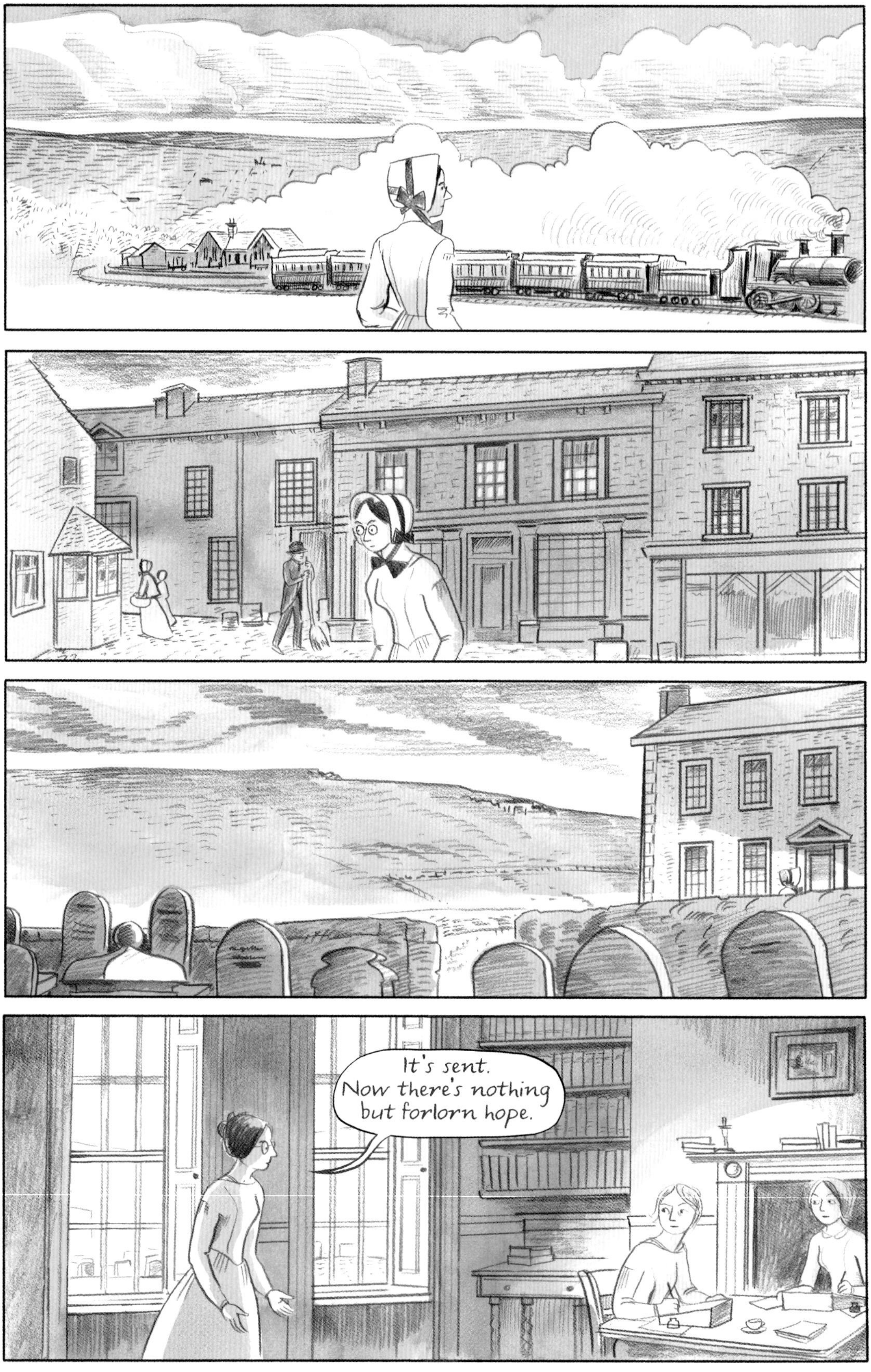
It's sent. Now there's nothing but forlorn hope.

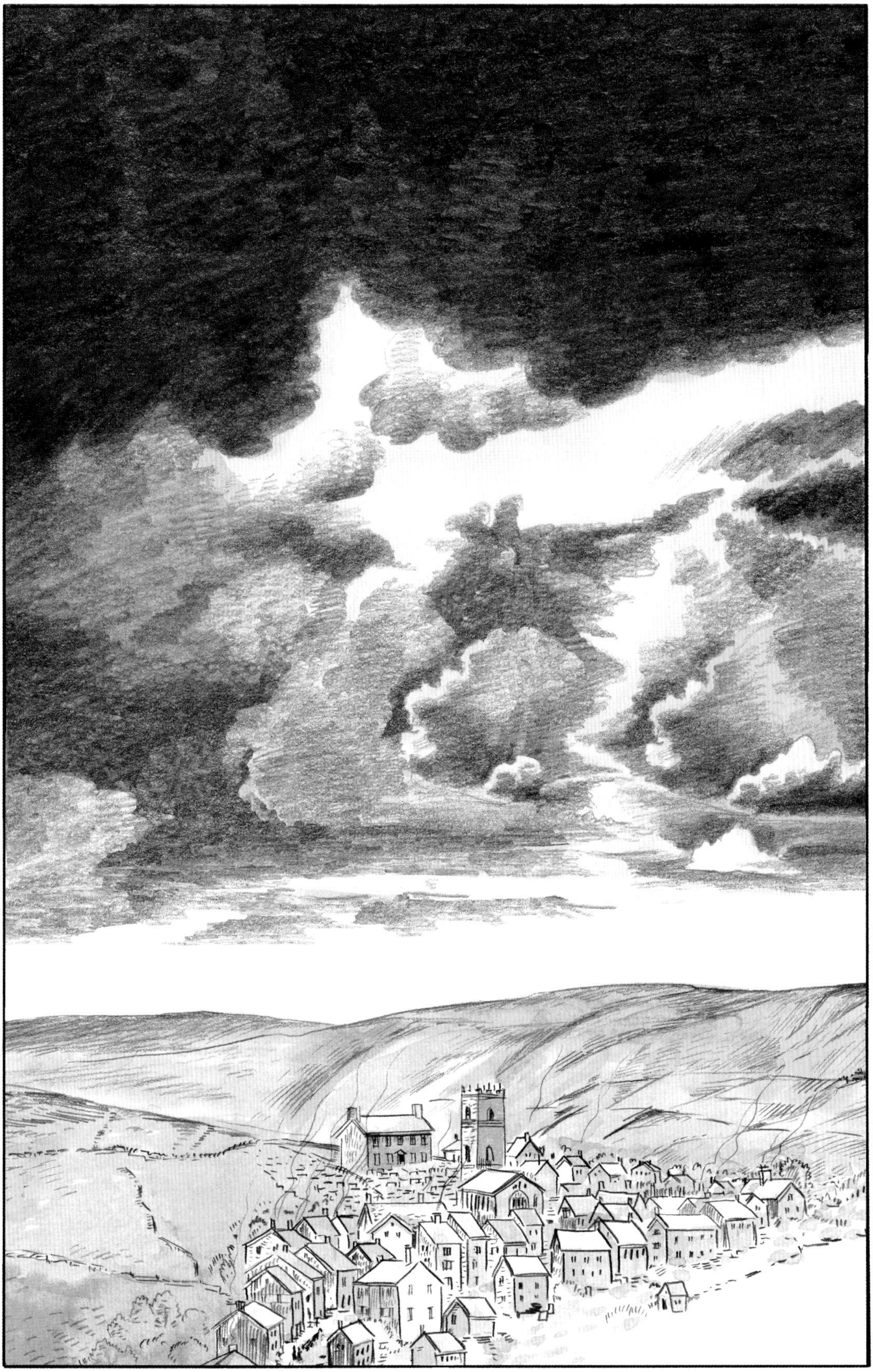

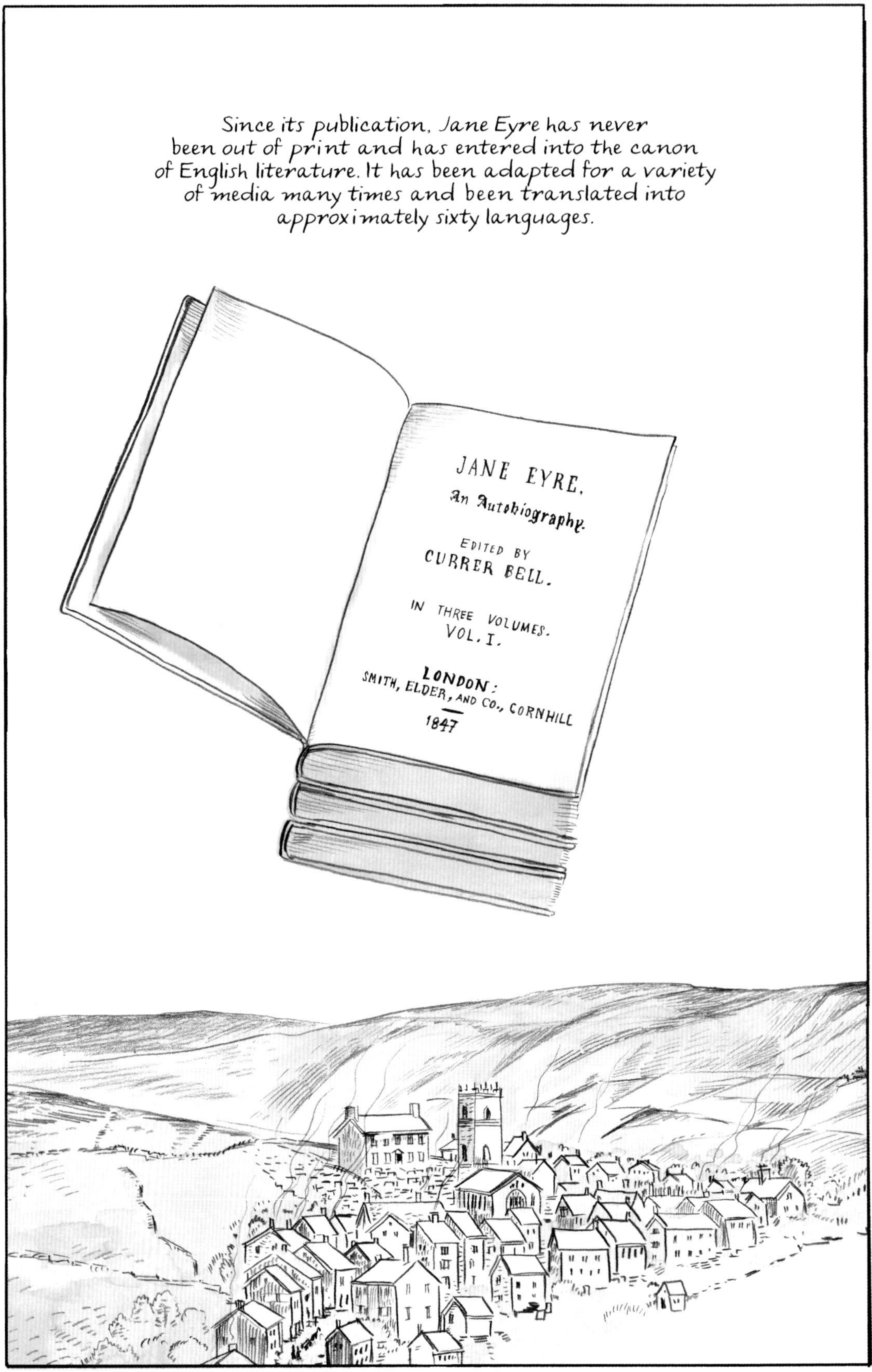
Since its publication, Jane Eyre has never been out of print and has entered into the canon of English literature. It has been adapted for a variety of media many times and been translated into approximately sixty languages.
JANE EYRE.
An Autobiography.
EDITED BY
CURRER BELL.
IN THREE VOLUMES.
VOL. I.
LONDON:
SMITH, ELDER, AND CO., CORNHILL
1847

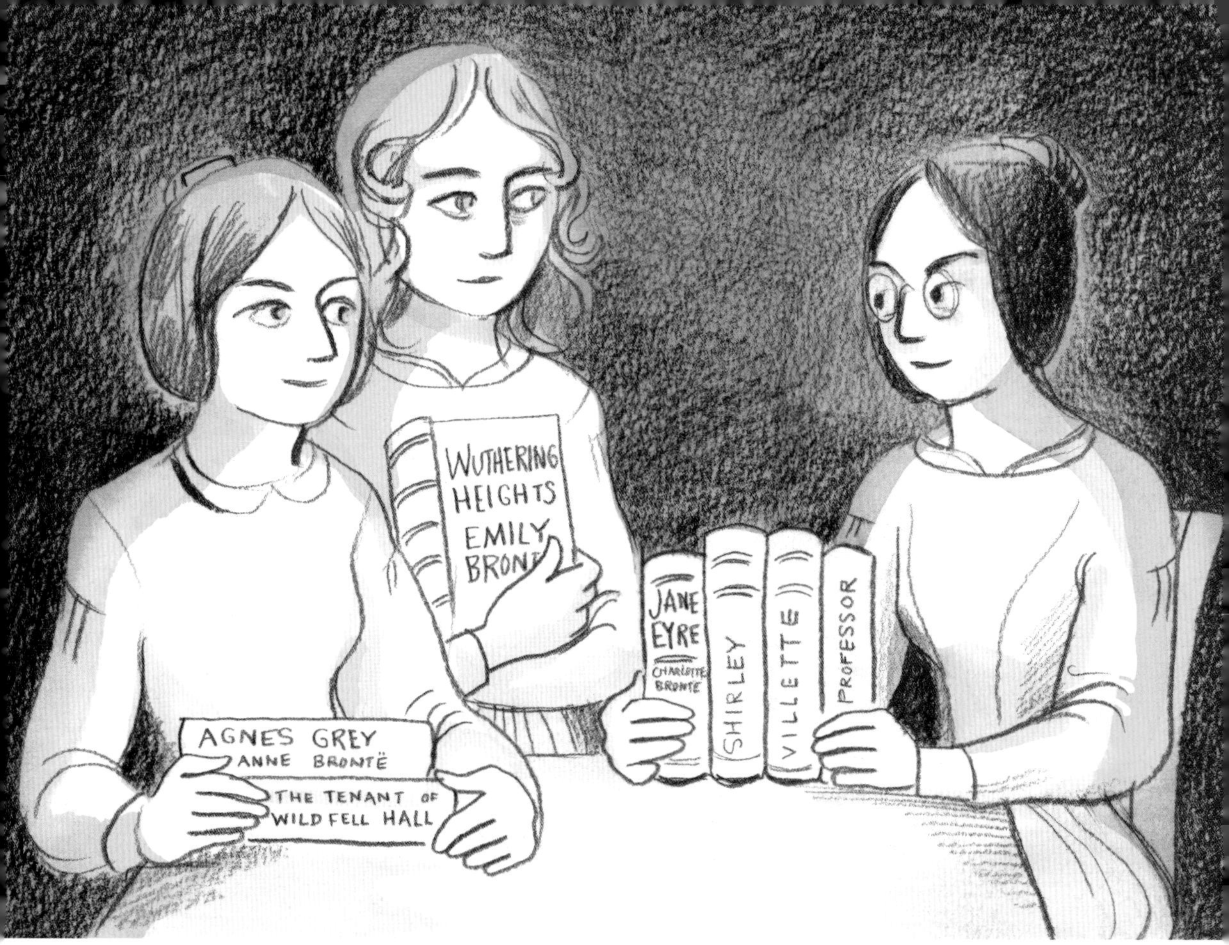
WUTHERING HEIGHTS
EMILY BRONT
JANE EYRE
CHARLOTTE BRONTE
SHIRLEY
VILLETTE
PROFESSOR
AGNES GREY
ANNE BRONTË
THE TENANT OF WILDFELL HALL

POSTSCRIPT

Why a biography of Charlotte Brontë? Working on this project allowed me to rediscover a writer whose work I had enjoyed earlier in life, but I wasn't prepared for the love and respect for Charlotte I've gained in the course of my research. Her persistence in pursuing her career against so many odds and facing such heartbreak, her imagination, from her earliest writing about the world of Glass Town to the shades of feeling she captures in *Villette*, are inspiring across the years. Charlotte's humor and depth of thought have sustained me in writing and drawing this book.

Why a biography of Charlotte, and not of all three Brontë sisters? Charlotte alone among her siblings left the most evidence in the form of letters, diaries, and novels. Starting at Roe Head School, Charlotte made friends outside the family with whom she corresponded for most of her life. Although Emily and Anne both also attended Roe Head, they did not carry on sustained letter-writing as Charlotte did. Charlotte also left insights into her time in Belgium through letters, as well as her first novel, *The Professor*, and her last, *Villette*, which reveal how her relationship with her teacher changed the course of her writing. Emily's writing does not reflect on her time in Brussels, and Anne never had the opportunity to travel. Also, both died shortly after the time frame of this book—Emily in 1848 and Anne in 1849—leaving them little time for their diary papers, fiction, or anything else. I tried to show in this book how the Brontë siblings' interactions sparked their imaginations and their writing, from when they were very young and imagining Glass Town, to when Charlotte found Emily's poems and decided to take the initiative to publish the work of all three. The lives and literary work of the Brontës were inevitably intertwined. Their story has a mythology of its own, growing from Charlotte's introduction to the second printing of *Wuthering Heights*

and *Agnes Grey*, where she described her sisters' isolated lives in the parsonage on the moors, and then their early deaths, and also from the first biography of Charlotte by Elizabeth Gaskell. Their story captured the romantic imagination of many, and it resonates still.

When writing, I attempted to use as many of Charlotte Brontë's own words as possible. Even so, perhaps inevitably, most of the dialogue is my invention, though I tried to keep with the spirit of the characters as I understood them from reading biographies of Charlotte, Emily, and the rest of the family, and from the sisters' writing. I often felt conflicted when I needed to edit a passage of Charlotte's in order to fit the space of the page or flow of the story: Who am I to intrude on a great writer's work? In the limited scope of this short book, we chose carefully which scenes to include, and therefore were forced to leave out many others.

CHARLOTTE BRONTË *before* JANE EYRE

PANEL DISCUSSIONS

 **PAGES 3–4:** This is an excerpt of a letter to Charlotte from the then–poet laureate of England, Robert Southey (1774–1843), written in response to Charlotte's letter asking him for advice about making a living as a writer. Southey's reply was forwarded to Roe Head School, where Charlotte was teaching. Although he wrote discouragingly that "Literature cannot be the business of a woman's life," in other ways he encouraged Charlotte, for example, telling her to "write poetry for its own sake, not in a spirit of emulation, and not with a view toward celebrity."

. . . .

 **PAGE 8:** The Brontë family lived in the parsonage in Haworth, a village in Yorkshire, in the North of England, where the sisters' father, Patrick (1777–1861), was the parson. There were six children in 1821: Maria (born 1814), Elizabeth (born 1815), Charlotte (born 1816), Patrick Branwell, called by his middle name (born 1817), Emily Jane (born 1818), and Anne (born 1820). Maria read to her younger siblings from newspapers and books from the Brontës' library, so the children knew local and national news, as well as stories from the Bible, Shakespeare's plays, and poetry. The books shown here are all known to have been in their collection (Barker, p. 169).

The children's father, Patrick Brontë, remembers that "dispute(s) [would] not infrequently arise amongst them regarding [the] comparative merits of [Wellington], Bonaparte, Hannibal, and Caesar," and he would "come in as arbitrator" (Barker, p. 125).

The mother of the Brontë children, Maria Branwell Brontë (1783–1821), died after months of pain caused by what was probably uterine cancer (Alexander and Smith, p. 63).

Elizabeth Branwell, (1776–1842) called by the children Aunt Branwell, came to stay with the family when her younger sister, Maria Branwell Brontë, became ill. When Maria Brontë died, Aunt Branwell remained in Haworth to help raise the children.

The servants in this scene are Sarah and Nancy Garrs, who stayed with the family until 1825.

The Church of St. Michael and All Angels in Haworth, located across a crowded graveyard from the Brontë

Parsonage, was renovated at the end of the nineteenth century, so it does not look today as it did in the Brontës' time. I relied on old photographs of the earlier church in drawing this book.

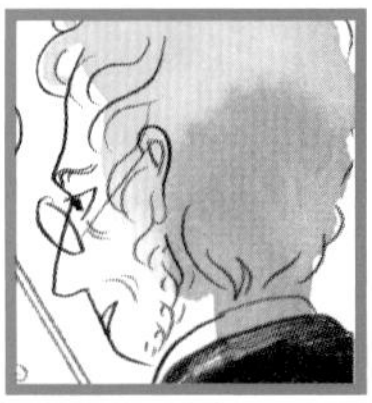

Page 10: Patrick Brontë was from a large Irish family and was the only one to leave Ireland and to study at Cambridge. He also knew that if he became too ill or died, his children would have no income and would have to leave the parsonage where they were all living. He wanted to ensure his daughters would be equipped with an education so that they would be able to support themselves. The advertisement for the Clergy Daughters School at Cowan Bridge appeared in the December 4, 1823, edition of the *Leeds Intelligencer*.

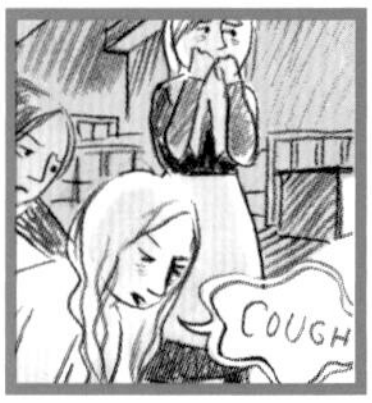
COUGH

Page 16: Clergy Daughters School had problems with the health of students from its opening. In 1824, when there were fifty-three pupils at the school, one girl died there and eleven went home sick—six of these died soon after. In 1825, twenty girls withdrew (including the four Brontës), nine of them in ill health. Typhoid caused many deaths, but Maria and Elizabeth Brontë died of what was then called consumption and now called tuberculosis (Barker, p. 147).

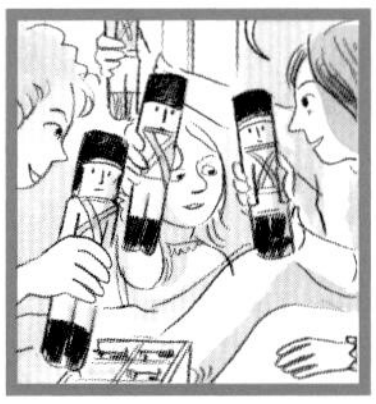

Page 20: Charlotte recorded how the gift of the box of twelve soldiers sparked the founding of the Glass Town Saga (which later focused on the country of Angria) in her *History of the Year* from 1829. In this short piece, written when Charlotte was thirteen, she described an event that had taken place three years previously.

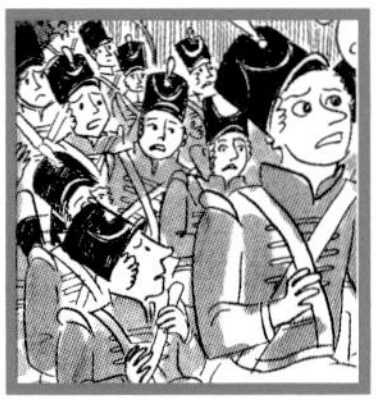

Page 21: This scene is based on Charlotte's tiny handwritten book *Two Romantic Tales* from 1829. The story describes battles the Twelve Soldiers fought against the African Ashantee and how they claimed the land for the building of the Great Glass Town. This story shows the influence of *Blackwood's Magazine* (printed between 1817 and 1980) and the colonialism of the time. The twelve young men also encounter the four genii: Tallii (Charlotte), Branii (Branwell), Emmii (Emily), and Annii (Anne) who govern the soldiers' fates, in

scenes inspired by *The Arabian Nights*. The Brontës used the word *genius* and not *genie* as the singular form of *genii*, and they were aware of the double meaning of *genius* as meaning someone very clever—a brilliant writer, for example. This story is the first of many Glass Town/Angrian tales that Charlotte wrote until she was in her early twenties.

The image of Glass Town (and subsequent images of it later in the book) is based on an 1816 engraving from a painting by J. M. W. Turner, *The Tenth Plague of Egypt*, first exhibited in 1802. It is probable that the Brontës had seen this engraving. The Brontës had prints of works by John Martin (1789–1854), a popular illustrator, engraver, and painter of dramatic Biblical scenes, including the *Seventh Plague of Egypt*, which is similar to Turner's painting.

· · · · · · · · · ·

PAGE 23: *Branwell's Blackwood's Magazine* was patterned after *Blackwood's Magazine*, and had prose, poems, and dialogues written by both Branwell and Charlotte, who took over "publishing" it—i.e., writing it out by hand—after a few months. Charlotte wrote in this tiny handwritten and hand-sewn book that it was available in all the Glass Towns, and in later manuscripts she and Branwell added "Paris," a fictional Paris, the capital of Sneakysland.

· · · · · · · · · ·

PAGE 24: Tabby is Tabitha Aykroyd, who was a servant at the parsonage from 1825 until her death in 1855. She took care of the children's daily needs and told them local fairy stories. In later life, when she was ill and injured, the sisters cared for her.

The dog in this scene is Grasper, an Irish terrier, who lived at the parsonage from about 1834–1838 and was the first of many pets. We know what he looked like because Emily drew his portrait.

· · · · · · · · · ·

PAGE 26: "A Day at Parry's Palace by Lord Charles Wellesley," by Charlotte, August 22, 1830, satirized Emily's preference for the local—as opposed to the exotic settings of Charlotte's and Branwell's stories. Emily and Anne eventually broke from their older siblings and created Gondal, an imaginative world with a northern climate, much like Yorkshire and the Scottish Highlands, influenced perhaps by the work of Sir Walter Scott. The characters and action of Gondal are known through Emily's and Anne's poetry and diary papers.

If they wrote prose narratives set in Gondal, they no longer exist.

• • • • • • • • • •

 **PAGE 31:** Milton's *Paradise Lost* was among the books the Brontë family owned. I don't know for certain whether Charlotte memorized these opening lines, but she may have. She did memorize many poems and passages from scripture.

• • • • • • • • • •

 **PAGE 33:** Charlotte got fined for telling a story about a sleepwalker—it is the only time she was ever in trouble at school—but the story itself is not recorded anywhere; this is my invention based on recurring themes in her early writing (for example "Mina Laury" and "Caroline Vernon") (Barker, p. 205). The girls are wearing curl-papers at night.

• • • • • • • • • •

 **PAGE 37:** Rogue is Branwell's troublemaking character. He was a former pirate, arch-demagogue, revolutionary, and first friend and then foe to the Duke of Zamora. Rogue also went by the name Northangerland, and he eventually married Lady Zenobia Elrington. Charlotte's drawing is "Zenobia Marchioness Elrington" from 1833.

• • • • • • • • • •

 **PAGE 39:** This page is based on Emily's diary paper from 1834. Emily and Anne wrote diary papers every four years and kept them in a tin box (on display at the Parsonage Museum). They are vivid accounts of daily life mixed with their private world of Gondal, Emily and Anne's shared fantasy world separate from Charlotte and Branwell's Angria. It isn't clear in Emily's diary paper what "Rainbow, Diamond, Snowflake" are—they may all be cats. I drew geese because she also had geese, and geese seemed most likely to eat at the same time as Jasper pheasant, but I may be wrong!

• • • • • • • • • •

 **PAGE 42:** Charlotte worked for a reduced salary to take into account that one of her sisters was receiving a free education, hence the need to replace Emily with Anne (Barker, p. 274).

 **PAGE 51:** Charlotte went back to Roe Head School (now located at Dewsbury Moor) in August 1838, which eventually led to her breakdown, possibly because Miss Wooler left Charlotte on her own for more than two weeks while she was called away to take care of family.

 **PAGE 53:** Henry Nussey proposed to Charlotte by letter, and recorded the fact in his diary. She wasn't the first of his proposals, nor the last; he mechanically wrote to eligible women he knew with the hope of securing a wife to help him in his work. Henry may be the basis for the character of St. John Rivers in *Jane Eyre*. He wrote in his diary after Charlotte's refusal: "Received unfavorable reply from CB. The Will of the Lord be done" (Barker, p. 353). Some of the text on this page comes from a letter Charlotte wrote to Ellen about her brother's proposal, explaining that the attraction of becoming Ellen's sister-in-law was not enough to entice her to marry Henry.

 **PAGE 54:** Anne wrote about the thrill of setting off to earn her own living as a governess in *Agnes Grey*. The scenes of children throwing their governess's desk out of the window and the governess tying her charges to a table also occur in the novel—and they aren't the worst of what happens.

 **PAGE 57:** Imprisonment is a recurring theme in Emily's poems. As early as "The Islanders Plays" (recorded by Charlotte in October 1829 [*Selected Writings*, p. xxxv]), Emily initiated the School Rebellion, where a mutiny takes place at a palace school and the leaders, including "Princess Victoria," are imprisoned. This is just the beginning of the appearance of dungeons in Emily's Gondal poems.

 **PAGE 59:** Charlotte, Emily, and their father traveled eleven hours by train from Leeds to London with Mary Taylor and her brother, and arrived late at night. They stayed at the Chapter Coffee House, and when Charlotte awoke, she had her

first view of the dome of St Paul's Cathedral. Charlotte's thoughts on this page are from *Villette*, when the character Lucy Snowe describes the same view from her hotel room: "My inner self moved; my spirit shook its always-fettered wings half-loose; I had a sudden feeling as if I, who had never yet truly lived, were about to taste life" (Brontë, p. 443). That day Charlotte acted as a tour leader and dragged her friends and family to Westminster Abbey and the British Museum (pictured here). Mary Taylor wrote years later: "[Charlotte] seemed to think our business was, and ought to be, to see all the pictures and statues we could" (Barker p. 443).

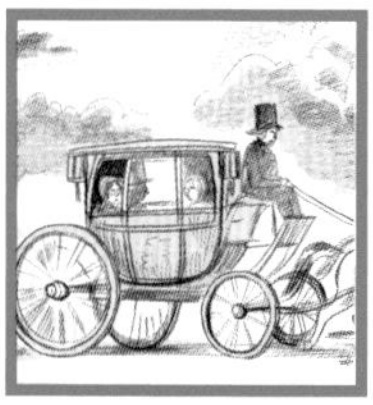

PAGE 60: The dialogue is from Charlotte's first novel, *The Professor*, and must have been based on Charlotte's experience of traveling to Brussels: "Don't call the picture a flat or dull one—it was neither flat nor dull to me when I first beheld it. When I left Ostend on a mild February morning and found myself on the road to Brussels, nothing could look vapid to me. My sense of enjoyment possessed an edge whetted to the finest, untouched, keen, exquisite . . . not a beautiful, scarcely a picturesque object met my eye along the whole route, yet to me, all was beautiful, all was more than picturesque."

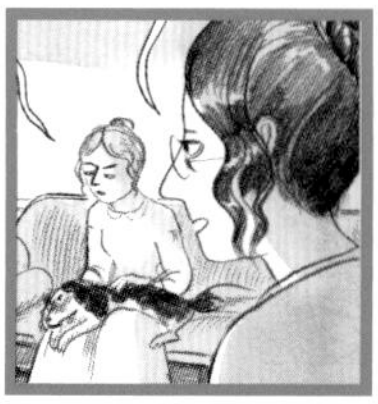

PAGE 68: The sisters each received a small legacy from Aunt Branwell of £30. It was not enough to sustain a living, but it allowed Charlotte to feel as if she could afford to return to Brussels.

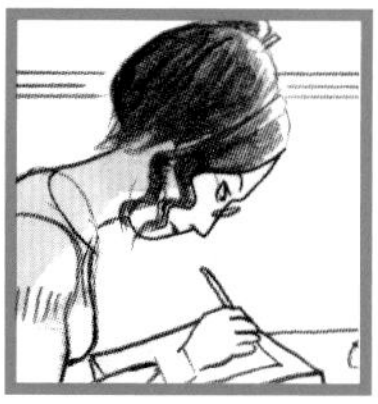

PAGE 74: Back in Haworth, Charlotte wrote repeatedly to M. Heger, but he never replied. Some of her letters to him were preserved by the Heger family, and brought to light by a daughter much later, after both Charlotte and M. Heger had died (in 1896). At least one of the letters was torn to bits, probably by M. Heger himself, and carefully restored—possibly by Madame Heger—who may have suspected that Charlotte would later become famous.

 **PAGE 76:** "Some very unpleasant and undreamt of experiences of human nature" is from Anne's diary paper of July 31, just after Branwell was dismissed earlier in July. We don't know whether she was aware of her brother's affair with Mrs. Robinson while she was working at Thorp Green, though it seems unlikely she didn't know, given how indiscreet they both were and that they were living in the same house with the family. Charlotte referred in letters to Branwell "making himself ill," when he got drunk—it amounts to the same thing!

 **NOTE ON THE BRONTË DOGS:** Grasper: (an Irish terrier) (c. 1833–1838). Emily's dog Keeper (c. 1838–1848) was a mix of mastiff and bulldog, and Anne's Flossy (c. 1846–1851) was a spaniel. We know what they looked like because both Emily and Anne drew portraits of their beloved dogs. Their collars are on display at the Parsonage Museum. The Brontë family also owned cats, but we have no images of them!

. . . .

 **PAGE 83:** *Poems by Currer, Ellis, and Acton Bell* was published May 1846, but they didn't know it had only sold two copies until June 1847.

Branwell wrote to a friend in 1845 that he was working on a three-volume novel, and that in the publishing world a novel is more salable than poetry. He never finished the novel, and his disappointment over the affair with Mrs. Robinson drove him to despair (Barker, p. 561).

SELECTED BIBLIOGRAPHY

Alexander, Christine and Jane Sellars. *The Art of the Brontës*. Cambridge: Cambridge University Press, 1995.

Alexander, Christine and Margaret Smith. *The Oxford Companion to the Brontës*. Oxford: Oxford University *Press*, 2003.

Barker, Juliet. *The Brontës: Wild Genius on the Moors: The Story of a Literary Family*. New York, London: Pegasus Books, 2010.

Brontës, The. *Tales of Glass Town, Angria, and Gondal: Selected Early Writings*. Edited by Christine Alexander. Oxford: Oxford University Press, 2010.

Gardiner, Juliet. *The Brontës at Haworth: The World Within*. New York: Clarkson Potter Publishers, 1992.

Harman, Claire. *Charlotte Brontë: A Fiery Heart*. New York: Vintage, 2017.

Lutz, Deborah. *The Brontë Cabinet*. New York and London: W. W. Norton & Company, 2015.

Miller, Lucasta. *The Brontë Myth*. New York: Penguin Random House, 2003.

To Walk Invisible, written and directed by Sally Wainwright, London, UK, BBC TV, 2016.

CREDITS

Author-Illustrator

GLYNNIS FAWKES is an Ignatz Award–nominated cartoonist and illustrator living in Burlington, Vermont. She has worked as an illustrator for archaeological excavations since 1998 on sites in Greece, Cyprus, and the Middle East, and her comics have appeared on TheNewYorker.com. She is currently at work on a book about her first trip to Greece, a draft of which received the MoCCA Arts Festival Award in 2016. Find out more about Glynnis and her work at glynnisfawkes.com.

Introduction

ALISON BECHDEL is an award-winning cartoonist known for her long-running comic strip *Dykes to Watch Out For* and graphic novel memoirs *Are You My Mother?: A Comic Drama* and *Fun Home: A Family Tragicomic*, which was adapted into a Tony Award–winning musical. Her comics have appeared in the *New Yorker*, *Slate*, *McSweeney's*, the *New York Times Book Review*, and *Granta*. In 2014, she was named a MacArthur Fellow. Alison lives in Vermont.

Series Editor

JAMES STURM is a cartoonist and the cofounder of the Center for Cartoon Studies. His graphic novels include *Satchel Paige: Striking Out Jim Crow*, *The Golem's Mighty Swing*, *Market Day*, and *Off Season*. His picture books for children include *Ape and Armadillo Take Over the World*, *Birdsong*, and the Adventures in Cartooning series (with Andrew Arnold and Alexis Frederick-Frost).

THANK YOU

I feel deep gratitude to Juliet Barker for reading my rough manuscript and carefully offering many corrections. Her depth of knowledge of quotations, chronology, and details of dress are invaluable. Her thorough and lively book *The Brontës: Wild Genius on the Moors: The Story of a Literary Family* was the main source for my research. Thank you to James Sturm, insightful, humorous, visionary editor, who made this project a tremendous learning experience and pleasure to write and draw. Thanks to Amy Burns for many hours of help preparing pages. Thanks to Darryl Cunningham (native of Keighley) who strongly recommended I make the trip to Haworth. I'm grateful to the volunteers in the Brontë Parsonage Museum who answered my many questions during my visit. Thanks also to La Maison des Auteurs in Angoulême, France, for a residency, and to Giorgia Marras, for sharing a studio and ideas about making comics set in the nineteenth century. Deep thanks to friends-in-comics Summer Pierre, Jennifer Hayden, and Ellen Lindner for continual encouragement. I'm grateful to my family, John, Sylvan, and Helen, who almost never got tired of my telling them what Charlotte did and said. Thanks also to my parents. My mother read *Wuthering Heights* to me when I was thirteen, when the image of Cathy's hand scratching at the window was etched into my memory, and a curiosity about the Brontë sisters began.

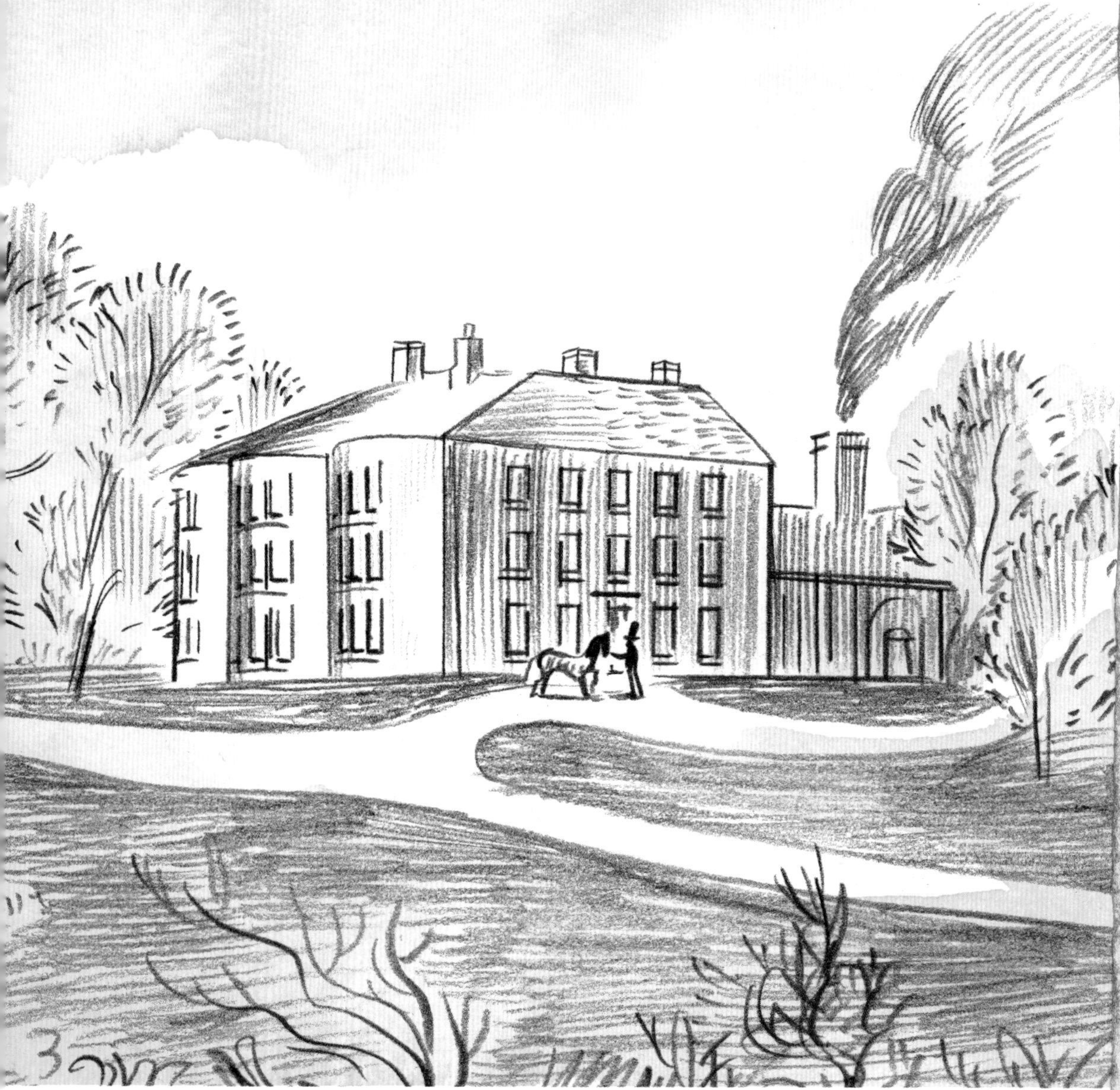

THE CENTER FOR CARTOON STUDIES produces comics, zines, posters, and graphic novels (like this book about Charlotte Brontë!). For those interested in making comics themselves one day, the Center for Cartoon Studies is also America's finest cartooning school—offering one- and two-year courses of study, master of fine arts degrees, and summer workshops.